W9-BXS-942

THE SOCCER ENCYCLOPEDIA

KINGFISHER
LONDON & NEW YORK

KINGFISHER
LONDON & NEW YORK

Published in 2022 in the United States by Kingfisher,
120 Broadway, New York, NY 10271
Kingfisher is an imprint of Macmillan Children's Books,
London
All rights reserved.

Copyright © Macmillan Publishers International Ltd. 2022
Distributed in the U.S. and Canada by Macmillan,
120 Broadway, New York, NY 10271

EU representative: 1st Floor, The Liffey Trust Centre,
117-126 Sheriff Street Upper, Dublin 1 D01 YC43

Author: Clive Gifford
Consultants: Simon Mugford and Anthony Hobbs
Illustrations: Peter Liddiard, Sudden Impact Media
Design: Darren Jordan, RockJaw Creative
Cover design: Jake Da'Costa

ISBN 978-0-7534-7834-9

Library of Congress Cataloging-in-Publication data has been
applied for.

Kingfisher books are available for special promotions and
premiums. For details contact: Special Markets Department,
Macmillan, 120 Broadway, New York, NY 10271.

For more information, please visit www.kingfisherbooks.com

Printed in China
9 8 7 6 5 4 3 2 1
1TR/0622/WKT/RV/128MA

Note to readers: The website addresses listed in this book are correct
at the time of publishing. However, due to the ever-changing nature of
the Internet, website addresses and content can change. Websites can
contain links that are unsuitable for children. The publisher cannot be
held responsible for changes in website addresses or content, or for
information obtained through third-party websites. We strongly advise
that Internet searches should be supervised by an adult.

MIX
Paper from
responsible sources
FSC® C116313

CONTENTS

THE BEAUTIFUL GAME

Soccer's dynamic action, breathtaking skills, and heartstopping drama are all crammed into 90 minutes of play. It is sport as drama, making heroes and villains out of its players, managers, and officials. Clubs and national teams inspire passion and loyalty in fans, and major competitions are watched avidly worldwide. From humble beginnings in the 1800s, soccer has grown to become a major industry that provides great moments of excitement, celebration, and despair. No other sport has quite the same power to unite and divide.

A CHANGING SPORT

As soccer has grown, dozens of changes have occurred. Some have involved the laws of the game—from the two-handed throw-in, introduced in 1883, to the back-pass law for goalkeepers that was adopted 99 years later. Other changes—such as the arrival of promotion and relegation up and down a league—have shaped the competitions of which matches are a part.

Soccer's adaptability has been one of its strengths. Another great part of its appeal is that people of all ages and skill levels can play the game. At its most basic, soccer is a simple sport that can be enjoyed without expensive equipment and played almost anywhere—from a sandy beach to an office or hallway with a crumpled ball of paper.

The simplicity of soccer is a big selling point with new fans. The finer details of rules and tactics may pass them by at first, but the basics of the game and the skills of star players—their pace, ball control, passing, shooting, and tackling—can be admired by almost anyone.

◀ Wendie Renard of France and Brazil's Cristiane at the 2019 FIFA Women's World Cup. Over 993 million people watched some of the tournament on TV—a record for the women's game.

◥ France's Kylian Mbappé battles for the ball with Bernardo Silva of Portugal at EURO 2020. Incredibly, Mbappé won the FIFA World Cup, the UEFA Nations League, four Ligue 1 titles, and three Coupes de France before the age of 23.

▲ Soccer is a sport that generates intensely strong bonds between fans and their teams. This fan, dressed in the national colors of Mali, celebrates during the 2021 African Nations Championship semifinal against Guinea.

▼ Soccer can be played practically anywhere, in almost any conditions. These Brazilian schoolchildren are enjoying a casual game just days before their country hosts the 2014 World Cup.

THE NUMBERS GAME

In its full version, soccer is a game in which two teams of 11 people play two halves of 45 minutes. Today more than 50 million players around the world participate in official competitions. Many millions more play the game on a regular basis—a survey by world soccer's governing body, the *Fédération Internationale de Football Association* (FIFA), estimates that figure to be more than 265 million. Top leagues, such as Serie A in Italy, Spain's La Liga, and Germany's Bundesliga, attract millions of viewers. In 2021, English Premier League games or highlights were broadcast to more than 190 countries. The final of the 2018 FIFA World Cup between France and Croatia, held in Russia, was watched by a staggering 1.12 billion people— a seventh of the entire human population

SOCCER'S ORIGINS

An alehouse in Victorian England seems an unlikely place to launch a sport that would become the world's biggest and most popular. Yet that is precisely what occurred in 1863 at the Freemason's Tavern in London, England. There, representatives of 12 clubs met to form the Football Association (FA) and draw up a single set of rules for the game.

HISTORY MYSTERY

No one knows where or when the first forerunner of soccer was played. Many nations claim early ball games as their own, from the ancient Greeks with episkyros to the Roman game of harpastum.

The ancient Chinese game of tsu chu (or cuju) was played more than 2,000 years ago and was even used as military training during the Ch'in dynasty (255–206 B.C.). Players tried to propel a ball made of animal skin stuffed with hair through bamboo posts or a circular hole in netting. Equally ancient is the mysterious Mesoamerican ball game played with a solid rubber ball in a stone court by the ancient peoples of Central America over 2,500 years ago.

In medieval Europe, games of mob soccer were so unruly and violent that the leaders of several countries, including Charles V in France and Oliver Cromwell in England, attempted to ban the sport. In contrast to mob soccer, the Italian game of calcio was first played in the 1500s by aristocrats and religious leaders, including three popes. Each team was made up of 27 players, and goals were scored by kicking or throwing the ball over a certain spot on the edge of the field.

▲ Illustrations from the very first international match, in 1872. Despite England fielding eight forwards and Scotland six, the game ended in a 0–0 tie.

GETTING ORGANIZED

By the late 1700s and early 1800s, a kicking-and-rushing ball game was played in private schools and universities across Britain, but rules varied from place to place. In 1848, players at Cambridge University drew up soccer's first set of rules. This attempt to bring order into the game had only limited success, and so in 1863 representatives of 12 clubs (including the Crusaders, No Names of Kilburn, and Crystal Palace) met in London. They formed the FA, developed the laws of the game, and—eight years later—set up the world's oldest surviving cup competition, the FA Cup. The first international match, between England and Scotland, was played in 1872, and in 1888 the first soccer league was founded in England.

◀ The Japanese game of kemari is at least 1,500 years old. Players had to keep the ball from touching the ground by juggling and passing it with their feet.

THE WOMEN'S GAME

Women's soccer struggled from the beginning against male prejudice that it was "unladylike" for females to play the game. Interest in women's soccer reached its first peak after World War I, thanks to the exploits of the Dick, Kerr Ladies team (see page 79). The women's game was then stifled for almost half a century following the introduction of a ban on women playing at the grounds of FA member clubs. Between 1969 and 1972, bans were lifted in a number of countries, and women's soccer slowly began to expand. The first European Championships for women were held in 1984, while an Olympic competition was launched in 1996. More than 60 nations entered the qualifying competition for the first Women's World Cup in 1991.

(see page 79)

WHAT'S IN A NAME?

Around the world, many teams have taken their names from European clubs. Here are just a few:

Arsenal Lesotho
Lesotho Cup winners 1989, 1991, 1998

Liverpool
Uruguay, Supercopa Uruguaya winners 2020

Barcelona
Ecuador, league champions '95, '97, 2012, 2016

Benfica de Macao
Macao, league champions 2018

Juventus
Belize, league champions 1999, 2005

Berekum Chelsea
Ghana, league champions 2011

◀ U.S. striker Alex Morgan leaps over Dutch goalie Sari van Veenendaal during the Tokyo 2020 Olympics quarterfinal. The United States won on penalties, on their way to a bronze medal.

SOCCER EXPORTS

Soccer spread rapidly around the globe in the late 1800s. The game was exported first by British players and then by converts from other European nations, particularly to their colonies. Soccer was introduced to Russia in 1887 by two English mill owners, the Charnock brothers, while resident Englishmen founded Italy's oldest league club, Genoa, six years later.

In 1885, Canada defeated the United States 1–0 in the first international match to be played in the Americas. In Argentina, British and Italian residents encouraged the formation of South America's first club, Buenos Aires, in 1865. The first league in South America was set up 28 years later.

In 1904, FIFA was founded in Paris, with seven members: Belgium, Denmark, France, Holland, Spain (represented by Madrid FC), Sweden, and Switzerland. Over time, FIFA became the dominant organization in world soccer. In 1930, it had 45 member nations; in 1960, that figure stood at 95. In 2016, FIFA welcomed Gibraltar and Kosovo as its 210th and 211th members.

◀ W. R. Moon of Corinthians, an English amateur team, in his uniform. Corinthians helped to spread soccer by touring the world. Their 1910 trip to South America inspired the formation of the famous Brazilian team Corinthians Paulista.

THEN AND NOW

Going back in time 150 years, a modern soccer fan would be surprised to find no referees, corners, or field markings at a game. Players wore coats and even top hats; they handled the ball in the air and wrestled with each other on the ground. Over time, soccer has evolved into the game that we know today.

▼ The referee's whistle was first blown at a soccer match in 1878. British firm Acme Whistles, astonishingly, has sold over 200 million Acme Thunderer whistles, which have been heard at World Cups and in top leagues around the globe.

THE FIELD

Unlike in most sports, the field in soccer can vary in size. Most are around 328 ft. (100m) long and 213–230 ft. (65–70m) wide. In the 1860s, a field could be as long as 590 ft. (180m). The first markings arrived in 1891, including a center circle and a line running the width of the field, 36 ft. (10.98m) in front of the goal line. A penalty kick could be taken from any point along that line. It was another 11 years before the field markings we know today were introduced. Since then only two additions have been made—the penalty arc at the front of the penalty area (in 1937) and the corner quadrants (in 1938).

GOALS

To score a goal, a team has to propel the entire ball over the goal line, between two posts that are set 24 ft. (7.32m) apart. On many occasions, controversy has raged over whether the ball crossed the line—from the 1966 World Cup final between England and West Germany to the DFB-Pokal Cup final in 2014 between Borussia Dortmund and Bayern Munich.

Early goals consisted of just two posts. Following arguments over the height of a shot, a white tape was fitted to the posts, 8 ft. (2.44m) above the ground. Wooden crossbars began to replace tape in the 1870s. Goal nets came later, invented by an engineer from Liverpool, John Alexander Brodie. They were first given a trial in January 1891, when Everton's Fred Geary became the first player to put the ball in the back of the net. Incidentally, that game was refereed by Sam Widdowson, who had invented shin pads 17 years earlier.

▲ Referee Anna-Marie Keighley tests the goal line technology before a 2019 Women's World Cup match. Fourteen 3D cameras track the ball to determine whether it crossed the goal line or not.

THE MEN AND WOMEN IN BLACK

Referees did not feature in early games of soccer because the sport's founders believed that gentlemen would never intentionally foul or cheat. Instead, each team had an umpire to whom they could appeal. By 1891, games were controlled by a referee in order to cut down on controversial decisions and long stoppages for debate, and the two umpires became linesmen. (Since 1996, linesmen have been known as assistants.) Despite often being described as the "men in black," referees have played in all sorts of colors. Early referees tried to keep up with play dressed in the popular fashions of the time—pants, a blazer, and even a bow tie.

▶ Hugo Guillamón of Valencia receives the first red card of the 2021–22 La Liga season after just three minutes of a match against Getafe. Red and yellow cards were first used at the 1970 World Cup.

CLEATS AND BALLS

No game is complete without a soccer ball, up to 60 million of which are sold every year. Early balls were made from the inflated bladder of a pig or sheep, covered in a shell of stitched pieces of brown leather held in place by laces. Brazilian club Santos pioneered the use of a more visible white ball, while today's balls—made from leather and synthetic materials—are often bright and colorful. A referee has to check that the match ball and spares are the correct size, weight, and air pressure before a game begins.

Early soccer shoes were heavy, above-the-ankle work boots, often with metal toe caps and metal or leather studs nailed into the sole. Modern cleats are lightweight and flexible, enabling players to feel the ball on their foot. Their soles come in a variety of customizable studs, blades, or dimples that players select depending on the condition of the field.

▼ A vintage ball and pair of boots at Barcelona's Camp Nou museum.

▲ Arsenal's Alex James tries out a muscle-enhancing machine in the 1930s. Today's players undergo carefully planned exercise regimes and eat a diet that is scientifically monitored by their teams.

▲ Brazilian players show off their multicolored cleats in training ahead of the 2018 World Cup.

ALL DRESSED UP

Today's lightweight soccer uniforms are the result of years of research and development. During the very first international match in 1872, the Scotland and England teams wore knickerbockers (long shorts), long shirts, and "bobble hats" or caps. Gradually, soccer uniforms developed to give players more freedom of movement, although shorts remained almost knee length until the 1960s. Numbers appeared on shirts regularly for the first time in the 1930s, but player names did not arrive until the late 1980s. In 1924 the English Football Association (FA) began to insist that teams have a second shirt (known as an away shirt) that could be worn in the event of a color clash. Today, uniform manufacturing is a highly profitable business. Teams often have two or even three away uniforms; they update their uniform design every season and sell many thousands of replica shirts to fans.

◀ High-profile transfers can send fans into a shirt-buying frenzy. When Lionel Messi's move to Paris Saint-Germain was confirmed in August 2021, the club website sold out of 150,000 "Messi 30" shirts within 30 minutes.

FACT FILE

The Belgian referee at the 1930 World Cup final, Jean Langenus, wore a dinner jacket, golfing plus fours, and a red striped tie.

THE GLOBAL GAME

FIFA is in control of world soccer, while the sport is organized regionally by six continental confederations. South America and Europe have been the traditional powerhouses, but the men's and women's games have boomed globally, and talented players now emerge from all over the world.

BALANCE OF POWER

Great advances have been made by the federations and national teams of regions outside Europe and South America. More and more national soccer teams have become truly competitive on the world stage, thanks to the emergence of dozens of high-quality players in Africa, Asia, Oceania, and North and Central America. Australia's 2018 World Cup appearance was its fourth in a row. Before 2006, it had last qualified in 1974. New Zealand was the only team at the 2010 World Cup not to lose a game. African nations have featured in three of the last six Olympic men's soccer finals, winning two golds and one silver. In December 2021, the continent had 11 men's teams ranked in FIFA's top 60. There have also been strong showings by Japan, Costa Rica, and the United States at recent international tournaments. As a reflection of this, African and Asian nations have been chosen to host many tournaments, including the World Cups of 2002 (South Korea and Japan), 2010 (South Africa), and 2022 (Qatar), and the Women's World Cup of 2007 (China). Additionally, Africa and Asia now enjoy more automatic places at the World Cup than ever before.

▲ Steve Mokone was the first black South African to play professionally in Europe. From the 1950s, he starred for Coventry City, Dutch team Heracles, Spain's Valencia, Marseille in France, and Italy's Torino. Mokone later played in Australia and Canada.

CONCACAF
CONFEDERATION OF NORTH, CENTRAL AMERICAN, AND CARIBBEAN ASSOCIATION FOOTBALL

FOUNDED: 1961 · MEMBERS: 41

Mexico and the U.S.—traditionally the strongest CONCACAF nations—have hosted three World Cups, while smaller nations such as Costa Rica have reached the tournament. CONCACAF teams have often been invited to play in South América's Copa America competition, and the federation actually includes two South American nations, Guyana and Suriname.

▶ The Copa América is South America's top international tournament. In 2021, Argentina beat Brazil to win its 15th title.

CONMEBOL
CONFEDERACIÓN SUDAMERICANA DE FÚTBOL

FOUNDED: 1916 · MEMBERS: 10

CONMEBOL teams have won nine men's World Cup finals, while the Brazilian women's national team was the World Cup runner-up in 2007. Argentina won the 2004 and 2008 Olympic men's finals and is rarely out of the top five of FIFA's world rankings. Domestic leagues, however, are suffering, with clubs in debt and most of the continent's top players heading for Europe and elsewhere to play.

OFC
OCEANIA FOOTBALL CONFEDERATION

FOUNDED: 1966 · MEMBERS: 11

Soccer has struggled for support in Oceania. In the larger countries, it has to compete with more popular sports, while smaller nations suffer from a lack of finance, facilities, and players. Australia, the OFC's biggest and most successful nation, became frustrated by the lack of an automatic World Cup place for the confederation. In January 2006 it left the OFC to join the Asian Football Confederation.

FACT FILE
Australia was the first OFC team to reach a World Cup, in 1974.

UEFA
UNION OF EUROPEAN FOOTBALL ASSOCIATIONS

FOUNDED: 1954 · MEMBERS: 55

As the most powerful confederation, UEFA was awarded 13 of the 32 places at the 2022 World Cup. It runs the two largest competitions after the World Cup: the UEFA European Championships and the UEFA Champions League. Thousands of foreign players play in Europe, but UEFA clubs may soon be forced to include a minimum number of homegrown players on their teams.

▶ Chelsea players celebrate their 2021 UEFA Champions League triumph over Premier League rivals Manchester City.

HAVE CLEATS, WILL TRAVEL

Professional players travel the world. Thousands of South American and African players in particular move continents, seeking out clubs that will employ them. The richest clubs are mostly found in Europe, partly because of the huge sums some receive from television rights, advertising, and prize money for appearing in competitions such as the UEFA Champions League. This revenue enables European clubs to pluck the very best talents from around the globe, even if it leaves another country's league bereft of its best players. None of the 23-man Algerian squad that won the 2019 African Cup of Nations, for example, played for Algerian clubs. Other nations also recruit large numbers of foreign players. Each MLS club in the United States is allowed up to eight international players, while the Chinese Super League has twice broken the $60-million barrier to bring Brazilian players into its competition (Hulk and Oscar).

AFC
ASIAN FOOTBALL CONFEDERATION

FOUNDED: 1954 · MEMBERS: 47

Asian soccer is booming. The highly successful Asian Champions League was set up in 2002, and national leagues are now very popular. Many foreign players play in Asia—for example, 63 Brazilians played in Japan's J.League in 2020–21. Australia joined the AFC in 2006, but all eyes are now turning to China, which has the world's largest pool of potential players and fans.

▶ Kawasaki Frontale's Leandro Damião celebrates with the J1 League trophy in 2021, his club's fourth league title.

CAF
CONFÉDÉRATION AFRICAINE DE FOOTBALL

FOUNDED: 1957 · MEMBERS: 54

Africa was not awarded an automatic World Cup place until 1970, but the CAF sent six teams to the 2010 World Cup, including the host nation, South Africa. While national teams continue to improve, the domestic game struggles because of a lack of finance and the movement of its best players out of Africa. In 2021, for example, more than 500 African players were playing in 11 of the top leagues in Europe.

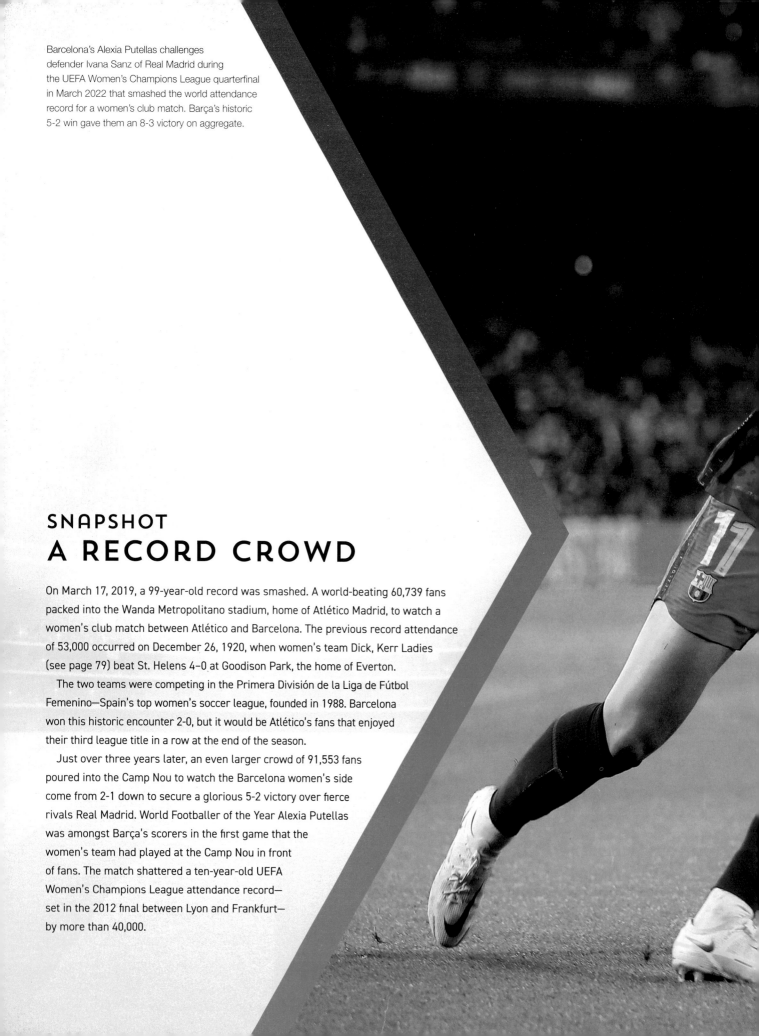

Barcelona's Alexia Putellas challenges defender Ivana Sanz of Real Madrid during the UEFA Women's Champions League quarterfinal in March 2022 that smashed the world attendance record for a women's club match. Barça's historic 5-2 win gave them an 8-3 victory on aggregate.

SNAPSHOT
A RECORD CROWD

On March 17, 2019, a 99-year-old record was smashed. A world-beating 60,739 fans packed into the Wanda Metropolitano stadium, home of Atlético Madrid, to watch a women's club match between Atlético and Barcelona. The previous record attendance of 53,000 occurred on December 26, 1920, when women's team Dick, Kerr Ladies (see page 79) beat St. Helens 4–0 at Goodison Park, the home of Everton.

The two teams were competing in the Primera División de la Liga de Fútbol Femenino—Spain's top women's soccer league, founded in 1988. Barcelona won this historic encounter 2-0, but it would be Atlético's fans that enjoyed their third league title in a row at the end of the season.

Just over three years later, an even larger crowd of 91,553 fans poured into the Camp Nou to watch the Barcelona women's side come from 2-1 down to secure a glorious 5-2 victory over fierce rivals Real Madrid. World Footballer of the Year Alexia Putellas was amongst Barça's scorers in the first game that the women's team had played at the Camp Nou in front of fans. The match shattered a ten-year-old UEFA Women's Champions League attendance record—set in the 2012 final between Lyon and Frankfurt—by more than 40,000.

BASIC SKILLS

In the words of former Liverpool manager Bill Shankly, soccer "is a simple game based on the giving and taking of passes, on controlling the ball, and on making yourself available to receive a pass." Shankly's words highlight the most fundamental skills in soccer.

BALL CONTROL

The world's top players, such as Cristiano Ronaldo and Lionel Messi, appear to control the ball effortlessly. Their easy command and movement of the ball hides thousands of hours of practice and training, often from a very early age. As children, many great players spent long hours playing games with a tennis ball, a crumpled wad of paper, or a battered piece of fruit.

Players can control the ball with any part of their body except their hands and arms. Cushioning is a technique in which a player uses a part of the body to slow down a moving ball and then bring it under control with his or her feet. High balls can be cushioned using the chest, thigh, or a gentle header to kill the ball's speed and bring it down. For a low, incoming ball, the foot is preferred—either the inside of the cleat or its instep (where the laces are). A ball that is rolling across the field can be stopped with the sole of the foot—a technique known as trapping.

◀ Achraf Hakimi uses the side of his foot to push the ball forward for Paris Saint-Germain in a 2021 Ligue 1 match.

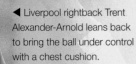

◀ Liverpool rightback Trent Alexander-Arnold leans back to bring the ball under control with a chest cushion.

▼ An instep cushion is used to control a ball arriving front-on. Here, the player meets the ball with his shoelaces and instantly pulls back his foot, killing the pace of the ball.

SHIELDING AND OBSTRUCTION

When players have the ball at their feet, they are said to be in possession and have a number of options. These include running with the ball, dribbling with the ball close to the feet, passing, shooting, and shielding the ball. Shielding or screening involves a player putting his or her body between the ball and an opponent in order to prevent the other player from gaining possession. This gives the shielding player crucial time to decide on the next move, which may be a pass backward to a teammate or a sharp turn and an attempt to play the ball around the opponent. Shielding players have to be careful not to hold, push, or back into the other player. They must also keep the ball close by and under control—otherwise the referee may award an indirect free kick for obstruction (in which a player unfairly blocks an opponent's path to the ball). An obstruction usually occurs when a player steps into the path of an opponent when the ball is several yards away.

▲ Venezuela's Salomón Rondón shields the ball from Uruguayan defender Diego Godin during a Copa América game.

◀ Crystal Dunn (left) of the United States challenges Australia's Hayley Raso for the ball during the Olympic bronze-medal match in 2021.

PASS MASTERS

Passes can be made with a thrust of the chest or a header. Usually, however, they are made with one of three parts of the shoe—the outside, the instep, or the inside. The inside or side-foot pass is the most common and accurate pass, allowing players to pass the ball with a high level of precision. Some players attempt as many as 60 or 70 passes in a game, most of which are side-foot passes. Italian midfielder Manuel Locatelli completed 2,749 passes in the 2020–21 Serie A season.

For longer passes, players tend to use the instep. This allows them to propel the ball with force. The instep can also be used for lofted drives that send the ball into the air as a cross or a clearance, as well as to stab down on the back of the ball. This makes the ball rise up at a steep angle, known as a chip. A pass's weight—the strength with which it is hit—is as important as accuracy in order for the pass to be successfully completed. At EURO 2020, strong passers such as Aymeric Laporte, Pedri, Pau Torres, and Jorginho and made hundreds of passes with over 90 percent success.

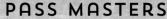

▼ Voted 2018 world soccer player of the year, Luka Modric of Croatia hits a long instep drive pass.

▶ Pedri González plays an accurate sidefoot pass. At EURO 2020 he won the young player of the tournament award and successfully completed 429 passes in just six games. Age 18, he was the youngest Spaniard to ever play at a EURO.

MOVEMENT AND SPACE

Soccer is a dynamic, fast-moving sport. Throughout a game, pockets of space open and close rapidly all over the field. Players who have great awareness of where space is or shortly will be, and who have the ability to pass or move into it, are a real asset to their team.

◀ PSG defender Paulina Dudek strikes a sidefoot pass. Top players play with their heads up, looking for teammates' moves and runs.

FACT FILE
At the 2018 World Cup, England completed 3,336 passes—more than any other team.

SPOTTING AND CREATING SPACE

The ball can zip around a field far more quickly than even the fastest of players. Good players make the ball do the work, moving it around with quick, accurate passes. Vision is the priceless ability to spot a pass, space, or goal-scoring opportunity that other players do not see, or to see it before they do. Players with good vision look to move into open space, timing their run to give a teammate who has the ball a chance to make a pass that cannot be intercepted by an opponent. Once the ball has left the passer's control, he or she often moves into a position to receive a return pass. All players, not just midfielders and attackers, must be capable of passing well and moving into space to receive passes in return.

Players can create space for themselves or for teammates through quick, agile movement and the use of feints or dummies, with which they attempt to fool a nearby opponent into thinking they are moving one way before sprinting off in another direction.

▼ A wall pass (also known as a one-two pass) is a classic way to cut out an opposing player. It involves two passes that must be hit quickly and accurately, with the first passer running on to collect the return ball.

▲ Making space can be crucial to winning the ball at a throw-in. Here, one player makes a decoy run toward the thrower, dragging a defender with him and creating space in which a teammate can collect the ball.

▶ Manchester City's Raheem Sterling attempts to drive around the outside of Tottenham defender Japhet Tanganga.

OFFSIDE

Players have to stay aware of Law 11—the offside law—throughout a game. This law causes controversy and has been altered throughout the sport's history. Today a player is offside if at the moment the ball is played he or she is in the opposition half and is closer to the opponent's goal line than both the ball and the second-from-last opponent. That opponent can be an outfield player or the goalkeeper. Players cannot be offside in their own half or if they receive the ball directly from a goal kick, throw-in, or corner.

Being in an offside position is not always an offense. Referees must judge whether the player in an offside position is involved in active play, moves toward the ball, or does anything to make it harder for an opponent to play the ball. This tests an official's judgment to the limit. Is a player offside but a long way from the ball involved in "active play"? Perhaps he or she is drawing defenders out as markers. If a referee does stop the game, an indirect free kick is awarded to the opposing team where the player was judged to be offside.

▲ French striker Djibril Cissé looks ruefully at the referee's assistant after being signaled offside in a French league match.

▶ Portugal defeated Argentina 2–1 to win the 2021 FIFA Futsal World Cup, their first title. Brazil tops the list of winners, with five titles.

▲ Here, the player at the top left of the picture is in an offside position when the ball is struck. The referee decides that he is not interfering with play, however, and awards the goal.

▶ You cannot be offside if you are behind the ball when it is played. This scorer receives the ball from a teammate who is ahead of him, so he is onside and the goal is given.

SMALL-TEAM GAMES

In many countries, children under the age of 11 play matches that feature six, seven, or eight players per team. These small-team games give young players an invaluable chance to see more of the ball and improve their control, passing, and movement. Futsal is FIFA's official five-on-five game. A match lasts for 40 minutes (two halves of 20 minutes) and is played on a field the size of a basketball court, without surrounding boards or walls.

Futsal was devised by a Uruguayan, Juan Carlos Ceriani, in 1930. The game has flourished since then, with continental competitions for clubs and national teams, including a UEFA Futsal Champions League and a 24-team men's World Cup. Kazakhstan team AFC Kairat has won the Champions League twice, while Sporting Lisbon won the title in 2021.

THE OFFICIALS

Frequently abused by players, managers, and fans, referees are soccer's guardians and the enforcers of its laws. Their job is to impose order on a match and prevent intimidation, injury, and cheating.

THE REFEREE'S ROLE

Referees perform a surprisingly large number of tasks before and after a game. These include checking the goals, nets, and balls and deciding whether the field and weather conditions are suitable for the game to go ahead. Afterward, they write a report containing details of disciplinary actions and other important incidents. On the field, the referee runs the game. His or her duties range from adding on time—because of injuries, other stoppages, and time wasting—to deciding whether the ball is in or out of play or has crossed the goal line. If a player commits a foul or breaks a law, referees must stop play and order a restart, such as a drop ball or a free kick. They can caution players and team officials and even abandon a game if weather, crowd trouble, or another factor makes the game unplayable. Referees have to follow the laws of the game, but they have a certain amount of freedom to interpret aspects of the rules as they wish. For example, if a player is fouled when his or her team is in a promising position, a referee may let the game continue, playing the advantage rule to keep the game flowing.

ASSISTANTS AND THE FOURTH OFFICIAL

A referee relies on his or her assistants as extra pairs of eyes. Referee's assistants indicate when the ball goes out of play and whether a goal kick, corner, or throw-in should be awarded. They also use flag signals to point out that a substitution has been requested or a player is offside, or whether an offense has taken place out of the view of the referee. A referee can consult with an assistant if he or she was closer to the action, but it is up to the referee to make the final decision. Fourth officials have duties before and after a match, as well as helping with substitutions and displaying the amount of time added on at the end of each half for injuries and other stoppages.

◄ A fourth official uses a digital board to signal the time added on to the first half of the Germany vs. France EURO 2020 match in 2021.

▼ Roma's head coach, Paulo Fonseca, receives a red card for arguing with the referee.

◣ Early in a game, a good referee talks to players to calm them down or issues verbal warnings rather than cards. Here, Nicole Petignat soothes AIK Solna's Krister Nordin in the first UEFA Cup game to be refereed by a woman, in 2003.

FACT FILE

In 1998, English referee Martin Sylvester sent himself off after punching a player during a match in the Andover and District Sunday League.

TOP-FLIGHT PRESSURES

Thousands of amateur referees give up their weekends and evenings for free, purely to give something back to the game they adore. Top referees have their performances assessed, attend training seminars, undergo regular medical checks, and are tested for fitness. A referee may run 5.6–7 mi. (9.5–11.5km) during a game (even further if extra time occurs) and often has to sprint to keep up with play. Referees work in a harsh, unforgiving environment in which footage from multiple cameras and slow-motion television replays are broadcast over and over again, highlighting each poor decision. However, the very technology that has put referees under the spotlight is now coming to their aid. Goal-line technology removes doubt about whether a goal has been scored by sensing if the whole of the ball has crossed the goal line.

◀ Referee Daniele Orsato brandishes the 26th red card of Spanish defender Sergio Ramos's career during a 2020 UEFA Champions League match. Although a record in Europe, other players elsewhere have more—Colombia's Gerardo Múnera received 46 during his career (1995–2015).

CAUTION!

A player is shown a yellow card if he or she:
- is guilty of unsporting behavior, such as simulation;
- shows dissent by word or action;
- persistently breaks the rules—for example, by making repeated foul tackles;
- delays the restart of play;
- fails to stand at the required distance at a corner kick or free kick;
- enters or leaves the field of play without the referee's permission.

A player is sent off if he or she receives two yellow cards or one red card. Red-card offenses include a very dangerous tackle, spitting, and stopping a goal with a deliberate handball.

VAR

In 2018, FIFA introduced the Video Assistant Referee (VAR) to the elite game. The VAR studies TV footage of contentious penalties, goals, straight red-card decisions, and cases of mistaken identity, and alerts the onfield referee. The referee can make a rectangle signal, race to the sideline, and review a moment of the game on a monitor to aid their decision.

VAR features in more and more league and cup competitions. It is designed to stop major mistakes in matches, but a referee must still stay alert for the many fouls and infringements that occur in a fast-moving game. Spotting contact in a crowded penalty area is a particularly difficult task, especially when some players fall to the ground with the slightest of contact or with no contact at all—a bookable offense known as simulation.

RED-CARD RECORDS

Fastest in a top league
Ten seconds—Giuseppe Lorenzo, Serie A, Bologna vs. Parma, 1990

Fastest in the World Cup
55 seconds—José Batista, Uruguay vs. Scotland, 1986

Most in one match
36—Claypole vs. Victoriano Arenas (Argentina), 2011

▼ Chile's Daniela Zamora is fouled by Pitsamai Sornsai of Thailand at the 2019 Women's World Cup.

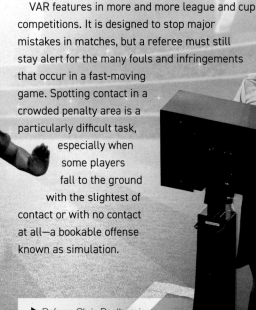

▶ Referee Chris Beath reviews VAR footage before awarding Brazil a penalty kick in the Tokyo 2020 Olympic men's final.

DEFENDING

Compared to strikers or creative midfielders, defenders are rarely praised as game winners. Yet the foundation of every successful team is a composed, secure defense. Defending consists of a range of individual skills allied to good teamwork and understanding between players so that they defend as a unit. Defenders require strength and excellent heading and tackling skills, along with intense concentration, quick reactions, and bravery. But in truth all players must defend if their team is to remain competitive in a match.

▶ French defender Raphael Varane shows expert timing to rob Turkey's Cenk Tosun of the ball. Tough, accurate tackling that wins possession is a crucial part of the game.

TRACKING AND TACKLING

The two keys to defending well are denying the opposing team the chance to score and winning the ball back. As soon as an opponent gets the ball, defenders try to get between the ball and their goal and eliminate space. Defenders spend much of a game tracking opponents as they make runs and closing down the player with the ball in order to delay his or her progress. This is called jockeying. The aim is to slow down an attack until the defending team is in a stronger position. The defender tries to guide the attacker into a weaker position, such as near the sideline, where there is little support. When a defender has cover from nearby teammates, he or she may make a tackle. The defender should stay on his or her feet in order to gain possession.

◀ This attacker has spotted a weak pass by an opponent and reacts quickly to make an interception. Sometimes attackers drop back to help their team defend.

◢ Philadelphia Union's Jakob Glesnes stretches to block a shot by América's Roger Martínez during a 2021 CONCACAF Champions League match.

FALLING FOUL OF THE LAW

Many of soccer's laws, such as obstruction, apply to defenders. A jockeying defender must be careful not to commit a foul, such as pushing, holding, or shirt-pulling. A poorly timed tackle may result in a foul. Tackles from behind are especially risky, often leading to a yellow or red card if the defender makes contact with the attacker. A professional foul is a deliberate foul made to deny an attacking team a clear goal-scoring chance. Two of the most common types are using the hands or arms to stop a goal-bound ball and bringing down an attacker with the ball when he or she has a clear path to the goal. Both should result in the offending player being sent off.

DEFENSIVE FORTRESS

During periods of open play, defending teams mark opponents man-to-man or with a zonal system (see page 60). At corners and free kicks from a wide position, they tend to mark man-to-man. A team may also try to catch out attackers by playing an offside trap (see page 61). Communication between defenders is crucial to prevent attackers from getting free and into open space to score. Certain teams equipped with highly skilled defenders who work well together have been able to squeeze the life out of opponents' attacks. Czech team Slavia Prague went through the entire 2020–21 league season unbeaten, tying eight of 34 games. The Juventus women's team did even better, winning all 22 games and conceding just ten goals in their march to the Serie A title.

◀ Virgil van Dijk (right) jockeys for the ball with Everton's Richarlison during a 2020 Premier League match. Van Dijk looks to secure possession of the ball or clear it away from danger.

◀ Australia's Alanna Kennedy rises high to head the ball clear and away from U.S. attacker Carli Lloyd during the Tokyo 2020 Olympic bronze-medal match in 2021.

SHUTOUTS

Goalkeepers and defenders are especially proud of a shutout—a game in which their team does not concede a goal. Shutouts are usually credited to goalkeepers, but in truth they depend on a solid defense as well as midfielders and strikers who are willing to chase, harry, track, and tackle. In 2021, Italy played 1,168 minutes without conceding a single goal, marshaled by their central defender Giorgio Chiellini and young goalkeeper Gianluigi Donnarumma. The record run was ended by a goal from Austria in the EURO 2020 Round of 16. The longest run without conceding in club soccer occurred in Brazil in 1977–78 when the Vasco da Gama goalie, Mazarópi, went 1,816 minutes unbeaten—that's more than 20 matches.

LONGEST UNBEATEN LEAGUE RUNS (IN GAMES)

108	ASEC Abidjan (Ivory Coast), 1989–94
104	Steaua Bucharest (Romania), 1986–89
88	Lincoln FC (Gibraltar), 2009–14
85	Esperance (Tunisia), 1997–2001
71	Al-Ahly (Egypt), 2004–07
63	Sheriff Tiraspol (Moldova), 2006–08
62	Celtic (Scotland), 1915–17
61	Levadia Tallinn (Estonia), 2008–09
60	Al-Hilal (Sudan), 2016–18
	Union Saint-Gilloise (Belgium), 1933–35
59	Boca Juniors (Argentina), 1924–27
	Pyunik Yerevan (Armenia), 2002–04
58	AC Milan (Italy), 1991–93
	Olympiakos (Greece), 1972–74
	Skonto Riga (Latvia), 1993–96

FACT FILE

Rangers went unbeaten during the 38-game 2020–21 Scottish Premiership season, conceding just 13 goals.

GOALKEEPING

Goalkeepers are different. Their role is unique. They are the only players allowed to handle the ball and must wear different shirts from their teammates. They act as the crucial last line of defense and can be match-winners thanks to their saves, decision-making, agility, bravery, and presence in the goal.

◄ Antonio Mirante of Roma makes a brave save at the feet of Udinese forward Rodrigo de Paul.

▲ Atlético Madrid's Jan Oblak stretches to make a diving save against Red Bull Salzburg.

KEEPING CONTROL

Goalkeepers can use their arms or hands to control the ball inside their own penalty area, but otherwise they must obey all the same rules as outfield players. They cannot handle the ball:

· after releasing it and without it touching another player;
· after receiving the ball directly from a throw-in;
· if it has been deliberately kicked to them by a teammate.

This last rule, known as the back-pass rule, came into effect in the 1990s to reduce time-wasting from goalkeepers and their defenders passing the ball back and forth to each other. If a goalie handles the ball in the above situations, the opposition is awarded an indirect free kick at the point where the offense occurred. This can be dangerously close to the goal.

In the past, goalkeepers could be barged into, but today they are well protected. Even so, they must be brave to contest a ball in a crowded penalty area or to dive at an opponent's feet. If a goalie fouls or brings down the attacker, they may give away a penalty kick and be sent off.

▲ Celta Vigo's Ruben Blanco punches away a dangerous ball.

A GOALIE'S SKILLS

To achieve a shutout, goalkeepers need more than supreme agility and the ability to make diving saves. Top goalies train hard to improve their handling skills, learning to take the ball at different heights and from different angles. They must be able to stay alert for the entire game. Many minutes can go by before, suddenly, they are called into action. Goalies need good decision-making skills too, since a cross or shot may call for them to choose whether to try to hold the ball in a save, punch it away, or tip it over the bar or around a post. Goalkeepers are in a unique position to see opposition attacks developing, and they must communicate instructions to their teammates. They line up walls at free kicks and command their goal area, urging defenders to pick up unmarked opponents. A defense and goalie that communicate well can be a formidable unit.

► VfL Wolfsburg's Katarzyna Kiedrzynek instructs her defenders, hoping to snuff out an opposition attack as early as possible.

DEFENSE INTO ATTACK

With the ball in their possession, goalies can distribute it either with their hands or feet. Goalies have three types of throws (underarm, overarm, and the javelin throw from the shoulder) with which to direct the ball to a teammate. A quick, accurate throw can release a wingback or midfielder to start an attack. Alternatively, a goalie with the ball in hand can kick the ball on the volley or half-volley to send it long upfield. Manuel Neuer, Marc-André ter Stegen, Ederson, and Alisson are examples of modern-day sweeper-keepers. These players are extremely comfortable with the ball at their feet and may adopt a high position out of their goal area to act as an extra outfield player.

▶ Washington Spirit's Aubrey Bledsoe, NWSL Goalkeeper of the Year in 2019 and 2021, pulls off a spectacular full-stretch save.

▲ Barcelona's Marc-André ter Stegen prepares to bowl out the ball underarm.

FACT FILE

The world's first black professional soccer player was a goalkeeper. Born in the Gold Coast (now Ghana), Arthur Wharton played in 1889 for Rotherham United in the English league.

GOAL-SCORING GOALIES

While goalkeepers strive to prevent goals, they occasionally score them as well. Some are scored from long goal kicks that have tricked the opposing goalkeeper through their flight path or a deceptive bounce. Others have been scored by a goalie running into the opponent's penalty area in the dying seconds of a game to try to force an equalizer or winning goal. This was the case in 2021, when Liverpool's Alisson Becker won an English Premier League game against West Bromwich Albion. A handful of goalkeepers have made a reputation for scoring from free kicks and penalty kicks, such as Germany's Hans-Jörg Butt, who scored 30 goals during his career. None can compare to Brazilian goalie Rogério Ceni, however, who scored an incredible 131 goals for São Paulo.

◀ In a one-on-one situation, many goalies come off their line to narrow the angle—reducing how much of the goal the attacker can see. They stay upright for as long as possible to increase the chance of the shot striking them.

◥ Liverpool goalie Alisson shows his skill with the ball at his feet, launching an attack with an accurate long kick.

ATTACKING

As soon as a team gains possession of the ball, with time and in space, its players' thoughts turn to attacking. There are many ways in which a team can launch an attack, from a fast drive into space by a player who is sprinting forward and pushing the ball ahead, to a slow, probing attack in which many players keep the ball securely in possession and look for an opening.

▼ Paul Pogba plays a diagonal pass behind Liverpool defender Andrew Robertson to set up an attack for Manchester United. Accurate, sharp passing can often open up an opponent's defense.

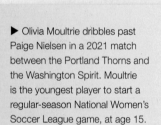

► Olivia Moultrie dribbles past Paige Nielsen in a 2021 match between the Portland Thorns and the Washington Spirit. Moultrie is the youngest player to start a regular-season National Women's Soccer League game, at age 15.

TEAM ATTACKS

Many attacks rely on two or more teammates working together to create a promising position. The wall pass (see page 16), for example, is a good way of propelling the ball past a defender with two quick movements. Attacking players also make decoy runs that pull defenders in one direction, creating space for another attacker to run into. Using the full width of the field can be vital to the success of an attack. Fullbacks, wingbacks, or wingers who are in space near the sideline may join an attack and make an overlapping run down the line. Receiving the ball, they may be able to head further forward to put in a cross or cut infield and move toward the goal. An overload is a situation in which the attacking team has more players in the attacking third of the field than the defending team. Classic ways of creating an overload are through a counterattack—in which one team's attack breaks down, and the opponent launches a rapid, direct attack—and an accurate long pass that is received by an attacker who is supported by teammates, with only an isolated defender to beat.

BEATING OFFSIDE TRAPS

Some teams play an offside trap (see page 61), in which defenders move up in a straight line to catch opponents offside. Beating an offside trap takes cunning, skill, and awareness. A perfectly weighted through pass can unlock the trap if the ball is collected by a player who stays onside until the moment the ball moves ahead of him or her. A long diagonal pass that switches play forward and across the field may also work. The receiver makes a run from a deep position, staying onside until the ball moves ahead, then collects the ball behind the defense. Individual brilliance—such as dribbling or playing a short "push and go" pass—can also beat some offside traps.

► Dutch winger Lieke Martens whips a cross into Australia's penalty area for a teammate to attack during a 2021 friendly. She was part of the Barcelona Femení team that in 2021 won a league-cup-UEFA Champions League triple.

Schollen

Ibrahimovic 4

Mendes da Silva 3

Mendes da Silva 2

Ibrahimovic 2

Mendes da Silva 1

Stam

Ibrahimovic 3

Zonneveld

Ibrahimovic 1

GAME ACTION

In a 2004 game against NAC Breda, Ajax's Zlatan Ibrahimovic scored a legendary solo goal. After receiving a pass with his back to the goal, Ibrahimovic won a tackle with Mike Zonneveld, twisted past David Mendes da Silva, and headed goalward. Weaving his way to the edge of the penalty area, Ibrahimovic's options looked limited with four defenders around him. Yet with supreme balance and a series of feints and turns, he avoided the lunging tackle of Ronnie Stam. At the very last moment, when a shot with his right foot looked likely, Ibrahimovic switched the ball to his left foot to slide a shot past goalkeeper Davy Schollen.

▼ New England Revolution's Antonio Delamea Mlinar (no.19) outjumps the Houston Dynamo defense to score with a header from a whipped-in corner kick.

SET PIECES

Set pieces are often planned in training. They are attacking moves made from a restart such as a free kick, corner, or throw-in. If a team has a player who can throw the ball a long way, it may treat a throw-in that is level with the penalty area as if it were a corner. Often, a target player just inside the penalty area will attempt to flick the throw into the goal area. Mostly, set pieces are planned from corners and attacking free kicks (see page 28). At a corner, a team's tallest players or its best headers of the ball move up, usually from defense, to join strikers and attacking midfielders in the penalty area. Corners are sometimes played short to catch the defending team off guard, but usually they are whipped into the goal area. The attacking team looks for a header or shot on goal or a flick-on to a teammate.

◄ An unexpected piece of brilliance—such as this acrobatic volley by Neymar —can open up a defense or result in a goal.

MATCH MAGICIANS

Some attacks are inspired by a piece of individual skill, trickery, or brilliance. A player may break free of a defense with a sudden change of pace and direction or a trick move such as a Cruyff turn or a dragback. Some players, like Kylian Mbappé and Romelu Lukaku, can simply outpace or outmuscle a defense, bursting through to score. Dribbling—jinking and moving with the ball under control—is an exciting way to beat defenders. Star dribblers such as Cristiano Ronaldo, Marta, Lionel Messi, and Neymar can open up games by themselves. They strike fear into defenders who know that one false move or a poorly timed challenge may allow the dribbler to go past or win their team a free kick or penalty kick.

GOAL SCORING

Players who score goals regularly are the most valuable of all. But scoring is not just reserved for the strikers. A successful team needs its midfielders to contribute a number of goals each season, while tall defenders who are experts at heading often score five or six goals per season from set pieces. For out-and-out strikers, goals are what they play for and are judged on. As Argentinian striker Gabriel Batistuta once said, "Goals are like bread. I need them to live."

OWN GOALS

An own goal is technically any goal in which the last person to touch the ball before it crossed the line was a player on the defending team. In practice, however, an own goal is awarded not only when the ball has been deflected, but also when a defending player has made a genuine error or caused a major change in the course of the ball. The history of professional soccer is littered with outrageous own goals. Among the most common are goalkeeping errors, skewed defensive clearances that are sliced into the net, and misdirected headers. In 2021, Portugal became the first team to score two own goals in a major championship game as they lost 4–2 to Germany in a EURO 2020 Group F game.

THE GOAL SCORER'S ART

Pace, power, accuracy, confidence, and a deadly eye for a chance are just some of the qualities required to be a top goal scorer. Some skills can be honed in training—close ball control or swerving a shot, for example. Other qualities, such as confidence and vision, are harder to master. Soccer has gotten quicker at the highest level, and most strikers need a lot of speed in order to break past increasingly mobile defenders or into space to receive the ball before anyone else. Strength to hold off a challenge can be an asset too. Some strikers, however, rely more on their intuition, fast reactions, and ball skills to dribble through a crowded penalty area. Others are taller, stronger players who can score with towering headers or blasted shots. Most crucially of all, strikers have to be able to spot a chance for a goal and go for it. They need to react instinctively, using their vision to time runs into a scoring position. Once on the ball, they rarely have long to shoot. In an instant, strikers have to weigh their options, know where the goal, defenders, and goalie are, and hit a shot with enough speed, bend, or accuracy to beat the goalkeeper.

◀ Canada's Christine Sinclair holds the world record for the most international goals, with 188 scored from 308 games.

FACT FILE

Seventeen women players have scored 100 or more goals for their national team. Seven of these are U.S. players.

◥ Tottenham's Harry Kane, one of the deadliest strikers in the world, has won three Premier League Golden Boots as well as the 2018 World Cup Golden Boot.

▶ France's Kylian Mbappé uses his strength and athleticism to score an acrobatic volleyed goal against Wales in 2021.

◀ Goal scorers need poise and accuracy to put away a chance. Here, the Netherlands' Vivianne Miedema lifts the ball over Zambia's goalie to score at the Tokyo 2020 Olympics.

GOAL-SCORING RECORDS

All-time leading goal scorers
Artur Friedenreich (Brazil)—1,329 goals (1909–39)

Pelé (Brazil)—1,281 goals (1956–77)

Most international goals (men)
115—Cristiano Ronaldo (Portugal), 2004–

Most international goals (women)
188—Christine Sinclair (Canada) 2000–

Most goals in one international match
13—Archie Thompson (Australia), 2001

Fastest international goal
8.1 seconds—Christian Benteke (Belgium) versus Gibraltar, 2016

Fastest international hat trick
Inside 3.5 minutes—Willie Hall (England), 1938

Most hat tricks in consecutive matches
4—Masashi Nakayama for Jubilo Iwata (Japan), 1998

Fastest goal
2 seconds—Vuk Bakic for GSP Polet (Serbia), 2012

Fastest own goal
8 seconds—Pat Kruse for Torquay United (England), 1977

FACT FILE
The world record for own goals in one game is a staggering 149! In the last match of the 2002 Madagascan league season, against champions AS Adema, Stade Olympique l'Emryne repeatedly scored own goals from the kickoff in protest at a refereeing decision in their previous game.

GOAL CELEBRATIONS
As fans celebrate a goal, so do players. For many years, celebrations were no more flamboyant than a punch of the air and a hug from a nearby teammate. That all changed in the 1980s and 1990s, partly thanks to the acrobatic backflips of Mexican striker Hugo Sanchez. Since then, players have rocked imaginary babies, danced the conga, and pulled off spectacular gymnastic moves. Icelandic team Stjarnan FC have gained fame for their elaborate team celebrations, which include all the team members pretending to row a boat and reel in a player acting as a fish. This performance clocked up over a million views on YouTube in 2011. Referees can penalize teams for time-wasting or removing shirts during such celebrations.

▼ Players from the Democratic Republic of Congo dance in line to celebrate a goal at the 2017 Africa Cup of Nations.

FREE KICKS AND PENALTY KICKS

▼ Referee Ravshan Irmatov marks out where Morocco's defensive wall can stand from a Spanish free kick at the 2018 World Cup. The spray marks a point 30 ft. (9.1m) from the ball, and vanishes in minutes.

Referees award a free kick when a player breaks one of the laws of the game. Common free-kick offenses are mistimed tackles, shirt-pulling, obstruction, and offside. There are two types of free kick—indirect, which cannot be scored from without a second player touching the ball, and direct, which can be scored from directly and is awarded for more serious fouls. If a direct free-kick offense is committed by the defending team inside its penalty area, the referee may award a penalty kick.

▶ Max Aarons lies behind the Norwich wall to guard against a low shot in a 2021 Premier League match. This allows the rest of the wall to jump if the free-kick taker aims high.

FREE KICKS

Both types of free kick are taken from where the foul or offense was committed, although a rule change means that in some competitions the referee can move a kick around 30 ft. (9.1m) closer to goal if the other team wastes time or shows dissent. Opposition players must move around 30 ft. (9.1m) away from the ball, giving the team taking the kick valuable possession in space and with time. Some free kicks are taken quickly to get the ball moving in the middle of the field. Wide free kicks are often crossed with pace toward the goal.

Attacking free kicks engage the two teams in a battle of wits. Players on the defending team mark attackers in the penalty area and form a defensive wall to block a direct shot. The kick taker may pass to a teammate in space or try to hit a cross or shot past the wall. Some free kick specialists rely on powerful and direct strikes, while others— such as Paulo Dybala, Hakan Calhanoglu, and Cristiano Ronaldo—are famous for the extreme bend they put on the ball.

◀ Liverpool's Trent Alexander-Arnold strikes across the back of the ball to make it bend over and around West Bromwich Albion's defensive wall.

PENALTY KICKS

Introduced in 1891, a penalty kick is an outstanding opportunity to score. The penalty kick taker is just 36 ft. (11m) away from goal with only the goalie to beat. All other players must stay outside the area until the taker has struck the ball, and a referee can order a penalty kick to be retaken if players encroach. Penalty kick takers must kick the ball forward and cannot touch the ball a second time until it has touched another player—a reason why the taker must stay alert in case it strikes the goalkeeper and rebounds. Some penalty kick takers favor accuracy over power, directing the ball into the corner of the goal. Others prefer a stuttering run to throw the goalie off, or blast the ball hard. For the goalie, trying to figure out where the ball will go is a crucial guessing game.

Germany's U21 goalie Finn Dahmen dives the right way but cannot reach Gustav Isaksen's perfectly placed penalty kick.

Stephanie Labbé holds her nerve to save a penalty kick during Canada's 3–2 shoot-out win over Sweden in the Tokyo 2020 Olympic final.

FACT FILE

During qualifying for the 1954 World Cup, Spain and Turkey tied 2–2 in a playoff. A blindfolded boy, Luigi Franco Gemma, drew lots to decide the winner. Spain was knocked out.

SHOOT-OUT!

Tense and unpredictable, penalty kick shoot-outs bring fans to the edge of their seats. Professional soccer's first shoot-out took place in a 1970 English cup competition between Hull City and Manchester United, with United winning 4–3. The 1972 Asian Nations Cup semifinal between Thailand and South Korea was its first appearance at a major tournament. Germany lost the first European Championships shoot-out to Czechoslovakia in 1976 but defeated France in the first World Cup shoot-out six years later.

SHOOT-OUT RULES

In a shoot-out, five players per team are chosen to take one penalty kick each, all at one end of the field. A shoot-out is not considered to be part of the actual match, meaning that a goal is not added to a player's season or career tally. Neither penalty kick takers nor teammates are allowed to score from a rebound—each player has just one shot at glory. The goalie knows this and often does his or her best to intimidate a penalty kick taker. If the scores are level after each team has taken five penalty kicks, the competition goes into sudden death. Teams take one penalty kick each until one side misses and the other scores.

Some shoot-outs really go the distance. Ivory Coast and the Democratic Republic of Congo contested a 22-penalty-kick shoot-out in the 2015 Africa Cup of Nations semifinal, as did Villareal and Manchester United in the 2021 UEFA Europa League final. In that shoot-out, the first 21 penalty kicks were scored before David de Gea, United's goalie, missed.

FACT FILE

The first ever penalty kick was given by mistake to Scottish club Airdrieonians in March 1891. The new law did not actually take effect until the following season.

MOST PENALTY KICKS IN A SHOOT-OUT

PENS	SHOOT-OUT SCORE	COMPETITION
48	KK Palace 17 Civics 16	Namibian Cup, 2005
44	Argentinos Juniors 20 Racing Club 19	Argentinian league, 1988
40	Obernai 15 ASCA Wittelsheim 15	Coupe de France, 1996

Italy's Gianluigi Donnarumma saves England's fifth and final penalty kick, taken by 19-year-old Bukayo Saka. Donnarumma, Italy's youngest goalkeeper ever, won UEFA's player of the tournament award—the first goalie ever to win the accolade.

SNAPSHOT
SHOOT-OUT SUCCESS

It was a dramatic end to a dramatic tournament in which only two of the 51 matches ended goalless. Italy, the favorite for the EURO 2020 crown, faced a resurgent young England team in a penalty kick shoot-out after the final ended 1–1 after extra time. Both teams had had their chances in open play but now were pitted against each other in the cauldron of an unbearably tense shoot-out watched by hundreds of millions on television.

There had been 21 penalty kick shoot-outs at European Championships before and Italy had taken part in six, more than any other team. It had suffered defeat on three occasions but had already enjoyed shoot-out success in this tournament, knocking Spain out at the semifinal stage. The team also had its EURO 2012 shoot-out win over England to bolster it.

England went ahead after Jordan Pickford's save from Andrea Belotti was sandwiched between two strong penalty kicks by Harry Kane and Harry Maguire. England manager Gareth Southgate had brought on two last-gasp attacking substitutes, Jadon Sancho and Marcus Rashford, with the aim of them taking penalty kicks. It was a bold move but it backfired, with both players failing to convert their attempts. A third miss by England handed Italy its second European Championship crown, 53 years after its victory at EURO 1968.

SOCCER SUPERSTARS

From France's Zinedine Zidane to Argentina's Lionel Messi, soccer has been lit up by the talents of thousands of highly committed and skilled players, all of whom have enthralled spectators and inspired their teams to great achievements. Packed into this section are profiles of more than 70 of the finest players to have graced the game.

FACT FILE
Gordon Banks won FIFA's Goalkeeper of the Year award a record six times.

KEY
COUNTRY = international team · CAPS = international games · GOALS = international goals (to April 2022)

GOALKEEPERS

PETER SCHMEICHEL
DENMARK · BORN 1963 · CAPS: 129 · GOALS: 1

After playing for Hvidøvre and then Brøndby, Schmeichel became one of the best goalies of the 1990s after Alex Ferguson took him to Manchester United in 1991 for the modest fee of $900,000. The high point of his international career came with winning the 1992 European Championships, while the silverware poured in at team level. The hugely committed Dane redefined one-on-one goalkeeping, standing menacingly tall and large or bravely sprawling at an attacker's feet. After winning a triple (Premier League, FA Cup, and UEFA Champions League) with Manchester United in 1999, he moved to Sporting Lisbon and helped the Portuguese team win its first league title in 17 years. He made a surprise return to the Premier League in 2001, with Aston Villa and then Manchester City, before injury forced him to retire.

IKER CASILLAS
SPAIN · BORN 1981
CAPS: 167 · GOALS: 0

Spain's number-one goalie for more than a decade, Casillas played over 700 times for Real Madrid, with whom he won five La Liga titles, before moving to Porto in 2015. In 2000, he became the youngest goalie to play in a UEFA Champions League final, which Real won 3–0. With his razor-sharp reflexes and superb positioning, Casillas was voted goalkeeper of the year five times and captained Spain to two European Championship titles and the 2010 World Cup. He retired in 2020 after suffering a heart attack.

◀ Peter Schmeichel won ten league titles in Denmark, England, and Portugal.

▶ Iker Casillas organizes his defense during a La Liga match between Real Madrid and Celta Vigo.

BEST GOALKEEPER AT THE WORLD CUP

Year	Winner
1994	Michel Preud'homme (Belgium)
1998	Fabien Barthez (France)
2002	Oliver Kahn (Germany)
2006	Gianluigi Buffon (Italy)
2010	Iker Casillas (Spain)
2014	Manuel Neuer (Germany)
2018	Thibault Courtois (Belgium)

GORDON BANKS
ENGLAND • 1937–2019
CAPS: 73 • GOALS: 0

"Banks of England" was as reliable a goalie as any nation could call upon in the 1960s. During his ten-year international career, he kept 35 shutouts and was on the losing team just nine times. His professional career began at Chesterfield, before a $20,000 move took him to Leicester City. In 1962 Banks made his debut for England, with whom he won the 1966 World Cup. The following year, he moved to Stoke City, but a car accident in 1972 caused Banks to lose the sight in his right eye. The accident ended his career in Great Britain, although he did play in the U.S. for the Fort Lauderdale Strikers in 1977–78.

◄ Gordon Banks in action for Stoke City in 1970. Throughout his career, Banks trained tirelessly on angles and repeat drills to improve his strength and agility.

SARAH BOUHADDI
FRANCE • BORN 1986
CAPS: 149 • GOALS: 0

After spells early in her career with CNFE Clairefontaine, Toulouse, and Juvisy, Bouhaddi joined Lyon. There she enjoyed an incredible era of success, playing more than 280 games for the preeminent French club and winning 11 league titles, eight Coupes de France Féminine, and seven UEFA Women's Champions League crowns. Bouhaddi made her debut for France in 2004 and was still playing for her country in 2020.

◄ Bouhaddi issues instructions at the 2019 Women's World Cup. The following year she won the Best FIFA Goalkeeper award.

JAN OBLAK
SLOVENIA • BORN 1993
CAPS: 46 • GOALS: 0

Oblak has been one of the world's best goalies ever since he was part of Benfica's 2013–14 triple-winning team. He became La Liga's most expensive goalkeeper when Atlético Madrid paid around $20 million for his services in 2014, and it has proved a wise investment. Oblak's slick positioning, safe handling, and unflappability saw him break a longstanding La Liga record in 2020 by becoming the fastest goalkeeper to reach 100 shutouts—a feat he managed in 189 matches.

◄ Jan Oblak captained the Slovenian national team for the first time in 2019.

◄ Lev Yashin makes a great save at the 1966 World Cup.

LEV YASHIN
SOVIET UNION • 1929–90
CAPS: 75 • GOALS: 0

In South America, Yashin was called the "Black Spider." In Europe he was the "Black Panther"; but everywhere he was regarded as the finest goalkeeper of his era and, possibly, of all time. Blessed with extraordinary anticipation and agility, Yashin made countless, seemingly impossible saves and stopped as many as 150 penalty kicks during his career, which was spent entirely at Moscow Dynamo. In 1954 he made his debut for the national team. Yashin's bravery, vision, and shot-stopping skills helped the Soviets to an Olympic title in 1956, the European Championship crown in 1960, and a semifinal place at the 1966 World Cup. With Moscow Dynamo, Yashin won six league titles and two Soviet Cups. In 1963 he became the first—and still the only—goalkeeper to win the coveted European Player of the Year award.

GIANLUIGI BUFFON
ITALY • BORN 1978
CAPS: 176 • GOALS: 0

Top goalkeepers can have long careers, but few can surpass the longevity or continued excellence of this Italian veteran, who spent six years at Parma before his world-record $40.5 million transfer to Juventus in 2001. A commanding and reassuring presence in the goal, Buffon spent an incredible 17 consecutive years at Juve (plus two further seasons later on). There, he won ten Serie A championships and five Coppa Italia, and played almost 700 games for the club. For Italy, he won the World Cup in 2006 and reached the EURO 2012 final. One season at PSG (2018–19) was followed in 2021 by an emotional return to his first club, Parma, now playing in Serie B.

▶ Gianluigi Buffon kisses the Serie A trophy in 2018. It was his seventh league title in a row for Juventus.

HOPE SOLO
U.S. • BORN 1981 • CAPS: 202 • GOALS: 0

The United States' best goalie from 2005 to 2016, Solo started her professional career with Philadelphia Charge in 2003 before having spells in Sweden and France and returning to the U.S. with a succession of WUSA and WPS teams. In 2013 she joined the Seattle Reign in the newly formed National Women's Soccer League. She has won Olympic gold twice (2008, 2012) and was a member of the U.S. team that was the runner-up at the 2011 World Cup. Solo was voted goalie of the World Cup—a feat she repeated four years later as her five shutouts helped her team become 2015 champions.

FACT FILE
At EURO 2016, Neuer set a record of 557 minutes without conceding a goal in a major tournament.

▶ Manuel Neuer was voted German player of the year for the 2014–15 season, a rare accolade for a goalkeeper.

MANUEL NEUER
GERMANY • BORN 1986 • CAPS: 109 • GOALS: 0

A dynamic sweeper-keeper, comfortable on the ball, and excellent in one-on-one situations, Neuer joined Schalke 04 in 1991 and didn't leave until 2011, when he moved for a record fee of around $30 million to Bayern Munich. He made an instant impact, notching up over 1,000 minutes without conceding a goal in a string of games in his first season, winning three Bundesliga titles and the 2012–13 UEFA Champions League. Debuting internationally in 2009, he only conceded one goal in Germany's EURO 2012 campaign. More was to come in 2014 when he became a World Cup winner and was voted goalkeeper of the tournament.

DEFENDERS

MARCEL DESAILLY
FRANCE • BORN 1968 • CAPS: 116 • GOALS: 3

Marcel Desailly is world-famous as one of the French players who won the World Cup and European Championship crowns in 1998 and 2000. He was born in the African nation of Ghana and came to France as a young child. A skillful and commanding central defender, Desailly began his career with FC Nantes and then Olympique Marseille. In 1993 he won the Champions League with Marseille, before moving to AC Milan and winning the Champions League again the following year. After a series of outstanding performances at the 1998 World Cup, Desailly moved to Chelsea, where he proved a popular leader. In 2004, Desailly retired from international soccer and left Chelsea to join Qatar's Al-Ittihad club.

FACT FILE
World Cup winner Marcel Desailly became the third player to be sent off in a World Cup final when he was dismissed against Brazil in 1998 after receiving two yellow cards.

▲ Marcel Desailly was nicknamed "The Rock" for his strength and consistency. Here, he holds off Marcus Bent of Ipswich while playing for Chelsea in 2002.

▼ Virgil van Dijk steps across Leeds United's Raphinha to seize possession in typically controlled fashion.

LUCY BRONZE
ENGLAND • BORN 1991
CAPS: 86 • GOALS: 9

Starting out on Sunderland's youth team, this tough-tackling yet skillful defender made her first-team debut at the age of 16. Moving to the United States in 2009, Bronze became the first English player to win the NCAA Cup with the University of North Carolina's Tar Heels. Time at Everton, Liverpool, and Manchester City followed before she signed for Lyon in 2017, where she won both the French league and the UEFA Women's Champions League in 2018. Arguably the most consistent all-around defender in women's soccer, her resolute displays and occasional goal threat helped propel England to third place at the 2015 Women's World Cup. In 2020, she returned to Manchester City and won the FIFA Women's Player award—the first defender to do so.

▶ Lucy Bronze hits a pass for Manchester City in the FA Cup. She has won the trophy twice, in 2017 and 2020.

VIRGIL VAN DIJK
NETHERLANDS • BORN 1991
CAPS: 46 • GOALS: 5

A towering yet calm presence in central defense, van Dijk has justified the enormous $97 million transfer fee Liverpool paid Southampton in 2018 for his services. The Saints had purchased him from Scottish club Celtic for around $20 million two and a half years earlier. Van Dijk began his senior career at Dutch team Groningen before moving to Scotland in 2013, but it was in England that he truly flourished. Powerful and skillful in the air, van Dijk is equally masterful on the ground, where his timing and clean tackling have seen him receive only 11 yellow cards in 186 Premier League appearances. A bad knee injury kept him out of most of the 2020–21 season, but he has returned with his old verve to the relief of his club and the Netherlands, which he has captained since 2018.

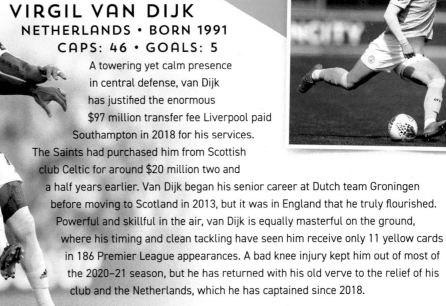

WENDIE RENARD
FRANCE • BORN 1990
CAPS: 129 • GOALS: 32

A defensive rock for club and country, Renard has played all her club soccer for Lyon, with whom she has won a remarkable 14 Division 1 Féminine league titles and seven UEFA Women's Champions Leagues. A strong, fast central defender, she was the tallest player at the 2019 Women's World Cup, at 6 ft. 2 in. (1.87m). She is extremely adept at snuffing out opponents' attacks and driving forward with the ball to link defense and attack. Renard also presents a serious goal-scoring threat herself, especially at set pieces. From 2017–18 onward, she scored a dozen or more goals a season for four consecutive seasons, an incredible feat for a defender.

◄ Wendie Renard uses her body to cushion the ball and bring it under control.

PAOLO MALDINI
ITALY • BORN 1968 • CAPS: 126 • GOALS: 7

One of the best defenders in world soccer, Paolo Maldini was a one-team player. He made his first-team debut for AC Milan in 1985 and played over 900 games for the Italian team, mostly at leftback, although he would also play as a central defender or as a sweeper. Maldini was able to read the game extremely well, tackle cleanly, and move the ball forward accurately. He debuted for Italy in 1988 and soon became a regular on the national team. He played in four World Cups and four European Championships, retiring from international soccer after the 2002 World Cup. Winning seven Serie A titles, Maldini also lifted the Champions League trophy in 2003 and 2007. He eventually retired just before his 41st birthday.

▼ Bobby Moore played more than 500 games on defense for West Ham between 1958 and 1974.

▶ Paolo Maldini, Italy's longest-serving defender, clears the ball out of his penalty area during the 1994 World Cup final against Brazil.

BOBBY MOORE
ENGLAND • 1941–93 • CAPS: 108 • GOALS: 2

England's finest ever defender, Moore appeared to lack the speed and commanding physique to be a great central defender. However, he was blessed with a wonderful eye for the game and always appeared to be one step ahead of opposition attackers. His tackling was clean and precise, and he was very rarely cautioned. One of soccer's truly outstanding captains, Moore led England in 90 games—a record shared with Billy Wright—including the 1966 World Cup triumph. He spent most of his career at West Ham, only joining Fulham (alongside George Best) at the age of 32, before finally moving to the United States to play for Seattle Sounders and San Antonio Thunder. His friendship with Pelé was cemented in 1970 when the two men played out an epic struggle for supremacy in England's World Cup game against Brazil. Pelé called Moore the greatest defender he had played against.

DANIEL PASSARELLA
ARGENTINA
BORN 1953
CAPS: 70 • GOALS: 22

Passarella was a gifted central defender who made surging runs into midfield to build attacks. He was exceptionally good in the air despite being of average height, and he struck devastating free kicks. In 298 Argentinian league matches he scored an astonishing 99 goals. Passarella had success with River Plate before a move to Europe in 1982, first to Fiorentina and then to Internazionale. In 1985–86, he scored 11 goals for Fiorentina, a record for a defender that lasted for 15 years. He won the 1978 World Cup, played in the 1982 tournament, and was chosen to play in 1986 but was sidelined through injury. After retiring, Passarella became a coach, managing Argentina at the 1998 World Cup.

FRANZ BECKENBAUER
WEST GERMANY • BORN 1945 • CAPS: 103 • GOALS: 14

Der Kaiser ("The King") made his debut for Bayern Munich in 1964 as an attacking inside-left. Only 27 games later, he was on the national team. At the 1966 World Cup, Beckenbauer played in midfield and scored four goals on the way to the final. By the 1970 tournament, he had moved into defense, where he revolutionized the ultradefensive role of sweeper with his astonishing vision and smooth on-ball skills. Time and again he would turn defense into attack, striding up the field to release teammates or to take a chance himself. With his stylish attacking play, it is sometimes forgotten that he was a masterful defender, always cool under pressure. In 1972 Beckenbauer won the European Championships with West Germany and was European Footballer of the Year. Two years later, he won the first of three consecutive European Cups with Bayern Munich and also captained his country to World Cup glory. In 1977, he made a surprise move to the United States, playing on a star-studded New York Cosmos team before returning to Germany in 1980 with Hamburg. He became West Germany's coach in 1984, leading the team to two World Cup finals and winning one.

THIAGO SILVA
BRAZIL • BORN 1984
CAPS: 105 • GOALS: 7

Tough and skillful, Silva can play in any position across the defense and actually started out as a midfielder in Brazil before moving to Europe in 2004. After spells at Porto and Dynamo Moscow, where he contracted tuberculosis and almost quit soccer, Silva joined Fluminense and helped them win their very first Copa do Brazil in 2007. AC Milan paid $14 million to bring him back to Europe in 2009, where he won the 2010–11 Serie A before becoming the world's most expensive defender with a move to Paris Saint-Germain. Silva won the 2013 FIFA Confederations Cup and the 2019 Copa América with Brazil, and in 2020 moved to Chelsea.

◄ Franz Beckenbauer at the 1974 World Cup. Sixteen years later, he became the second man—after Brazil's Mario Zagalo—to have won the World Cup as both a player and a manager.

▼ Thiago Silva strikes a long, accurate crossfield pass during Chelsea's UEFA Champions League game against Zenit St. Petersburg.

RUUD KROL
NETHERLANDS • BORN 1949
CAPS: 83 • GOALS: 4

Krol was a vital part of the great Ajax and Dutch "total soccer" teams of the late 1960s and 1970s, comfortable playing in almost any defensive position. With Ajax he won six league titles and two European Cups (1972 and 1973). Krol was the last of the Ajax greats to move away when, in 1980, he played for Vancouver Whitecaps in Canada. He returned to Europe the following year to play for Napoli and later for Cannes in the French second division, where injury forced him to retire in 1987. He has since managed in a variety of countries, including Switzerland, Egypt, and Belgium.

▶ Ruud Krol evades a sliding tackle from France's Didier Six in a World Cup qualifier in 1981.

LINDA MEDALEN
NORWAY • BORN 1965 • CAPS: 152 • GOALS: 64

Medalen started her career as a striker, making her debut for Norway in 1987 and going on to win the 1988 unofficial Women's World Cup and the 1993 European Championships. At the 1991 World Cup she was her team's top scorer, with six goals, as Norway finished runner-up. As Medalen's career progressed, she moved into defense, where her skill in the air and strong tackling helped Norway win the 1995 World Cup, conceding just one goal in six games. Medalen played in the 1999 tournament, but a knee injury kept her out of the 2000 Olympics, which Norway won. At club level, she won five league championships and three cup competitions for the Norwegian team Asker SKK.

▲ John Charles (center) leaps for the ball. Charles's name is still revered by Juventus fans, who nicknamed him *Il Buon Gigante*—the Gentle Giant.

▶ Linda Medalen tackles China's legendary midfielder Sun Wen at the 1999 World Cup.

JOHN CHARLES
WALES • 1931–2004 • CAPS: 38 • GOALS: 21

The gloriously talented Charles was equally skilled as a bustling, powerful center-forward or as a hugely commanding central defender. In both positions, he was world class. Appearing on attack for Leeds United, he scored a record 42 goals in one season, while playing internationally as a central defender. On the Welsh team, Charles was joined by his brother, Mel, and teammates Ivor and Len Allchurch—the first time that any national team had included two pairs of brothers. In 1957 the British transfer record was smashed as he moved to Juventus for $185,000. Charles became a genuine legend in Italy for his towering performances, generous behavior toward fans, and his sportsmanship. In a highly defense-minded league he scored an astonishing 93 goals in 155 matches, helping Juve win three Serie A titles and two Coppa Italia. He later moved back to Leeds, then on to Parma, Cardiff City, and Hereford United before retiring.

GEORGIO CHIELLINI
ITALY • BORN 1984
CAPS: 116 • GOALS: 8

Strong, aggressive, and streetwise, Chiellini has been a mainstay of the Juventus defense either at leftback or in central defense since the mid-2000s. He formed a strong defensive partnership with Leonardo Bonucci, with whom he played for club and country through most of the 2010s. During that decade, Chiellini won nine Serie A titles and numerous other trophies. At international level, he was part of Italy's EURO 2012 team that reached the final and captained his country for the first time later that year. Nine years later, he led Italy to EURO 2020 glory.

▶ Georgio Chiellini celebrates Italy's dramatic EURO 2020 final win over England on penalties.

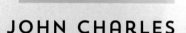

MIDFIELDERS AND WINGERS

KEVIN DE BRUYNE
BELGIUM • BORN 1991 • CAPS: 88 • GOALS: 23

A complete, modern midfielder, de Bruyne is comfortable striding forward in possession, delivering telling passes and assists, and making shots himself. He started at Genk before he was bought by Chelsea, which moved him on loan to Werder Bremen and then sold him to Vfl Wolfsburg. There, he set a new Bundesliga record with 21 assists in the 2014–15 season. Weeks after assisting for the winning goal that defeated Bayern Munich in the 2015 DFL-Supercup, de Bruyne moved to Manchester City for around $84.7 million. He has since become the lynchpin of a team that won three league titles between 2018 and 2021 and reached the final of the 2020–21 UEFA Champions League.

◄ Manchester City's Kevin de Bruyne controls the ball with the outside of his foot.

CARLOS VALDERRAMA
COLOMBIA • BORN 1961
CAPS: 110 • GOALS: 10

Famous for his flamboyant style of play and hairstyle, Carlos Valderrama was an exquisite passer of the ball in midfield, who would often link with the attack for a devastating effect. He played for three Colombian teams—Union Magdalena, Millionarios, and Deportiva Cali—before moving to France in 1988, where he won the league title with Montpellier. In 1996 he moved to the United States to play for Tampa Bay Mutiny and then Miami Fusion. Valderrama captained Colombia to three World Cup tournaments in a row (1990–98) and retired from international soccer after the 1998 tournament. Yet, even past his 40th birthday, Valderrama was still one of the biggest stars in the MLS.

◄ Landon Donovan prepares to pick out a teammate with a pass during an MLS game between LA Galaxy and FC Dallas.

► Carlos Valderrama on the ball during Colombia's 1998 World Cup game against England.

LANDON DONOVAN
U.S. • BORN 1982
CAPS: 157 • GOALS: 57

Donovan came to prominence early when he was voted the best player of the 1999 FIFA Under-17 World Championship and was signed the same year by Bayer Leverkusen. Returning to the United States on loan with the San Jose Earthquakes, Donovan would later have short loan spells with Bayern Munich and Everton, but in 2005 he joined LA Galaxy. He won five MLS Cups, three with LA Galaxy and two with the San Jose Earthquakes, as well as winning the CONCACAF Gold Cup three times with the U.S. team. Two-footed and capable of devastating attacking bursts from midfield, Donovan's eye for a goal saw him score more than 160 times in the MLS and other U.S. club competitions. His 57 goals make him far and away the U.S. national team's most prolific goal scorer.

FACT FILE

Andrés Iniesta's consistency saw him voted into FIFA's World XI nine seasons in a row (2009–19).

XAVI HERNÁNDEZ
SPAIN • BORN 1980
CAPS: 133 • GOALS: 12

Rising through the ranks of youth and reserve teams at Barcelona, Xavi made his first-team debut in 1998 and played over 750 games for the Spanish club before moving to Qatar in 2015 to play for Al Sadd. With Barcelona, he won eight La Liga titles and four Champions Leagues and enjoyed EURO 2008, 2012, and 2010 World Cup glory with Spain. Brilliant at finding space even in the most crowded parts of the fields, Xavi was known as a passing maestro—enabling his team to keep possession and attack.

ANDRÉS INIESTA
SPAIN • BORN 1984
CAPS: 131 • GOALS: 13

Quick feet and an even quicker soccer brain enabled this slight midfielder to become one of the most celebrated players in world soccer. Joining Barcelona as a youth teamer, Iniesta later formed a formidable central midfield partnership with Xavi Hernández for both club and country. With Barcelona, he won nine La Liga titles, four Champions Leagues, and six Spanish Super Cups. Internationally, he scored the winning goal in the 2010 World Cup final.

◀ Xavi and Andrés Iniesta celebrate winning the UEFA Champions League in 2015.

DAVID BECKHAM
ENGLAND • BORN 1975
CAPS: 115 • GOALS: 17

David Beckham is one of the most recognizable soccer players on the planet. He began his career as a youth-team player at Manchester United and then had a short loan stint with Preston North End, before announcing his arrival in English soccer with a Premiership goal from inside his own half against Wimbledon. At the 1998 World Cup he was heavily criticized for kicking out at Argentina's Diego Simeone and receiving a red card. But Beckham's excellence for team and country, particularly his trademark swerving free kicks, won back public support—notably when he ensured England's qualification for the 2002 World Cup with a last-gasp free kick against Greece. He also won "the triple" of Champions League, Premiership, and FA Cup with Manchester United in 1999. When David Beckham joined Paris Saint-Germain in 2013, he donated his entire salary to a local children's charity. He became the first English player to win the league in four different countries (England, Spain, the U.S., and France). He is now a co-owner of MLS team Inter Miami CF.

◀ David Beckham salutes the crowd during a 2019 friendly between the triple-winning 1999 Manchester United team and their rivals in the 1999 Champions League final, Bayern Munich.

HRISTO STOICHKOV
BULGARIA • BORN 1966
CAPS: 83 • GOALS: 37

As an attacking midfielder or a striker, the strong, stocky Stoichkov was surprisingly quick over a short distance and possessed unstoppable power, particularly in his left foot. He emerged as a skillful young player at CSKA Sofia before moving to Barcelona. Unpredictable and with a fiery temper, Stoichkov became dissatisfied with Barcelona coach Johan Cruyff when he was asked to play out wide. He later moved to Italy's Parma, Japanese team Kashiwa Reysol, and the Chicago Fire in the MLS. He arrived at the 1994 World Cup as the star player on an underrated Bulgarian team that sensationally knocked out Germany before losing the semifinal to Italy. Stoichkov finished the tournament as joint top scorer.

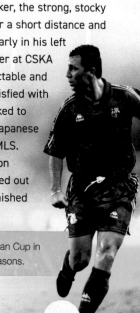

▶ At Barcelona, Stoichkov won the European Cup in 1992 and five La Liga titles in just seven seasons.

MICHEL PLATINI
FRANCE • BORN 1955 • CAPS: 72 • GOALS: 41

A truly great attacking midfielder, Platini was the glittering jewel on a French team that suffered semifinal heartbreak at the 1982 World Cup. Two years later he was top scorer at the European Championships (nine goals) as France won the title. In partnership with Alan Giresse and Jean Tigana, Platini exhibited immense skill and vision. At club level, Platini played for AS Joeuf, Nancy, and Saint-Étienne before turning down a transfer to Arsenal in favor of Italian giants Juventus in 1982. He was Serie A's leading marksman three times and was crowned European Footballer of the Year three times in a row (1983–85)—a unique feat. Retiring in 1987, he went on to coach France and then led his country's bid to host the 1998 World Cup. In 2007, he became president of UEFA.

◀ Michel Platini during France's 4–1 win over Northern Ireland at the 1982 World Cup.

GARRINCHA
BRAZIL • 1933–83
CAPS: 50 • GOALS: 12

Manuel Francisco dos Santos was nicknamed Garrincha—meaning "little bird"— at a young age. A small player at only 5 ft. 6 in. (1.69m) tall, a childhood illness had left his legs distorted, with one bent inward and the other 2.4 in. (6cm) shorter. Yet those who saw Garrincha play remember him as the greatest dribbler in the history of soccer. He played for Botafogo in Brazil but also for clubs in Colombia and Italy, and in France for Red Star Paris. It was on the international stage, however, that Garrincha became famous. He starred in the 1958 World Cup, which Brazil won, but eclipsed those performances at the 1962 competition. Voted player of the tournament, he was joint leading scorer as he struck two goals to knock out England in the quarterfinal, and then two more to beat Chile in the semifinal. Sadly, his life away from soccer was troubled, and he died of alcohol poisoning at the age of 49.

▶ Garrincha perfected the bending banana kick, which he used to great effect for Brazilian team Botafogo, scoring 232 goals in 581 matches.

DZSENIFER MAROZSÁN
GERMANY • BORN 1992
CAPS: 109 • GOALS: 33

Born in Hungary, Marozsán moved to Germany when she was a child so that her father could play for FC Saarbrücken. She played for the women's team there, and in 2007, at the age of 14 years and 7 months, became the youngest player to appear in the women's Bundesliga. In 2009, she moved to FFC Frankfurt, winning the UEFA Women's Champions League in 2014–15. A skilled and relentless passer, Marozsán is unflashy but very effective, and she became a vital cog on a star-studded Lyon team after her transfer in 2016. In 2021, after winning four league titles with Lyon, she went on loan to the OL Reign of the U.S. National Women's Soccer League.

FACT FILE
Garrincha retired in 1966, after Brazil's loss to Hungary in the World Cup. Astonishingly, in his 50 matches it was the only time he was on the losing team for Brazil.

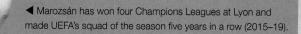

◀ Marozsán has won four Champions Leagues at Lyon and made UEFA's squad of the season five years in a row (2015–19).

ZINEDINE ZIDANE
FRANCE • BORN 1972
CAPS: 108 • GOALS: 31

The son of Algerian immigrants, Zidane grew up in Marseille with posters of his idol, Uruguayan striker Enzo Francescoli, on his wall. His first club was Cannes, followed by Bordeaux, where he won France's Young Player of the Year award in 1992. On his international debut in 1994, he scored both of France's goals in a 2–2 tie with the Czech Republic. In 1995–96, Zidane played 57 games—more than any other French player—and he appeared jaded as he underperformed at EURO '96. But a move to Juventus in the same year saw him regain his best form, as he helped the Serie A giants win two league titles. Zidane was a key part of the world-beating French team that captured a double of World Cup (1998) and European Championships (2000). As the best midfielder in the world, he won World Player of the Year titles in 1998, 2000, and 2003. Zidane's last tournament, the 2006 World Cup, was memorable as he led France to the final, scoring three goals on the way and being voted FIFA's player of the tournament. He was sent off in the final, however, for a headbutt to the chest of Italy's Marco Materazzi.

◀ Zidane in action during France's 3–1 win over Spain at the 2006 World Cup.

CRISTIANO RONALDO
PORTUGAL • BORN 1985
CAPS: 186 • GOALS: 115

A winger who, in his later years, has played more as a center forward, Ronaldo began his career on the Portuguese island of Madeira before joining Sporting Clube de Portugal. After impressing in a preseason friendly (exhibition game), he joined Manchester United in 2003, where he blossomed into one of the world's greatest attackers, bewildering defenders with tricks and speed, outstanding ball control, and masterful free kicks. His team performances helped propel Manchester United to three successive Premier League titles as well as the Champions League crown in 2008. Ronaldo joined Real Madrid in 2009 for a world-record fee of $130 million. He made a huge impact, scoring 450 goals in just 438 games as he won four Champions League and two Spanish league titles with the Spanish giants. He captained Portugal to EURO 2016 and UEFA Nations League 2019 glory, by which time he was freely scoring for Juventus, netting 101 goals in 138 games before returning to Manchester United in 2021.

▶ Cristiano Ronaldo has captained Portugal since 2008 and is his country's most-capped player and leading scorer.

WORLD-RECORD TRANSFERS

PLAYER	FROM	TO	FEE	YEAR
Neymar	Barcelona	Paris Saint-Germain	$263 million	2017
Kylian Mbappé	Monaco	Paris Saint-Germain	$216 million	2018
Philippe Coutinho	Liverpool	Barcelona	$195.5 million	2018
Ousmane Dembélé	B. Dortmund	Barcelona	$158.5 million	2017
João Félix	Benfica	Atlético Madrid	$142 million	2019
Jack Grealish	Aston Villa	Manchester City	$138 million	2021
Antoine Griezmann	Atlético Madrid	Barcelona	$135 million	2019
Romelu Lukaku	Inter Milan	Chelsea	$135 million	2021
Cristiano Ronaldo	Manchester Utd.	Real Madrid	$130 million	2009
Paul Pogba	Juventus	Manchester United	$120 million	2016
Cristiano Ronaldo	Real Madrid	Juventus	$117 million	2018

PAUL POGBA
FRANCE • BORN 1993
CAPS: 91 • GOALS: 11

This powerhouse central midfielder can play further forward or wide, where his surging runs open up defenses. He joined Manchester United from Le Havre in 2009, but limited opportunities to play saw him move to Juventus on a free transfer in 2012. There, he turned games with bursts of rapid skill, power, and audacity as Juve won Serie A in all four seasons he was part of the squad. Transfer rumors swirled near the end of his time in Italy, but it was still a surprise when Manchester United broke their own transfer record to pay $120 million to bring him back. At club level, he has both inspired and infuriated teammates and fans, while on the international stage he has a World Cup winners' medal after France's triumph in 2018.

◀ Paul Pogba looks for an opening in attack for France against Wales in 2021.

MICHAEL LAUDRUP
DENMARK • BORN 1964 • CAPS: 104 • GOALS: 37

The peak of Michael Laudrup's international career came in the quarterfinals of the 1998 World Cup, when Denmark lost narrowly to Brazil 3–2—despite his younger brother, Brian, scoring a goal. Laudrup was much in demand as an attacking midfielder, playing for Lazio and Juventus in Italy and winning five league titles in Spain with Barcelona and Real Madrid. Sadly, he missed out on Denmark's finest hour—its EURO '92 championship triumph, when he argued about tactics with the coach and was dropped from the team.

FACT FILE
Michael Laudrup is the only player to have appeared for Real Madrid in a 5-0 win over Barcelona and also for Barcelona when they have beaten Real 5-0.

▲ Michael Laudrup drives effortlessly forward during a 1996 friendly match against Germany.

CARLI LLOYD
U.S. • BORN 1982 • CAPS: 316 • GOALS: 134

A livewire attacker with stamina, pace, and a lethal shot, Lloyd played for W-League team New Jersey Splash while still in high school. She made her international debut at age 23 and became a fixture on the U.S. women's team that won two Olympic gold medals and the 2015 World Cup. In that competition, Lloyd was at her peak, scoring six times, including a hat trick in the final that featured a goal from the halfway line. Lloyd was made player of the tournament and was also voted the world's best female soccer player in both 2015 and 2016. Except for a short spell in 2017–18 with Manchester City, Lloyd's club career was spent entirely in the U.S. with teams including Chicago Red Stars and Western New York Flash. In 2021 she announced her retirement, going out with a bang by scoring five goals in a friendly against Paraguay.

▶ Carli Lloyd celebrates a 4–3 U.S. victory over Australia to win Olympic bronze in 2021.

AMANDINE HENRY
FRANCE • BORN 1989
CAPS: 93 • GOALS: 13

Henry's first season in senior soccer saw the bustling midfielder score 11 goals in 20 games for Henin-Beaumont—an outstanding return considering she was just 15. After two years at France's female soccer academy, Clairefontaine, she joined Lyon. Severe injuries blighted her early time there before she got the chance to shine. Henry mostly operates as a central or defensive midfielder, intercepting attacks and setting up her own team's forward play using her expert eye for a pass. She has been a valuable asset for title-winning Lyon and France, with whom she won the Silver Ball as the second-best player at the 2015 Women's World Cup.

▶Amandine Henry moves upfield against Brazil at the 2019 World Cup. She scored the extra-time winner.

MOHAMED SALAH
EGYPT • BORN 1992 • CAPS: 84 • GOALS: 47

The "Egyptian King" is beloved by neutrals and Egypt and Liverpool fans alike for his exuberant play and humble personality. A seemingly slight frame disguises his strength, sudden acceleration and excellence in dribbling, creating chances for teammates, and scoring audacious goals. After three seasons in the Egyptian Premier League and a spell in Switzerland with Basel, Salah was signed by Chelsea in 2014 but was given little chance to make an impact, playing just 13 league games before he was loaned out to Fiorentina and then Roma, who signed him permanently. A season later he joined Liverpool for $49 million, making an immediate impact with 44 goals in his debut season. He has barely let up since, taking just 151 games to notch 100 league goals.

► Salah won the Champions League in 2019 and the Premier League in 2020.

JAIRZINHO
BRAZIL • BORN 1944
CAPS: 82 • GOALS: 34

Jair Ventura Filho, better known as "Jairzinho," was an electrifying right-winger in a similar mold to his childhood hero, Garrincha. First capped for Brazil in 1964, he was moved to the left wing to accommodate Garrincha in the 1966 World Cup. At the 1970 tournament Jairzinho was moved back to his favored right side, where he shone, scoring in each of the six rounds of the competition—a record to this day. At club level, Jairzinho spent most of his career at Brazil's Botafogo, also having short stints with Marseille in France, Portuguesa in Venezuela, and the Brazilian team Cruzeiro, with whom he won the Copa América in 1976.

▲ Jairzinho worked as a ball boy at Botafogo before going on to make over 400 appearances for the Rio-based team.

SUN WEN
CHINA • BORN 1973
CAPS: 152 • GOALS: 106

A legend in women's soccer, Sun Wen won seven regional championships with Chinese team Shanghai TV before moving to the United States in 2000 to play for Atlanta Beat. Playing in midfield or attack, she became one of the world's leading international goal scorers, thanks to her strong shooting, vision, and eye for a goal. Sun Wen won both the Golden Boot (top scorer) and the Golden Ball (top player) awards at the 1999 Women's World Cup, where China was narrowly beaten on penalties in the final by the United States. In 2000, she was named FIFA World Player of the Century alongside the U.S. player Michelle Akers. After China's surprise World Cup exit at the hands of Canada in 2003, she retired.

LUKA MODRIC
CROATIA • BORN 1983
CAPS: 148 • GOALS: 21

A finalist with Croatia at the 2018 World Cup, where he was voted the tournament's best player, Modric is a skilled playmaker with an eye for the perfect pass. After long stints with Dinamo Zagreb and Tottenham Hotspur, Modric joined Real Madrid in 2012, with whom he has won four UEFA Champions Leagues. In 2018, he won the Ballon D'Or as the world's best soccer player.

◄ Luka Modric makes a typically slick and accurate sidefoot pass for Croatia.

STRIKERS

JOHAN CRUYFF
NETHERLANDS • 1947–2016
CAPS: 48 • GOALS: 33

Cruyff was one of the game's finest ever players and a pivotal part of the Dutch "total soccer" revolution. Blessed with great vision and remarkable ball skills, he is the only player to have a move named after him—the Cruyff turn. He won three European Cups in a row at Ajax before following his ex-boss, Rinus Michels, to Barcelona in 1973 and helping them win Spanish league and cup titles. Cruyff played as a center forward but would drift around the field, creating confusion among defenders. His total of 33 goals for the Netherlands would have been higher were it not for his refusal to play in the 1978 World Cup (see page 110). Cruyff later managed both Ajax and Barcelona to success in Europe.

▲ After Barcelona, Cruyff played for two seasons in the U.S.

◄ George Best won two First Division titles and the European Cup in 11 seasons at Manchester United.

GEORGE BEST
N. IRELAND
1946–2005
CAPS: 37
GOALS: 9

Best was only 17 when he made his first-team debut for Manchester United. He was the most gifted player to emerge from the British Isles—and its first superstar. Best's goal-scoring exploits and his eye for an outrageous pass or move quickly made him a legend. He was also a fearless tackler and great dribbler and was Manchester United's leading scorer five seasons in a row. Sadly, he was denied the biggest stage of all as Northern Ireland failed to qualify for the World Cup during his career. In 1974 Best sensationally retired from the game. He made a series of comebacks in England, the U.S., and, finally, Australia, where he appeared for the Brisbane Lions in 1983.

ROBERT LEWANDOWSKI
POLAND • BORN 1988 • CAPS: 129 • GOALS: 75

An absolute goal machine, Lewandowski has scored wherever he has played. He started out on Polish lower league teams before two seasons at Lech Poznań earned him a move to Borussia Dortmund. A quiet first season was contrasted by an explosion of goal scoring in the three that followed. His record since joining Bayern Munich in 2014 is outstanding—333 goals in 361 matches. In 2020–21 he broke Gerd Muller's record of most Bundesliga goals in a season with 41 in just 29 games. In 2021 his talent finally received the recognition it deserves with FIFA's Best Male Player award.

FERENC PUSKAS
HUNGARY • 1927–2006 • CAPS: 84
(4 FOR SPAIN) • GOALS: 83

A star for his club, Kispest (which became Honved), and his country, Puskas was short, stocky, and an average header of the ball. But his sublime skills, vision, and thunderbolt of a left-foot shot made him a devastating striker. After the Hungarian revolution in 1956, Puskas searched for a club in western Europe for more than a year. In his thirties and overweight, he was eventually signed by Real Madrid in 1958. He repaid Real's faith by heading the Spanish goal-scoring table four times, netting four goals in the 1960 European Cup final and a hat trick in the 1962 final. In 1966 he began a coaching career, which saw him take Greek team Panathinaikos to the 1971 European Cup final.

◄ Poland's Robert Lewandowski lines up a tricky sidefoot volley during a World Cup qualifier against Andorra.

LIONEL MESSI
ARGENTINA • BORN 1987
CAPS: 160 • GOALS: 81

Locals in the Argentinian city of Rosario knew they were seeing a special talent when Messi, not yet in his teens, powered his local children's soccer team to lose just one game in four years. Moving from Argentina to Spain at the age of 13, Messi was schooled on Barcelona's youth teams before making his official debut for the first team at the age of 17. He won ten La Liga, seven Copa del Rey, and four UEFA Champions League titles with the Spanish giants, as well as 2008 Olympic gold with Argentina. His close control, vision, and flair is almost unparalleled in the modern game. The 2009–10 season saw Messi score 47 goals, and the following season he upped this to a staggering 73 goals in all competitions. By 2021, Messi had scored 30-plus goals every season for 13 seasons in a row. In that year, he failed to agree a deal with Barcelona and moved to Paris Saint-Germain.

▶ Lionel Messi surges forward for Argentina, perfectly balanced, looking for an opening to attack.

▶ Dennis Bergkamp made more than 400 appearances for Arsenal, scoring 120 goals.

FACT FILE
A 2021 hat trick versus Bolivia made Lionel Messi South America's leading international goal scorer, beating Pelé's record.

DENNIS BERGKAMP
NETHERLANDS • BORN 1969
CAPS: 79 • GOALS: 37

Named after the Scottish striker Denis Law, Bergkamp was a product of the famous Ajax youth academy. He played in the Dutch league for the first time in 1986. The most technically gifted Dutch soccer player since Cruyff, Bergkamp often played in the space between midfield and attack, where he used his eye for an unexpected pass, plus world-class technique, to create as many goals as he scored. After an unsuccessful spell at Internazionale, Bergkamp moved to Arsenal for $12 million in 1995. In his 11 years at the club, he won three Premier League titles and scored or set up more than 280 goals. He retired in May 2006 after the final of the Champions League against Barcelona.

GAME ACTION
Dennis Bergkamp broke the deadlock in a tense 1998 World Cup quarterfinal against Argentina with a sensational goal. On the stroke of 90 minutes, Frank de Boer hit a 164 ft. (50m) pass into the penalty area. Controlling the ball with one delicate touch of his right foot, Bergkamp took a second touch to turn Argentinian defender Roberto Ayala, before shooting powerfully past goalie Carlos Roa. The goal saw Bergkamp become the Netherlands' leading international scorer.

ANDRIY SHEVCHENKO
UKRAINE • BORN 1976 CAPS: 111 • GOALS: 48

Shevchenko scored just one goal in 16 games in his first season at Dynamo Kyiv, but his perfect blend of speed and power propelled Kyiv to five Ukrainian league titles and strong showings in the Champions League. A multimillion-dollar transfer to AC Milan followed in 1999. On three occasions Shevchenko scored 24 goals per season in the ultratough Italian league. In 2004 he was voted European Footballer of the Year. Two years later he moved to Chelsea for around $59 million but returned to Milan on loan for the 2008–09 season. He then returned to Kyiv, where he made more than 80 appearances before retiring in 2012.

◀ Shevchenko on the move for Ukraine in a World Cup qualifier in 2005.

▶ Spain's Raúl was the top scorer in qualifying for EURO 2000, with ten goals from eight games. Here, he evades a tackle during EURO 2004.

RAÚL
SPAIN • BORN 1977
CAPS: 102
GOALS: 44

Raúl González Blanco made his debut for the Real Madrid first team at 17—their youngest player ever—and went on to score six times in his first 11 games. In the years that followed, Raúl became the biggest star in Spanish soccer and the country's all-time leading goal scorer. At club level, he won two Spanish league titles and three Champions Leagues with Real Madrid. Top scorer in the Spanish league twice, Raúl's goals in the 2003–04 Champions League campaign saw him become the first player to net more than 40 times in the competition.

GERD MÜLLER
WEST GERMANY • 1945–2021
CAPS: 62 • GOALS: 68

"The Bomber," as Gerd Müller was nicknamed, holds a series of goal-scoring records. From 1963, he scored a club record of 365 goals in 427 league matches for Bayern Munich. During 16 years with Bayern, he won four Bundesliga titles, four German Cups, and three European Cups. For his country, Müller held one of the greatest international striking records, scoring more than a goal every game. His two strikes against the Soviet Union helped West Germany win the 1972 European Championships. Müller's tally of 14 World Cup goals remained a record until 2006, while his final international goal won West Germany the 1974 World Cup on home soil.

▶ Gerd Müller (right) battles Konrad Weise of East Germany in 1974.

ROBERTO BAGGIO
ITALY • BORN 1967 • CAPS: 57 • GOALS: 27

Blessed with great skill and vision, Roberto Baggio made his professional debut with Vicenza (in the Italian third division) at just 15 years of age. He broke into Italy's Serie A with Fiorentina in 1985, and when Baggio was transferred to Juventus in 1990, three days of rioting by Fiorentina fans ensued. The fee of $13 million made him the world's most expensive player at that time. Crowned World Footballer of the Year in 1993, Baggio scored spectacular goals for his country and his clubs, AC Milan, Bologna, Inter Milan, and Brescia. In 2004, while playing for Brescia, he scored his 200th Serie A goal. He appeared in three World Cups and scored five out of Italy's eight goals in the 1994 competition. However, Baggio will always be remembered for his costly penalty kick miss in the final of the tournament. The striker was given an emotional sendoff in 2004 when he played for Italy for the first time in five years, in an exhibition game against Spain.

ERLING HAALAND
NORWAY
BORN 2000
CAPS: 17 • GOALS: 15

The son of Alf-Inge Håland, who played for Leeds United, Manchester City, and Norway, Haaland began at his father's home club, Bryne. He moved to Molde under the management of Ole Gunnar Solskjær and, in 2019, to Red Bull Salzburg. There he scored three hat tricks within months of arriving and a further three goals on his UEFA Champions League debut. Haaland is an explosive, lethal striker, fully exploiting his height—6 ft. 4 in. (1.94m)—mobility, aggression, and incredible finishing skills. A big-money move to Borussia Dortmund did not stem his flow of goals. In his first two and a half seasons, he averaged over a goal a game, making him one of the hottest properties in world soccer.

BOBBY CHARLTON
ENGLAND • BORN 1937 • CAPS: 106 • GOALS: 49

Except for a final season with Preston North End, Charlton was a one-team player with Manchester United, for whom he made his debut in 1956. Known around the globe for his trophy-winning exploits in both the World Cup and the European Cup, Charlton was one of the few survivors of the devastating Munich, Germany, airplane crash, which claimed the lives of many of his Manchester United teammates. As a player he showed great sportsmanship and dedication—in training, he even wore a slipper on his right foot to encourage him to pass and shoot with his weaker left foot. Operating as a deep-lying center forward with a phenomenal shot from either foot, Charlton scored 245 times from 751 appearances in total for the club. He was knighted in 1994.

▶ Bobby Charlton's 1970 World Cup campaign was his fourth in a row as part of the England squad.

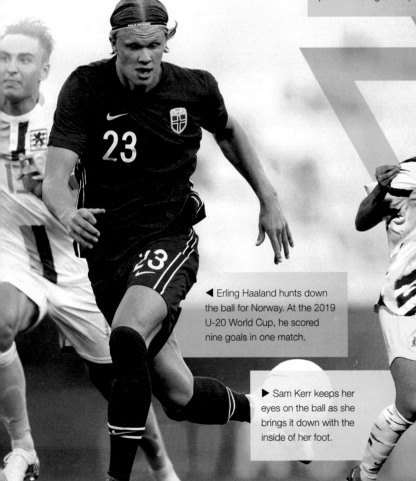

◀ Erling Haaland hunts down the ball for Norway. At the 2019 U-20 World Cup, he scored nine goals in one match.

▶ Sam Kerr keeps her eyes on the ball as she brings it down with the inside of her foot.

SAM KERR
AUSTRALIA • BORN 1993
CAPS: 108 • GOALS: 56

Astonishingly, Sam Kerr made both her W-League debut for Perth Glory and her national team debut at the age of 15. A prodigious talent, Kerr has developed into a reliable goal scorer who does her best work in and around the opponent's penalty area. Most of her goals are followed by her trademark backflip celebration. Much in demand, Kerr played for Sydney FC and three U.S. clubs—Western New York Flash, Sky Blue FC, and Chicago Red Stars—before moving to Chelsea in 2019. Internationally, Kerr has appeared at three Women's World Cups and in 2019 became the first Australian, male or female, to score a World Cup hat trick.

DIEGO MARADONA
ARGENTINA • 1960–2020
CAPS: 91 • GOALS: 34

Diego Armando Maradona was a phenomenal player. Stocky and with a low center of gravity, he conjured mesmeric, weaving runs through the tightest defenses, lightning turns that left opponents kicking at thin air, and sublime shots, chips, and flicks. Maradona debuted at the age of 15 for Argentinos Juniors. Calls for his inclusion in the 1978 World Cup team were ignored by Argentina's coach, Cesar Luis Menotti, but he would appear at the next four tournaments. His finest hour came in 1986, when Maradona was the player of the tournament as he skippered an unremarkable team to World Cup victory (see pages 54–55). Maradona captained Argentina at the 1990 World Cup, where he reached the final, but the following year he failed a drug test and was banned for 15 months. A further failed test during the 1994 World Cup saw him sent home after playing the first two games. His international career was over. After retiring, Maradona battled with drug addiction, but in 2000 he was the joint winner of FIFA's Footballer of the Century award with Pelé.

▶ Maradona holds the Argentinian record for most World Cup appearances—21 games.

ZICO
BRAZIL • BORN 1953
CAPS: 72 • GOALS: 52

Artur Antunes Coimbra (known as Zico) was given a special diet and training regime to build him up when he first arrived at the Brazilian club Flamengo. Sharp, quick-witted, and with the ability to hit an explosive shot or a deadly free kick, Zico won four league titles with Flamengo, as well as the Copa Libertadores and the World Club Cup in 1981. He scored a staggering 591 goals in his first 11 seasons with Flamengo. He went on to play in Asia for Kashima Antlers, and in 2002 he became manager of Japan's national team.

FACT FILE
Diego Maradona's moves to Barcelona in 1982 (for $7 million) and then to Napoli in 1984 (for $9 million) were both world-record transfers. After nine years at Napoli and a spell at Sevilla, he returned to Argentina with Newell's Old Boys and Boca Juniors.

RUUD GULLIT
N'LANDS • BORN 1962
CAPS: 66 • GOALS: 17

In 1978 the dreadlocked Gullit started out as a sweeper for Dutch team Haarlem. He possessed great attacking flair, stamina, a tough tackle, and a powerful pass. He was the subject of feverish transfer activity, moving to Feyenoord, PSV Eindhoven, and AC Milan, with whom he won European Cups in 1989 and 1990. After a season at Sampdoria he moved to Chelsea, and in 1996 he was appointed player-coach of the London club. By winning the 1997 FA Cup he became the first non-British coach to obtain a major domestic trophy in England.

◀ Ruud Gullit initiates an attack at EURO '88.

ALFREDO DI STEFANO
SPAIN • 1926–2014 • CAPS: 31 • GOALS: 23

To many people, Di Stefano was the "complete" player, years ahead of his time. His astonishing energy helped him play all over the field—defending, tackling, unselfishly distributing the ball, and creating chances for others as well as for himself. Born in a poor suburb of Buenos Aires, he played for River Plate in a relentless forward line known as La Máquina ("the Machine"). A move to Europe in 1953 saw him become part of the legendary Real Madrid team that dominated Europe in the 1950s and early 1960s. Di Stefano formed a deadly partnership with Ferenc Puskas, scoring in five European Cup finals in a row. Real Madrid player and coach Miguel Muñoz explained: "The greatness of Di Stefano was that with him in your side, you had two players in every position."

▶ As well as appearing for Real Madrid (pictured) and Spain, Di Stefano also played seven unofficial games for Argentina and four for Colombia.

EUSEBIO
PORTUGAL • 1942–2014 • CAPS: 64 • GOALS: 41

Eusebio da Silva Ferreira was the first African soccer superstar. Lethal in the air and equipped with a power-packed right-foot shot, he scored an incredible 727 goals in 715 professional games. Eusebio played his early soccer for Sporting Lourenço Marques in his home country of Mozambique—a Portugese colony at the time. The striker was at the center of one of the fiercest transfer disputes when he arrived in Portugal. He was virtually kidnapped by Benfica to keep him away from rivals Sporting Lisbon. Benfica's $21,000 purchase proved to be one of the buys of the century. Over a 15-year career with Benfica, Eusebio scored at an awe-inspiring ratio of more than a goal per game. He was the Portuguese league's top goal scorer seven times, twice the leading goal scorer in all of Europe and the 1966 World Cup's top scorer, with nine goals for Portugal.

▲ Eusebio won the Portuguese league title with Benfica an incredible 11 times in 15 seasons between 1960 and 1975.

VIVIANNE MIEDEMA
NETHERLANDS • BORN 1996
CAPS: 106 • GOALS: 85

Losing her two front teeth at age six in a collision with a goalkeeper did not diminish Miedema's appetite for attacking soccer. She began her senior career with SC Heerenveen, where she scored at a rate of more than a goal per game. This attracted the attention of more than 30 clubs, including Bayern Munich, which she joined in 2014 and helped propel to their first league title since 1976. Her international goal record, not far short of a goal per game, is astonishing. It includes her setting a new Olympic record in 2021 when scoring ten goals in just four games.

◣ Miedema moved to Arsenal in 2017 and by the start of 2022 had struck 109 goals in just 116 games.

JÜRGEN KLINSMANN
WEST GERMANY / GERMANY
BORN 1964 • CAPS: 108
GOALS: 47

Sharp and athletic around the penalty area and an outstanding goal poacher, Klinsmann was German Footballer of the Year in his first spell at VfB Stuttgart. He then moved to Internazionale, where he won the 1989 Serie A title. He was part of West Germany's 1990 World Cup-winning team, scored five goals in the 1994 competition, and captained the team at the 1998 tournament. Klinsmann enjoyed spells with Monaco and, in 1994, the first of two stints with Tottenham Hotspur. After 29 goals in his first Premiership season, Klinsmann was voted England's Footballer of the Year in 1995. The striker moved to Bayern Munich, Sampdoria, and Tottenham once more, before retiring in 1998. In 2004, he was appointed Germany's manager and coached an exciting team to third place at the 2006 World Cup.

◤ Jürgen Klinsmann is in sixth place on the World Cup scoring list, with 11 goals over three tournaments.

GEORGE WEAH
LIBERIA • BORN 1966 • CAPS: 61
GOALS: 22

In 1988 the Monaco manager Arsène Wenger shrewdly plucked the young, raw Weah from Cameroon team Tonnerre Yaoundé. Weah exploded onto the European scene, winning the French league with Monaco in 1991 and Paris Saint-Germain in 1994, before moving to AC Milan. A truly devastating finisher, Weah scored many spectacular goals to help AC Milan win two Serie A titles. He was voted African Footballer of the Year four times, and also won European and World Player of the Year awards in 1995 and FIFA's Fair Play Award the following year. He had short spells at Chelsea, Manchester City, and in the United Arab Emirates late in his career, before retiring in 2002. A UNICEF ambassador since 1997, Weah entered politics and was elected president of Liberia in 2018.

► An outstanding playmaker as well as goal scorer, Marta was voted best player of the 2007 Women's World Cup.

MARTA VIEIRA DA SILVA
BRAZIL • BORN 1986 • CAPS: 171 • GOALS: 115

Short for a striker, at 5 ft. 3 in. (1.6m) tall, Marta is a goal-scoring dynamo who was voted the world's best female player six times (2006–10, 2018). She played her early soccer for several Brazilian clubs before two spells in Sweden, either side of three seasons in the U.S., where she won the Women's Professional Soccer (WPS) championship twice with two different clubs—FC Gold Pride and Western New York Flash. A truly prolific finisher, Marta has scored more World Cup finals goals (17) than any other player, male or female. She has also won seven Swedish league titles, two Olympic silver medals, and three Copa América Femenina titles with Brazil, the latest in 2018. After her three goals at the Tokyo games in 2021, she became the first soccer player to score in five consecutive Olympics.

RONALDO
BRAZIL • BORN 1976
CAPS: 98 • GOALS: 62

Ronaldo Luis Nazario de Lima became a hot commodity as an 18-year-old by scoring 58 goals in just 60 games for Brazil's Cruzeiro. Ronaldo moved to PSV Eindhoven and then Barcelona, where his close control and devastating bursts of speed helped him become Europe's top scorer in 1996–97, with 34 goals. He was sold to Internazionale and was its top scorer in his first season. He then endured four injury-ravaged years. After a poor World Cup final in 1998, many doubted his ability, but he bounced back in 2002 as the tournament's top scorer. A month later, Real Madrid paid $46 million for the Brazilian, and in 2006 Ronaldo became the highest scorer in World Cup history, with 15 goals. In 2007, he moved to Italian giants AC Milan, and in 2009 to Brazilian team Corinthians.

NEYMAR
BRAZIL • BORN 1992
CAPS: 117 • GOALS: 71

Heralded as the heir to Ronaldo and Pelé when he debuted for Santos at age 17, Neymar has spent his entire career under the pressure of expectation. He won the Copa Libertadores as well as the South American Footballer of the Year twice as a teenager before moving to Barcelona, where his trickery and vision saw him score 105 goals. Two of these came in an electric display in 2017 when he masterminded Barça's 6–1 victory over PSG, overturning a 4–0 first-leg loss—the biggest comeback in UEFA Champions League history. Within six months he was a PSG player after a world-record $263 million transfer. Injuries and disciplinary issues have affected his later career, but he is still capable of magical dribbling and goal scoring moments that can turn the course of a game.

MIA HAMM
U.S. • BORN 1972 • CAPS: 276 • GOALS: 158

Born with a partial club foot that had to be corrected by casts, Mia Hamm went on to become the world's most famous female soccer player. She was the youngest player ever for the U.S. women's team when she debuted against China at the age of 15, and the youngest member of the U.S. team that won the 1991 World Cup. Hamm played in three more World Cups and won two Olympic gold medals and one silver. A phenomenal all-around player with an icy-cool finish, she was the leading scorer in the history of women's international soccer for a decade. Hamm was also a founding member of WUSA, playing for Washington Freedom when the league began in 2001.

FACT FILE
Ronaldo's ex-wife, Milene Domingues, broke the world record for keeping a soccer ball off the ground in 1995. She kept the ball in the air for nine hours and six minutes, making 55,187 touches in the process.

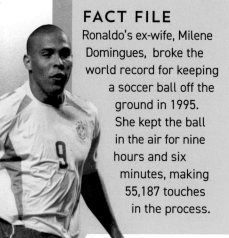

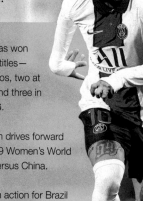

► Neymar has won eight league titles—three at Santos, two at Barcelona, and three in a row at PSG.

◤ Mia Hamm drives forward during a 1999 Women's World Cup game versus China.

◄ Ronaldo in action for Brazil in 2002, the year he won his third FIFA World Player of the Year award.

PELÉ
BRAZIL • BORN 1940 • CAPS: 92 • GOALS: 77

Edson Arantes do Nascimento simply had it all. Considered the finest soccer player of all time, Pelé was a masterful attacker with seemingly limitless skills, creativity, and vision. He was magnificent in the air, lethal on the ground, could dribble, pass, and take swerving free kicks, and saw passes and opportunities that other players could not. At age 11, Pelé was spotted by a former Brazil player, Waldemar de Brito, who took him to Clube Atletico Bauru. Four years later, Pelé made his debut for Santos at age 15. He would play for the São Paulo team for the next 18 years. Pelé was only 17 when he appeared at the 1958 World Cup, scoring a hat trick in the semifinal and two superb goals in the final as Brazil won their first World Cup. A pulled muscle cut short Pelé's involvement in the 1962 competition, and he had to be content with winning the World Club Cup for Santos. Injured by brutal tackling in the 1966 World Cup, Pelé was outstanding at the 1970 tournament. He retired from international soccer in 1971—in front of around 180,000 fans at the Maracanã Stadium—and from club soccer in 1974. In tribute, Santos removed the number ten shirt from its team lineup. Pelé later came out of retirement to play in a star-studded lineup at New York Cosmos. He went on to become Brazil's minister of sports and a United Nations (UN) and UNICEF ambassador. One of the most respected figures in world soccer, he was voted Athlete of the Century by the International Olympic Committee in 1999.

BIRGIT PRINZ
GERMANY • BORN 1977
CAPS: 214 • GOALS: 128

Apart from a stint in the United States in 2002, where her 12 goals in 15 games helped Carolina Courage win the WUSA championship, Prinz played all her club soccer for FFC Frankfurt. Here, she won six German league titles and eight German Cups, and scored over 250 goals (at a rate better than a goal a game). With Germany, she won two World Cups (2003, 2007), five European Championships, and three Olympic bronze medals—a staggering haul. She was also awarded the FIFA World Women's Footballer of the Year on three occasions and finished second a further four times, the last in 2010, a year before she announced her retirement.

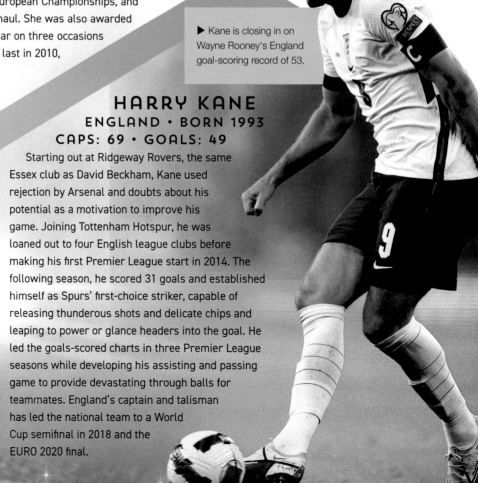

▶ Kane is closing in on Wayne Rooney's England goal-scoring record of 53.

HARRY KANE
ENGLAND • BORN 1993
CAPS: 69 • GOALS: 49

Starting out at Ridgeway Rovers, the same Essex club as David Beckham, Kane used rejection by Arsenal and doubts about his potential as a motivation to improve his game. Joining Tottenham Hotspur, he was loaned out to four English league clubs before making his first Premier League start in 2014. The following season, he scored 31 goals and established himself as Spurs' first-choice striker, capable of releasing thunderous shots and delicate chips and leaping to power or glance headers into the goal. He led the goals-scored charts in three Premier League seasons while developing his assisting and passing game to provide devastating through balls for teammates. England's captain and talisman has led the national team to a World Cup semifinal in 2018 and the EURO 2020 final.

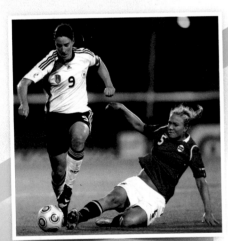

▲ Germany's Birgit Prinz is challenged by Norway's Anneli Giske during the UEFA Women's EURO 2009.

▲▲ Pelé at the 1970 World Cup, where he was Player of the Tournament.

KYLIAN MBAPPÉ
FRANCE • BORN 1998 • CAPS: 54 • GOALS: 26

Courted by Real Madrid and Chelsea while still a boy, Mbappé played for AS Bondy, where his father was coach, often in age groups older than himself. He joined Monaco's B team in 2015 but was thrown into first-team action as a 16-year-old and quickly established himself as a phenomenal attacking talent. Mbappé's explosive acceleration, pace, and power couple with tactical intelligence and a wicked shot. PSG came calling, making him the world's most expensive teenager in 2017. He repaid the investment rapidly with 100 goals for PSG before the end of 2020. His international debut came a year before the 2018 World Cup, where he became the first teenager since Pelé to score two World Cup goals in a match. At the same tournament he won FIFA's Best Young Player award.

◀ Kylian Mbappé kisses the World Cup trophy. The striker scored four goals in the tournament.

LEADING INTERNATIONAL GOAL SCORERS

PLAYER	COUNTRY	CAPS	GOALS
Men			
Cristiano Ronaldo	Portugal	186	115
Ali Daei	Iran	149	109
Mokhtar Dahari	Malaysia	142	89
Ferenc Puskás	Hungary	84	83
Lionel Messi	Argentina	160	81
Godfrey Chitalu	Zambia	111	79
Women			
Christine Sinclair	Canada	306	188
Abby Wambach	U.S.	256	184
Mia Hamm	U.S.	276	158
Carli Lloyd	U.S.	316	134
Kristine Lilly	U.S.	352	130
Birgit Prinz	Germany	214	128

MARCO VAN BASTEN
N'LANDS • BORN 1964
CAPS: 58 • GOALS: 24

One of the coolest finishers in world soccer, van Basten was just 29 when an ankle injury in the 1993 European Cup final effectively ended his playing career—although he struggled on until 1995. Renowned for spectacular goals in crucial contests, van Basten was European Footballer of the Year three times (1988, 1989, and 1992), and in 1988 he hit the headlines as the Netherlands won the European Championships. He scored a hat trick against England in the quarterfinal, the semifinal winner versus Germany, and a breathtaking volley from the tightest of angles in the final against the Soviet Union. With Ajax he won three league titles, scoring 128 goals. He then moved to AC Milan, hitting 90 goals in 147 games and winning three Serie A titles and two European Cups.

▶ Marco van Basten on the rampage in the Netherlands' 3–1 win over England at EURO '88.

HUGO SANCHEZ
MEXICO
BORN 1958
CAPS: 57 • GOALS: 26

Mexico's most famous player, Sanchez spent the peak of his playing career in Spain, scoring over 230 goals for Atlético Madrid and Real Madrid. He formed a lethal partnership with Emilio Butragueno at Real as they won five league titles in a row. Sanchez was La Liga's top scorer in five different seasons, and in 1990 he won the European Golden Boot for a record 38 goals in one season. Sadly, his commitments to European soccer and frequent bust-ups with Mexican soccer officials meant that he appeared in only a fraction of the international games played by his home country. He had a disappointing tournament at the 1986 World Cup on home soil, scoring just one goal.

SNAPSHOT
MARADONA'S WORLD CUP

Diego Maradona, the Argentinian striker with magical balance and touch, ended the 1986 World Cup with his hands on the trophy, and a highly impressive five goals and five assists. Yet these statistics do not tell the story of his true impact, for Mexico '86 was Maradona's tournament. He roused a relatively ordinary Argentinian team into recapturing soccer's biggest prize (the South Americans had won the trophy on home soil in 1978) and wiped out the memory of a disappointing tournament in 1982. In a tense quarterfinal against England, controversy raged over Maradona's infamous "Hand of God" goal (see below), but his second and winning goal was pure genius. The Argentinian collected the ball in his own half, then dribbled, twisted, and turned through the English defense to score what was later voted the goal of the century. He would score a goal of similar brilliance in the semifinal versus Belgium. At this point, at the age of just 25, Maradona was without doubt the greatest soccer player on the planet.

◄ Diego Maradona, clutching the World Cup after his team's epic 3–2 victory over West Germany in the 1986 final, is carried around the Azteca Stadium on the shoulders of ecstatic Argentinian fans.

▼ Maradona uses his hand to get the ball past England goalkeeper Peter Shilton to score Argentina's first goal in a 2–1 victory.

THE BRAIN GAME

Soccer is a sport that calls for pace, power, stamina, and skill, but it also demands mental agility. Players with the ability to think one step ahead of their opponents are highly prized, and such skills can win a match for their team. The same applies to managers and coaches. In the run-up to a match, they have many key decisions to make. They must decide who to select, which formation to play, and choose the tactics they will use in their bid to outwit the opposing team.

TEAM SELECTION

With large squads of players and endless analysis of opponents, managers fret over picking their starting 11 in the days ahead of a big game. Teams need flair, skill, composure, aggression, sound defensive skills, and goal-scoring abilities—all in the right quantities. Some players, despite being superstars, may not play well with each other or work with the rest of the team, while other, less-heralded players may actually perform a more effective job in a particular game. The way the opponent plays can dictate which players are selected, as can the fitness and performances of individuals. Star players, who would normally be first on the team sheet, may not be picked if they are recovering from injury or suffering from a lack of confidence or form. Both young, talented players emerging from the reserve team and experienced veterans at the end of their careers will have strong cases for a place on the team. It all adds up to a complex puzzle that managers must solve.

◀ In November 2021, Canada beat CONCACAF giants Mexico for the first time since 2000. Manager John Herdman brought onto his team 38-year-old veteran Atiba Hutchinson and striker Cyle Larin (left), who scored both goals in the famous victory.

▼ In the past, club squads were much smaller. In 1983–84, Liverpool's league- and European Cup-winning team (below) played 66 games with a squad of just 16. Bruce Grobbelaar, Alan Kennedy, Sammy Lee, and Alan Hansen played in every game.

FACT FILE
In a 2021 World Cup qualifier versus Poland, Gareth Southgate became the first England manager since 1996 not to make a single substitution. His opposing coach, Paulo Sousa, made five.

REST AND ROTATION

With large squads and matches coming thick and fast in the middle of a season, coaches for the top teams often rest and rotate players to keep them fresh and fit. They may also adjust their team game by game to counter the opponents' strengths and prey on their weaknesses.

Some coaches, such as Pep Guardiola, are particularly eager to tinker and rarely field the same starting 11 two or three times in a row. Other coaches prefer a more settled team, resting key players only against weaker opponents such as lower-league teams in cup competitions—but even this can come with a risk. In 2021, Leeds United manager Marcelo Bielsa rested his first-choice goalkeeper and striker only to crash out of the FA Cup, losing 3–0 to Crawley Town, three divisions below.

SUBSTITUTIONS

Replacing a player with a substitute was not a part of the competitive game for almost a century. Richard Gottinger became the first official World Cup substitute, for example, in a 1953 qualifier when he came on for West Germany. The lack of subs made for some amusing and heroic moments, with strikers having to play in the goal and teams occasionally reduced to eight or nine players through injury. Gradually, the number of substitutions a manager can make has risen. In the UEFA Champions League, for example, managers can make five substitutions. The timing and choice of substitutes can be crucial. Coaches use them to change tactics and the shape of the team or to seek a match-winning impact. At the 2018 World Cup, Belgium manager Roberto Martinez made two attacking substitutions with his side down 2–0 to Japan, bringing on Marouane Fellaini and Nacer Chadli. Both scored in a memorable 3–2 turnaround.

▶ Netherlands coach Sarina Wiegman prepares a sub. During her reign, the Dutch lost just 11 of 72 games, won EURO 2017, and reached the 2019 World Cup final.

◤ 150 of Ole Gunnar Solskjaer's 366 appearances for Manchester United were as a substitute. He scored 33 goals in the last 15 minutes of matches, including the memorable winner in the 1999 UEFA Champions League final.

◤ Christophe Galtier managed Lille to a surprise Ligue 1 title in 2021 with a team built around a core of promising young players.

FORMATIONS

The way in which a team lines up is known as its formation. In the first soccer international, in 1872, Scotland set up in a 2-2-6 formation, with two backs, two halfbacks (similar to midfielders), and six attackers. England went even further, playing 1-1-8 (eight forwards), but crowded goalmouths saw the game end 0–0.

▶ Marcela Bielsa is famous for playing unusual formations such as 4-1-4-1 and 3-3-1-3 as coach of Leeds United, Marseille, and Chile.

CHANGING SHAPES

Attack-heavy formations persisted until 1925, when Arsenal's Herbert Chapman capitalized on changes to the offside law with an innovative new W-M formation. Similar to a modern-day 3-2-2-3, W-M was adopted by many other teams, and it was only the arrival of a flat back four that changed things. Sometimes thought of as negative, the flat back four was employed by a Brazil team that dazzled at the 1958 World Cup with a 4-2-4 formation. Up front, the team's two wingers fed into two central strikers, one of whom was a teenage Pelé.

In the World Cups that followed, many teams kept the back four defenders but adjusted the rest of the formation to less-attacking 4-3-3 and 4-4-2 shapes. These are still employed today—the United States won the 2019 Women's World Cup playing 4-3-3—but they are just two of a large selection of different formations at a manager's disposal. Teams may even change formation once or twice during a game.

FORMATION VARIATIONS

Some modern coaches, such as Jürgen Klopp, favor four at the back but expect their wide defenders to be a major attacking threat as well. To cover for them, defensive midfielders may be employed. Some teams adopt a 3-5-2 formation with three central defenders and two wingbacks who need exceptional stamina, as they are expected to both attack and defend throughout the game. Up front, different shapes and roles drift in and out of fashion, such as split strikers with one playing ahead of the other and the "false 9." This innovation was championed by Vicente del Bosque's EURO 2012–winning Spain team and by Pep Guardiola at Barcelona. He moved Lionel Messi from playing wide in attack to the center but expected him to head back into midfield to drag defenders out of position, receive the ball, turn, and dribble. Other common false 9s include Roberto Firmino, Paulo Dybala, and Nabil Fekir.

▲ Wingbacks, such as Bayern Munich's Alphonso Davies, play on the flanks. They act like fullbacks on defense but also make attacking runs upfield.

PROTECTING THE DEFENSE

Made popular by Italian teams from the early 1950s onward, a sweeper plays behind the main bank of defenders to offer further protection. German legend Franz Beckenbauer turned the sweeper role from ultra-defensive to attacking, moving forward with the ball and linking defense with attack. Today few teams play with a sweeper. Instead some teams rely on a goalkeeper who is skilled with their feet to do the job, or they prefer one or more holding midfielders who are stationed in front of the defense. Their job is to close down attacks, tackle, and intercept the ball. This role is so important that top holding midfielders—from Declan Rice and Rodri to Julie Ertz and N'Golo Kante—are highly prized.

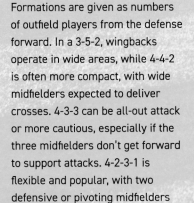

▲ U.S. holding midfielder Julie Ertz stops the Netherlands' Jill Roord. Ertz is excellent at denying opponents time and space.

FORMATIONS

Formations are given as numbers of outfield players from the defense forward. In a 3-5-2, wingbacks operate in wide areas, while 4-4-2 is often more compact, with wide midfielders expected to deliver crosses. 4-3-3 can be all-out attack or more cautious, especially if the three midfielders don't get forward to support attacks. 4-2-3-1 is flexible and popular, with two defensive or pivoting midfielders in front of four defenders.

FLUID SOCCER

Inspired by Rinus Michels when he was in charge of Ajax and the Netherlands in the 1960s and '70s, "total soccer" saw gifted players swap positions with dizzying regularity all over the field. A defender might pop up in attack, a wide midfielder could cover in defense, or a striker would drift into midfield. For most teams—who played rigidly in their formations, often with man-to-man marking—it could be a nightmare to defend against. It did, however, require players with great energy and intelligence to work. Today many top teams play fluid soccer that is not strictly total soccer but in which players do regularly exchange positions and roles.

◀ Nabil Fekir of Real Betis can be a devastating false 9, finding gaps between an opposing team's banks of defenders and midfielders.

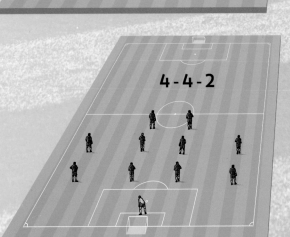

4-3-3

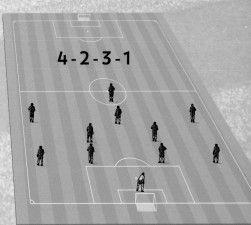

3-5-2

4-4-2

4-2-3-1

TACTICS

Teams may kick off a game in one of several common formations, but there can be great variation in how they play within that formation and in the tactics they use. For example, a team that lines up as a 4-4-2 team may choose to play defensively, with midfielders tucking in, or aggressively, with one or more midfielders joining the strikers in attack.

TAILORING TACTICS

Managers start a game with what they feel are the best tactics for the players available and the opponents they face. They watch how a match unfolds closely, knowing they can change tactics at any time to exploit an opponent's weakness or to fix problems in their own team's play. Most top players can play in several positions. A manager may switch formations using the same players or bring on a substitute with different attributes and skills. Some managers take this to extremes. In the 2021 UEFA Super Cup final against Villareal, Chelsea coach Thomas Tuchel substituted his world-class goalie, Edouard Mendy, with Kepa Arrizabalaga in the 119th minute with the scores tied. Tuchel felt that Kepa would have more success in the penalty kick shoot-out. The coach's hunch proved inspired as Kepa saved two penalty kicks and Chelsea won.

◀ Liverpool's Mohamed Salah dribbles at speed. Salah can play on the wing, as a second striker, or as a central attacking midfielder and can even switch positions throughout a match.

▼ Atlético Madrid's Stefan Savic lunges to block a shot from Real Sociedad's Alexander Isak, confident that he has support from teammates behind him.

TACTICS IN DEFENSE

Teams have several choices about how they defend. Some managers prefer defenders to patrol areas of space that overlap, a system known as zonal marking. This tactic is often used by Argentinian clubs and many national teams. It requires good communication between defenders. Some coaches set their team up to perform a low block. This is stationing eight, nine, or ten outfield players in two banks deep inside their own penalty area. The idea is to restrict the time and space available for their opponents in dangerous areas. Alternatively, a coach may opt for each of their defenders and, sometimes, their defensive midfielders as well, to mark individual opponents, tracking their attacking runs and positions when the defenders' team does not have the ball. Sometimes a coach asks a player to mark a particularly dangerous opponent—such as a midfield playmaker who controls the opposing team's attacks—for an entire game. Denying them the ball or the space to move forward can reduce their threat greatly.

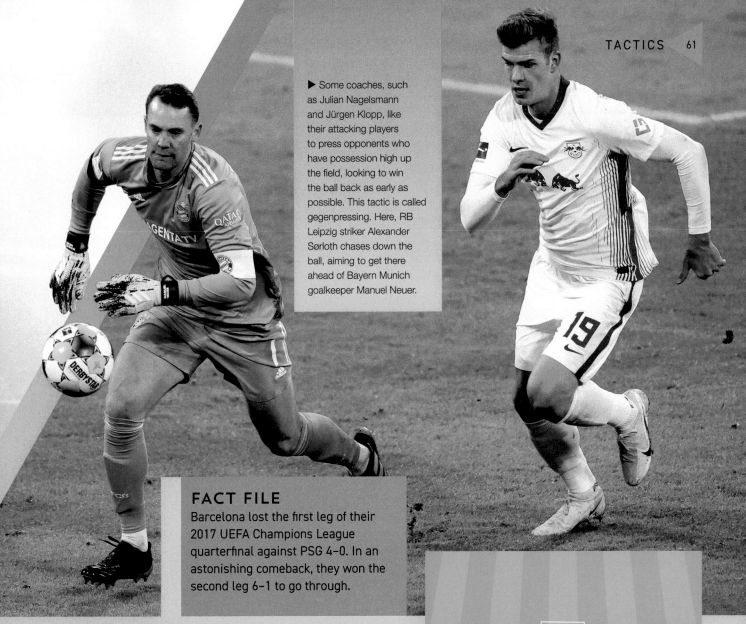

▶ Some coaches, such as Julian Nagelsmann and Jürgen Klopp, like their attacking players to press opponents who have possession high up the field, looking to win the ball back as early as possible. This tactic is called gegenpressing. Here, RB Leipzig striker Alexander Sørloth chases down the ball, aiming to get there ahead of Bayern Munich goalkeeper Manuel Neuer.

FACT FILE

Barcelona lost the first leg of their 2017 UEFA Champions League quarterfinal against PSG 4–0. In an astonishing comeback, they won the second leg 6–1 to go through.

LONG OR SHORT

All teams seek to pass and move the ball into the attacking third of the field, where goal-scoring chances can be fashioned. For many decades, British managers believed that hitting long balls toward tall strikers created more goal chances, often through a defensive mistake. In continental Europe and South America, a shorter, pass-and-move game was preferred, with teams keeping possession for relatively long periods as they looked for an opening. Another tactic is to rely on pinpoint passing and skillful dribbling to get into the opposition penalty area. Some teams play a counterattacking game, defending in large numbers and soaking up pressure. When they retrieve the ball, they move it rapidly out of defense with a long pass or by running with the ball. Fast counterattacking can catch opponents off guard and outnumbered but requires speedy, aware players. Many coaches mix up their passing and movement tactics—if their team is behind with only minutes to go, they may switch to a direct style, pushing extra players up into the opposition penalty area to look for headers and knockdowns.

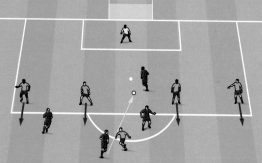

▲ The offside trap is a defensive tactic in which the back three or four players move upfield in a straight line to catch an opponent offside. It can be very effective but may be beaten by a player dribbling through the line or by a well-timed through pass combined with an attacking run.

THE COACH'S ROLE

A successful team needs more than great tactics. It needs to be prepared, instructed, and inspired to produce great performances. This is the role of the manager or head coach.

INS AND OUTS

A manager may seek to change the shape and performance of their team by bringing in new players. If money is tight, they may have to bring in loan players, promote youth-team players, or shop around lower leagues. At the other end, top soccer clubs are huge businesses and buy and sell players for many tens of millions of dollars. Bargains can still be had, though. Riyad Mahrez and Jamie Vardy cost Leicester City just $520,000 and $1.6 million respectively, while Borussia Dortmund bought striker Robert Lewandowski for a mere $7 million. Mahrez was eventually sold to Manchester City for 135 times the fee Leicester paid! Lewandowski, on the other hand, eventually left Dortmund for free.

◀ Belgium coach Roberto Martinez oversees a training session at EURO 2020.

◢ Thomas Tuchel celebrates winning Ligue 1 with PSG in 2020, alongside his assistant coaches and a video analyst.

ON A FREE

Many clubs swoop for free transfers of players who are out of contract, offering high wages. In summer 2021, for example, Paris Saint-Germain secured Lionel Messi, Gianluigi Donnarumma, Achraf Hakimi, Sergio Ramos, and Georginio Wijnaldum all on frees. On occasion, it's the manager instead of a player who is subject to a transfer fee! The record fee is $30 million paid by Bayern Munich in 2021 to RB Leipzig for their coach, Julian Nagelsmann. It's all a far cry from the women's game where, according to FIFA, just $1.2 million was spent globally on transfer fees in 2020.

THE TEAM BEHIND THE TEAM

A manager or head coach is in charge of an increasingly large staff, all devoted to ensuring the team performs at its best. They include assistant coaches, some of whom may specialize in training goalkeepers or strikers, while others might focus on set-piece moves. Fitness coaches, dieticians, masseurs, physiotherapists, and other medical staff prepare players for training and games and work with injured players on their recovery. Teams often work with sports psychologists, coordination and balance specialists, and sprint or strength trainers.

Performance, data, and video analysts are increasingly influential at top clubs. They compile detailed breakdowns of players' strengths and weaknesses, and where they can make better decisions during play. Analysts often prepare a detailed dossier on upcoming opponents. The manager digests the report and then communicates the key points to their players. Knowing that an opposing defender makes a particular pass when under pressure or that a striker always feints to the left before shooting can be the crucial detail that wins a game.

◀ Top managers, such as France's Didier Deschamps, talk to the press before and after every game.

▶ Lyon coach Sonia Bompastor passes on new instructions—which might include a change of tactics—to Amandine Henry.

◀ Leicester City paid around $8.5 million for N'Golo Kanté in 2015, then sold him for $42 million a year later. Despite that price tag, he's proved to be a bargain, helping Chelsea to Premier League and UEFA Champions League titles.

MANAGERIAL MIGRATIONS

More and more clubs and national teams look beyond their borders when seeking a new manager. Top coaches may switch countries and continents frequently, especially as the time they are likely to spend in charge of a team gets shorter and shorter. Former England manager Roy Hodgson has managed 17 clubs in eight different nations, but even he cannot compete with globetrotting Luiz Felipe Scolari, who has managed 21 clubs everywhere from China to Uzbekistan—including four spells in charge of Brazilian club Gremio in four different decades.

▶ Afshin Ghotbi has coached in the U.S., South Korea, Iran, China, Thailand, and Japan.

UNDER PRESSURE

Few people in sports are under as much pressure as the manager of a major club or national team. Managers stand or fall by their results. In the past, some managers stayed at clubs for season after season. Miguel Munoz, for example, managed Real Madrid for 417 games during the 1960s. At the top level today, few coaches stay in charge of the best teams for more than a handful of seasons. In the short summer period between seasons in 2021, 37 clubs in the top five European leagues changed managers. Many more went on to switch managers during the season. Club owners, chairpersons, and some fans have short memories, and even recent success does not guarantee job stability. Maurizio Sarri was let go days after winning the 2019–20 Serie A title with Juventus, while Unai Emery was fired as PSG boss in 2018 right after securing the Ligue 1 championship with a record points-per-game tally. In such an unforgiving climate, Alex Ferguson's remarkable record of 1,500 games in charge of Manchester United across 26½ years may never be beaten.

FACT FILE

In 2015, Chan Yuen Ting became the world's first female coach of any men's top division team when she took charge of Hong Kong team Eastern SC and coached them in the Asian Champions League.

GREAT MANAGERS

There have been dozens of truly great managers in soccer. Some have been masters at putting together successful teams on tight budgets; others are visionaries who have improved the skills of the world's biggest stars. Below are profiles of seven of the finest managers in the history of soccer.

▲ Rinus Michels at Barcelona, where he won La Liga in 1974.

JOSEP "PEP" GUARDIOLA
BORN 1971

Guardiola played over 380 games for Barcelona after making his debut under manager Johan Cruyff in 1990 as a deep-lying midfielder. He retired in 2006 and went on to manage three European heavyweights: Barcelona (2008–12), Bayern Munich (2013–16) and Manchester City (since 2016) with great success. At each club, Guardiola's obsessive preparation and mostly possession-based tactics led to long winning runs and at least three league titles per club. He lost a mere 19 out of 161 games at Bayern and just 21 out of 247 at Barcelona. UEFA Champions League glory has only come twice so far, in 2009 and 2011, although he led Manchester City to the final in 2021.

RINUS MICHELS
1928–2005

The man behind "total soccer," which revolutionized both Ajax and the Dutch national team, Marinus "Rinus" Michels had been a center forward as a player, winning five caps for the Netherlands in the 1950s. As coach of Ajax in the mid-1960s, he gave 17-year-old Johan Cruyff his debut. Michels later managed Cruyff at Spanish giants Barcelona and on the Dutch team that finished runner-up at the 1974 World Cup. Michels returned to Ajax in 1975 and became coach of German team Cologne five years later. He rejoined the Dutch national team in 1984 and, with a star-studded lineup, won the 1988 European Championships —the Netherlands' first major trophy. Michels's achievements were acknowledged in 1999, when he was named FIFA's Coach of the Century.

HELENIO HERRERA
1917–97

The well-traveled Argentinian Helenio Herrera was a tough manager who liked to control almost every aspect of a club. At Spain's Atlético Madrid, he won back-to-back league titles. After spells with Malaga, Valladolid, and Sevilla, he joined Barcelona. Under his management, they won two Spanish titles and two Inter-Cities Fairs Cups. Internazionale headhunted him in 1960. Herrera's reign and his use of defensive *catenaccio* tactics coincided with Inter's most glorious era, in which they won three Serie A titles, two European Cups, and two World Club Cups. Herrera was also in charge of Italy during qualification for the 1962 World Cup, but by the time the tournament began, he was manager of Spain.

► Pep Guardiola has set many Premier League records at Manchester City, including most points (100) and most goals scored (106) in a season.

FACT FILE
Alex Ferguson was fired only once, in 1978, when St. Mirren dismissed him for a range of offenses that included "unpardonable swearing at a lady."

► Helenio Herrera poses with two soccer balls in 1971, while coach of Italian team Roma.

◀ Alex Ferguson celebrates his final Premier League title in 2013, finishing 11 points clear of Manchester City.

ALEX FERGUSON
BORN 1941

As European soccer's longest-serving top-flight manager, Alex Ferguson took Manchester United to a record 13 Premier League titles and the 1999 and 2008 Champions League crowns. A ruthless and highly driven manager, Ferguson won three Scottish league titles and the 1983 European Cup-Winners' Cup with Aberdeen. He managed Scotland at the 1986 World Cup before joining Manchester United. Ferguson developed young talents such as David Beckham and Ryan Giggs and proved to be a masterful player of mind games with rival managers. Knighted in 1999 for his services to the game, Sir Alex announced his retirement at the end of the 2012–13 season, after 26 years with United.

JÜRGEN KLOPP
BORN 1967

The Best FIFA Football Coach winner in 2019 and 2020 began his career as a striker-turned-defender with German lower league club Mainz 05. Becoming Mainz's manager in 2001, Klopp guided them to the top tier of German soccer for the first time in their history. He moved to Borussia Dortmund in 2008, where his brand of pressing and rapid counterattacking reestablished the club as a dominant force. He won three major cups and two Bundesliga titles (2011, 2012) before joining Liverpool. Passionate and popular, Klopp built an attractive team with a three-pronged attack of Mo Salah, Sadio Mané, and Roberto Firmino. He endured three losses in major finals before winning the 2018–19 UEFA Champions League and the Club World Cup. Liverpool's first league title in 30 years followed the next season.

▶ Under Jürgen Klopp, Liverpool won 18 league games in a row starting in October 2019—a joint record in the English top league.

ANTONIO CONTE
BORN 1969

A Juventus legend with over 400 games as a player, Conte managed the club in 2011 after spells at S.S. Arezzo, Bari, Atalanta, and Sienna. He is a famously hard taskmaster whose intense coaching style does not suit every player, but his well-drilled teams have enjoyed great success, often in 3-5-2 formation with attacking wingbacks. He won three Serie A titles in a row at Juve, coached Italy at EURO 2016, and managed Chelsea to a Premier League title in 2017. Joining Inter Milan, he broke Juventus's Serie A dominance with a momentous title win in 2021. He left after disagreements over future player transfers, but later in 2021 he was appointed manager of Tottenham Hotspur.

▶ Antonio Conte issues instructions to Tottenham's players during a training session.

EMMA HAYES
BORN 1976

With her own playing career cut short by injury at 17, Hayes turned to coaching, first with U.S. college teams and then as assistant coach at Arsenal Women. After spells advising several U.S. clubs on transfers, she was appointed Chelsea Women's manager in 2012. There, she has enjoyed a 69 percent win rate as Chelsea won four Women's Super League titles in six seasons, as well as three FA Cups and two League Cups. The longest-serving manager in Women's Super League history, Hayes also led Chelsea to the UEFA Women's Champions League final in 2021, the first female coach in 12 years to do so.

▶ Emma Hayes lifts the WSL trophy in 2021, the same year she won the Best FIFA Women's Coach award.

U.S. attacker Megan Rapinoe celebrates scoring the opening goal against the Netherlands in the 2019 Women's World Cup final. Rapinoe was the star of the tournament, winning the Golden Ball as best player, the Golden Boot as top scorer with six goals, and becoming the first woman to start three World Cup finals in a row.

SNAPSHOT
ON THE DOUBLE

The U.S. Women's National Team had entered the 2015 FIFA Women's World Cup hurting from not winning the competition for 16 years and losing out to Japan in the final of the 2011 edition. The two teams met in a riveting 2015 final, in which a stunning hat trick from Carli Lloyd ensured the U.S. gained revenge with a 5–2 victory and secured its third Women's World Cup.

Only Germany had ever successfully defended the Women's World Cup, but the U.S. arrived in France in 2019 in good shape and began the tournament in emphatic style, hammering Thailand by a record score of 13–0, with five goals for Alex Morgan. Games tightened up during the knockout stages, and the U.S. recorded three successive 2–1 victories over Spain, France, and England to reach the final. There, they met a talented Netherlands team but came out on top thanks to a penalty kick from the tournament's Golden Boot winner, Megan Rapinoe, and a 69th-minute strike from dynamic midfielder Rose Lavelle. It could have been more were it not for heroics from the goalkeeper of the tournament, Sari van Veenendaal. The victory made the U.S. the only four-time winner of the competition and also made Jill Ellis the first coach to win two Women's World Cups. She retired after the tournament, leaving with an exceptional record of just seven defeats in 132 games.

GREAT TEAMS

Great players, managed well and playing with spirit and intelligence, can make a great team. Sometimes less-heralded individuals gel together to form an unstoppable team, such as the Leicester City squad that won the English Premier League in 2016. Other teams made up of stellar players form a powerful dynasty with long runs of success. This section focuses on teams that at one point in their history were especially exciting, revolutionary, or dominant in the competitions in which they played.

NATIONAL TEAMS

HUNGARY
FOUNDED: 1901

The Hungary team of the 1950s changed the way many teams played soccer. Hungary brimmed with talented attacking players, and coach Gusztáv Sebes devised a simple but devastating alternative to the W-M formation to get the best out of them. Nándor Hidegkuti was the team's nominal center forward, but he played deep, allowing Ferenc Puskás, Sándor Koscis, and others to raid ahead of the striker into open space. Opponents couldn't cope, and the team recorded an incredible run of 50 matches with only one defeat, scoring 220 goals along the way. They won the 1952 Olympics, and in the following year they thrashed England 6–3 and 7–1. However, their one defeat was heartbreaking, as it came in the 1954 World Cup final, where they lost to West Germany 3–2.

SWEDEN WOMEN
FIRST INTERNATIONAL
MATCH: 1973

Sweden won the first Women's European Championship in 1984 and have shown remarkable consistency since then, finishing second or third on seven occasions. World Cup and Olympic glory has evaded their grasp, with two back-to-back Olympic silver medals (2016, 2021), one World Cup runner-up spot (2003), and three World Cup third places (1991, 2011, 2019). They remain a very difficult team to beat, and after going undefeated for 18 matches in open play in 2020–21, find themselves placed second in the world at the start of 2022 according to the FIFA rankings.

◀ Hungarian goalkeeper Gyula Grosics gathers the ball under pressure from England's Stan Mortensen. Hungary's 6–3 win condemned England to their first home defeat to a team from the continent.

▶ Swedish defender Magdalena Eriksson (right) challenges U.S. forward Carli Lloyd. Eriksson has played over 80 times for the Blue-and-Yellows.

WEST GERMANY
FOUNDED: 1900

West Germany staged a major shock when they courageously toppled the favorite, Hungary, to win the 1954 World Cup thanks to two goals from Helmut Rahn. Their team of the mid-1960s finished runner-up at the 1966 tournament and third in 1970. Manager Helmut Schön then rebuilt the team shrewdly, keeping the superb Sepp Maier in the goal and moving Franz Beckenbauer from midfield into defense, where he played alongside Hans-Georg Schwarzenbeck and one of the best fullbacks of the 1970s, Paul Breitner. Schön incorporated the talented Günter Netzer into midfield and often played a 4-3-3 formation, with Uli Hoeness in attack alongside goal machine Gerd Müller. West Germany's players had a very strong team spirit because they came almost exclusively from just two clubs—Bayern Munich and Borussia Mönchengladbach. Their self-confidence was evident as they powered to the 1972 European Championships title and then went a step further, winning the 1974 World Cup on home soil. By this time the talented but outspoken Netzer had been replaced by Wolfgang Overath, while midfielder Rainer Bonhof had also played his way onto the team. A defeat to Czechoslovakia in the 1976 European Championships final signaled the end of a remarkable period in which West Germany had become the first team to hold the European and World crowns at the same time.

◄ Right back Benjamin Pavard in action for France against Hungary in a Group F match at EURO 2020.

▲ West German striker Uli Hoeness powers toward Spain's goal in a 2–0 quarterfinal second-leg win over Spain at the 1976 European Championships.

FRANCE
FOUNDED: 1919

France has a long and illustrious soccer pedigree. It has produced several superb teams, particularly in the late 1950s—the era of Raymond Kopa and Just Fontaine—and in the early 1980s, with an impressive team led by Michel Platini. But it was the team of the late 1990s that finally translated great promise into World Cup success.

As world champion, France entered Euro 2000 with the majority of its key players still at their peak, including flamboyant goalie Fabien Barthez and strong, skilled defenders in Marcel Desailly, Lilian Thuram, and Bixente Lizarazu. In midfield, a blend of flair and dynamism was headed by the world's best attacking midfielder, Zinedine Zidane. Up front, young livewires such as Sylvain Wiltord and Thierry Henry were intent on making their mark. Five players scored two or more goals in their six-match Euro 2000 campaign, which ended with France beating Italy 2–1 to become the second team (after West Germany in 1974) to hold European and World titles at the same time.

UNITED STATES WOMEN
FIRST INTERNATIONAL MATCH: 1985

Women's international soccer came of age during the 1990s and early 2000s, with the arrival of World Cup and Olympic competitions. The period's most successful nation was the United States, which won two Olympic titles (1996 and 2004) and two Women's World Cups (1991 and 1999). Their record in World Cup games during the 1990s was remarkable, with 20 wins, two ties, and just two defeats. Mia Hamm was considered to be the world's finest female striker, while Kristine Lilly became the first female player to pass 300 international caps in 2006. For a number of the U.S. women's team, 2004 proved a successful swan song, with victory over Brazil to win Olympic gold—a feat that a new generation of U.S. players such as Carli Lloyd, Christie Rampone, and Abby Wambach repeated in 2008 and 2012. The team has dominated the Women's World Cup in recent years, finishing as runner-up in 2011, lifting the trophy for the third time in 2015, and going unbeaten in 2019 when it defeated the Netherlands 2–0 to become world champion for the fourth time.

◄ U.S. midfielder Sam Mewis shoots during a 4–0 victory over Mexico in 2021. It was the 43rd game in a row that the U.S. team had gone unbeaten.

FACT FILE

Ahn Jung-Hwan struck the goal that knocked Italy out of the 2002 World Cup. Ahn played for Italian team Perugia, whose president was so enraged that he terminated the South Korean midfielder's contract.

▼ South Korea celebrates a famous victory over Spain in the quarterfinals of the 2002 World Cup. The match ended at 0–0 after extra time, with the Koreans winning the penalty shoot-out 5–3.

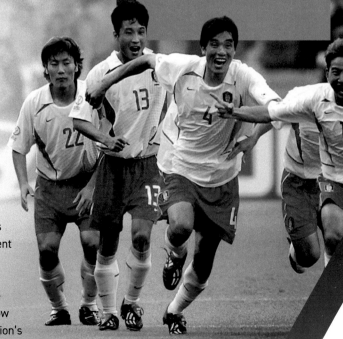

SOUTH KOREA
FOUNDED: 1928

At the 2002 World Cup, cohost South Korea was given little chance of success by many people. In truth, the country boasted an improving team and had qualified for the previous three World Cups. Under the guidance of Guus Hiddink—a former Real Madrid and Netherlands coach—the South Koreans beat Poland 2–0 to record their country's first win at the World Cup. After a 1–1 tie with the United States, South Korea knocked a strong Portugal team out of the tournament thanks to Park Ji-Sung's goal. An extraordinary second-round game versus Italy saw South Korea miss a penalty kick, then fall behind, only to tie two minutes before the final whistle. Urged on by an entire country, the hardworking team defended resolutely and attacked with energy, skill, and surprise. A "golden goal" three minutes before the end of extra time knocked Italy out of the tournament and sent the country into raptures. The drama was not over, however. A tense quarterfinal against Spain ended in a thrilling penalty shoot-out, with goalie Lee Woon-Jae pulling off a magnificent save from Joaquin before captain Hong Myung-Bo slotted home the winning penalty kick. A narrow 1–0 defeat to Germany in the semifinals did not dampen the cohost nation's enthusiasm, and attendances at club level rocketed in the following seasons.

SPAIN
FOUNDED: 1904

Spain had been the perennial underachievers on the international stage, producing dozens of world-renowned players—from Ricardo Zamora and Andoni Zubizarreta in the goal to Raul and Emilio Butragueño in attack—yet rarely producing the goods at major tournaments. The 2000s, however, saw a major change with the arrival of a clutch of supremely talented, technically gifted players, many from Barcelona, who thrived on a style of play—dubbed tika-taka—where control of the ball, frequent short passing, and quick, nimble movements are paramount. Players like Xavi Hernández and Andrés Iniesta in midfield kept possession of the ball in front of no-nonsense defenders such as Carles Puyol and Gerard Piqué. It yielded great results. Between November 2006 and June 2009, Spain went unbeaten in 35 international games—until suffering a surprise defeat by the U.S. at the Confederations Cup. Spain won EURO 2008 and became the first champions to successfully defend their European title in 2012. In between came Spain's very first World Cup triumph, achieved after qualifying with a perfect record (ten wins out of ten) and victories over Portugal, Paraguay, Germany, and the Netherlands at the tournament.

◥ Xavi Hernández unleashes a shot during Spain's comprehensive 4–0 victory over Italy in the final of the 2012 European Championships.

FACT FILE

In the semifinal of the 1938 World Cup, the string of Giuseppe Meazza's shorts broke and they fell to the ground just as he went to take a penalty kick. Holding his shorts up with one hand, Meazza calmly stroked the penalty kick home past the bemused Brazilian goalkeeper, Valter.

ITALY
FOUNDED: 1898

Italy and Uruguay emerged as the leading teams during the first decade of the World Cup. The Italians chose not to enter the first tournament, in 1930, but were hosts of the second, where they were managed by Vittorio Pozzo, who was nicknamed the "Old Maestro."

Pozzo deployed several oriundi—Argentinians of Italian descent—including Raimundo Orsi and the captain, Luisito Monti. His team also included one of the world's finest attackers of the inter-war years, Giuseppe Meazza. Italy won the 1934 World Cup under Pozzo's leadership and also triumphed at the 1936 Olympics. Recognizing the fact that his team was aging, the wily Pozzo introduced more and more young players, so that by the time of the 1938 World Cup, only two members of the 1934 team, Meazza and Giovanni Ferrari, remained. Pozzo's overhaul of the team proved a triumph, as Italy beat the popular French, Brazilian, and Hungarian teams to reclaim the trophy and make Pozzo the only manager in men's soccer to have won two World Cups.

◀ Italy's national team pictured after their 1938 World Cup victory, with coach Vittorio Pozzo holding the trophy. The Italians comfortably beat Hungary 4–2 in the final.

ENGLAND
FOUNDED: 1863

As an England player, Alf Ramsey's last game had been the 6–3 demolition by Hungary in 1953—the game that punctured English belief in its soccer superiority. Ramsey was made England coach in 1962, and for the 1966 World Cup he had assembled a powerful team with a strong spine—Gordon Banks as goalkeeper, Jackie Charlton and Bobby Moore in central defense, Bobby Charlton in midfield, and, up front, Roger Hunt and the free-scoring Jimmy Greaves (who was injured during the tournament and replaced by Geoff Hurst). Propelled by goals mainly from Hunt and Bobby Charlton, and by a prudent defense that did not concede a goal until the semifinal, England beat Mexico, France, Argentina, and Portugal. In the final at Wembley Stadium a memorable hat trick by Geoff Hurst and a goal from Martin Peters saw England beat West Germany 4–2 to win the trophy. After reaching the semifinals of the 1968 European Championships, England was one of the favorites for the 1970 World Cup. In the quarterfinal they were leading 2–0 with just 20 minutes left to play, before West Germany struck back to win 3–2. They would only reach two semifinals in the next 12 World Cups (1990 and 2018).

▶ England captain Bobby Moore sits on the shoulders of Geoff Hurst (left) and Ray Wilson (right) as he holds the World Cup at Wembley.

▲ Nigerian forward Daniel Amokachi is tackled by Flavio of Brazil at the Centennial Olympic games in 1996.

NIGERIA
FOUNDED: 1945

In 1985 Nigeria's youngsters captured the World Under-17 Championship to become the first African nation to win a world tournament. Eleven years later, the "Super Eagles" were the stars of the Atlanta Olympics thanks to their attacking verve, team spirit, and will to win. Featuring talented players such as Celestine Babayaro, Emmanuel Amunike, and Daniel Amokachi, Nigeria beat Hungary 1–0 and Japan 2–0, before losing to Brazil 1–0 in the group stages. They then beat Mexico 2–0 in the quarterfinals, setting up a second meeting with Brazil. That match is considered to be the finest in Olympic history. With 13 minutes to go, Nigeria were losing 3–1, but they pulled back one goal before their captain, Nwankwo Kanu, scored a last-gasp goal to tie. In a frenetic period of extra time, Kanu struck again to seal a 4–3 victory. Another great comeback in the final saw Nigeria win gold by defeating Argentina 3–2.

NETHERLANDS
FOUNDED: 1889

Rinus Michels, a former Netherlands center forward, masterminded a revolution in Dutch soccer in the mid-1960s. First at club team Ajax, and then with the national team, he developed a system in which all his players were comfortable on the ball and would switch positions, often with devastating results. Called "total soccer" (see page 59), the system revolved around such world-class talents as Johan Cruyff, Johan Neeskens, and Ruud Krol. With Michels at the helm, the Dutch powered to the 1974 World Cup final, scoring 14 goals and conceding only one in qualifying. They soared through the rounds, demolishing Argentina 4–0 and beating Brazil 2–0 on the way to the final against West Germany. Despite taking a one-goal lead within 80 seconds, the Netherlands suffered heartbreak, losing 2–1. Two years later, they reached the semifinal of the 1976 European Championships, going out to the eventual winners, Czechoslovakia, in extra time. The Dutch entered the 1978 World Cup without Cruyff, but could still call upon many of the 1974 squad, including Neeskens, Krol, and strikers Johnny Rep and Robbie Rensenbrink. They reached the final again, this time losing 3–1 to Argentina. Considered the most talented team never to win the World Cup, the Dutch enthralled millions of fans with their exploits and flair.

▶ Alexandra Popp can play anywhere in attack or midfield. By 2022, this versatile player had scored 53 goals for Germany.

GERMANY WOMEN
FIRST INTERNATIONAL
MATCH: 1982

Germany struggled to be competitive in the 1980s but received a huge boost in 1989 when they won the first of their eight European Championships. The 21st century proved remarkably fruitful for the team as they won the 2003 Women's World Cup and continued their European dominance with their sixth championship crown in a row in 2013. Before retiring in 2011, Germany's goal machine, Birgit Prinz, scored an incredible 128 goals for her country. In the 2007 World Cup, Germany's 11–0 spectacular defeat of Argentina—and feat of not conceding a goal throughout the tournament—were undoubted highlights. The Olympics eluded this talented team until Brazil 2016, when the team defeated China, Canada, and Sweden to win the gold medal.

◀ The Netherlands line up before the 1978 World Cup final, which was held at River Plate's home stadium.

MEXICO
FOUNDED: 1927

Having reached the quarterfinals of the two World Cups it has hosted (1970 and 1986), the soccer-crazy nation of Mexico had much to cheer about in the 1990s, when its national team dominated the continental championships, the CONCACAF Gold Cup. In the inaugural competition of 1991, Mexico lost to the U.S. at the semifinal stage, but in the next three competitions it was unstoppable. It was rampant in 1993, beating Canada 8–0 and Jamaica 6–1 before humbling the U.S. 4–0 in the final. At the 1996 Gold Cup, it defeated invited guests Brazil to win the title and, four years later, beat the U.S. again to secure a hat trick of wins. At the heart of Mexico's authoritative displays was the defender Claudio Suarez, nicknamed the "Emperor" for his commanding performances. Suarez made his national debut in 1992 and played his 177th game in 2006 against the Netherlands. A new generation of Mexican talent has added to this success, winning the Gold Cup in 2009 and 2011, and beating Brazil to grab more gold at the 2012 London Olympics.

FACT FILE
Mexico striker Javier Hernandez was timed as the fastest player at the 2010 World Cup—reaching a speed of 19.97 mph (32.15km/h).

◀ Mexican defender Dárvin Chávez at the 2012 Olympics. Chávez played 31 times for the Mexican under-23 team, which won Olympic gold.

BRAZIL
FOUNDED: 1914

The 1958 World Cup signaled the arrival of Pelé and the start of a magnificent era for Brazil in which they won three out of four World Cups. The squad that claimed the 1970 World Cup is considered by many to be international soccer's greatest team. In attack, few nations before or since have been able to field a team so blessed with flair and skill on the ball, as well as superb vision and movement off it. Opponents sometimes tried to mark Pelé out of the game, but this would only give opportunities to marvelous players such as center forward Tostao, the bustling Roberto Rivelino, midfield general Gerson, or powerful winger Jairzinho. At the back, high-class players such as Carlos Alberto maintained a solid defense, but this team was all about attack. After going a goal down to Czechoslovakia in their first match at the 1970 World Cup, Brazil responded by scoring four times. They scored three to beat Uruguay in the semifinal and four in the final, in which they outclassed a strong Italy with one of the greatest displays of attacking soccer. Brazil dazzled with their wit and invention, and the 4–1 score was completed by a marvelous team move ending in a thunderous shot by Carlos Alberto. In his last match for Brazil, Pelé was chaired off the field by his teammates. The departure of other members of the team meant that by the 1974 World Cup, only Rivelino and Jairzinho remained from the squad that had captured the imagination of millions.

◄ Brazil's team that beat England at the 1970 World Cup. Back row, left to right: Carlos Alberto, Brito, Wilson Piazza, Félix, Clodoaldo, Everaldo, Mario Zagalo (coach); front row: Jairzinho, Roberto Rivelino, Tostao, Pelé, Paulo Cesar.

FACT FILE

Brazil's first international match was in July 1914, when it played English league team Exeter City. In 2004, the 1994 Brazilian World Cup-winning team played a rematch against Exeter, winning the game 1–0.

▲ Pelé kisses the Jules Rimet trophy after Brazil's 1970 triumph. He was the first World Cup winner to score in four successive tournaments.

▼ Mo Salah celebrates with Essam El Hadary as Egypt progresses to the 2017 African Cup of Nations final.

EGYPT
FOUNDED: 1920

In 1934, Egypt became the first African nation to appear at a World Cup, but it has made only two further appearances since. In between, there was the brilliance of twin brothers Hossam and Ibrahim Hassan, and a spell of dominance in Africa underpinned by the excellence of Essam El Hadary in the goal and Ahmed Hassan as captain. The Pharaohs won three Africa Cup of Nations in a row (2006, 2008, 2010), without losing a single game in all three tournaments. El Hadary was voted the competition's best goalie in all three editions and Ahmed Hassan the best player overall in two. In 2012, Hassan became Egypt's most capped player, while El Hadary's story took a remarkable twist when he helped Egypt to another Cup of Nations final in 2017 and played at the 2018 World Cup at the age of 45, making him that competition's oldest player ever. Most of the national team today plays in Egypt, but fans of the Pharaohs also enjoy the exploits of foreign-based stars, including Mohamed Salah, their current captain.

JAPAN WOMEN
FIRST INTERNATIONAL MATCH: 1985

Japan enjoyed a rich spell of form in the 2010s that saw them challenge the dominance of Germany and the U.S. as women's soccer's preeminent teams. With a world-class midfield pairing of Homare Sawa and Aya Miyama at the heart of the team, Japan won a silver medal at the 2012 Olympics but the year before had shocked the soccer world with victories over Mexico, England, Germany, and Sweden to reach the final of the Women's World Cup. There, they defeated the U.S. to become the first Asian nation to win the ultimate prize in women's soccer. They came close to repeating the feat in 2015, reaching the final again, only to suffer a heavy defeat to the U.S. The retirement of much of the golden generation, including Sawa in 2015 and Miyama a year later, saw Japan undergo a lengthy rebuild. Within their continent, however, they remain peerless. Japan went unbeaten through two Asian Cups to be crowned double champions (2014, 2018) and never finished outside of the top four in the previous 12 tournaments—a remarkable record.

◀ Japan's inspirational captain Homare Sawa shoots during a group game against Mexico at the 2011 Women's World Cup. Sawa scored a hat trick as Japan won 4–0.

FACT FILE

Idriss Carlos Kameni was only 16 when he played goalkeeper for Cameroon in the 2000 Olympic final. He was a hero as early as the fifth minute, when he saved a Spanish penalty kick. Cameroon went on to win gold in a penalty shoot-out, making the coach, Jean-Paul Akono, the first African coach to win a major world soccer competition.

LONGEST UNBEATEN INTERNATIONAL RUNS (IN GAMES)

36	Brazil 1993–96
35	Spain 2007–09
31	Argentina 1991–93
	Spain 1994–98
30	France 1994–96
	Hungary 1950–54
29	Brazil 1970–73
28	South Korea 1977–79
27	Colombia 1992–94
	Spain 2016–18
26	Spain 2011–13
25	Italy 2004–06
	Netherlands 2008–10

CAMEROON
FOUNDED: 1960

Cameroon threatened a major shock at the 1982 World Cup, tying against Italy (the eventual winners) and Poland, yet narrowly failing to reach the second round. In 1990 a team led by Roger Milla lit up the tournament, winning a tough group containing the Soviet Union, Argentina, and Romania, beating Colombia in round two, and taking England to extra time before losing 3–2. Many of Cameroon's players have played for Europe's top clubs—Geremi at Real Madrid, Samuel Eto'o at Barcelona, and Salomon Olembe at Marseille, for example. After a disappointing 1998 World Cup, Cameroon roared back in 2000. They won the African Nations Cup, beating Nigeria. They then triumphed at the Olympics, stunning Brazil in the quarterfinals, Chile in the semis, and Spain in the final to win gold.

◀ Roger Milla races past Romania's Gheorghe Popescu to score his first goal at the 1990 World Cup. Milla struck again to give Cameroon a 2–1 victory.

CLUB TEAMS

BARCELONA
SPAIN • FOUNDED: 1899
STADIUM: NOU CAMP

With their own bank, radio station, and one of the most impressive stadiums in the world, Barcelona can easily claim to be one of the world's largest soccer clubs. Barcelona's domestic achievements are impressive—their sixth-place finish in the Spanish league, La Liga, in 2003 was their worst since 1942. The club has won 26 league titles, finished runner-up 26 times, and top the list of Copa del Rey winners, with 31 victories. Barcelona smashed the world transfer record in 1973 when they paid $2 million for Dutch maestro Johan Cruyff. Fifteen years later, he returned as the club's coach. In his first season, Cruyff steered the club to second place in La Liga and to victory over Sampdoria to collect the European Cup-Winners' Cup. Dutchman Ronald Koeman and Denmark's Michael Laudrup were signed to play alongside Spanish stars such as goalie Andoni Zubizarreta and midfielder José Bakero. In 1991 Barcelona won the first of four league titles in a row and one year later won their first European Cup, beating Sampdoria. Their second triumph in the competition came in 2006, along with the Spanish league title. Barcelona have won the prized double of La Liga and Champions League three times (2009, 2011, and 2015).

▲ Al-Ahly's Waled Suleiman (left) and Hossam Ashour (center) in action against Zamalek in a 2018 local-rivalry match in Cairo.

AL-AHLY
EGYPT • FOUNDED: 1907
STADIUM: AL-AHLY WE STADIUM

Cairo-based Al-Ahly can lay claim to being the most successful club in Africa. They have notched up 42 Egyptian Premier League titles, 37 Egypt Cup wins, and ten African Champions League triumphs—five more than the next best club, their fierce domestic rivals, Zamalek. After winning the first Egyptian league competition in 1949, Al-Ahly enjoyed a long spell of league success until the 1960s, and another period of supremacy in the 1980s. Intent on continuing their dominance after being named CAF's African Club of the 20th Century, Al-Ahly won 13 out of 15 league titles up to 2021. The year 2020 also saw Al-Ahly record their seventh CAF Super Cup victory and their second third-placed finish at the Club World Cup.

FACT FILE

Two of Al-Ahly's youngest stars during the 1990s were the twins Hossam and Ibrahim Hassan, the most-capped players in Egyptian soccer. The brothers were idolized as they helped Al-Ahly to four league titles, but turned from heroes to villains when they sensationally quit the club to join rivals Zamalek in 2000.

▶ Barcelona midfielder Frenkie de Jong in action against Napoli in the Champions League round of 16 in 2020. Barcelona won 4–2 on aggregate to progress to the quarterfinals.

FLAMENGO
BRAZIL • FOUNDED: 1895
STADIUMS: GÁVEA, MARACANA

Brazil is full of famous soccer teams, including Vasco da Gama, São Paulo, Botafogo, and Corinthians. Flamengo are the most heavily supported of them all, having recorded 42 attendances of 100,000 or more at their games. Many gifted players have worn the team's distinctive black-and-red striped shirts. One of the greatest was Léonidas da Silva, known as the "Black Diamond" and the star of the 1938 World Cup. After a successful period in the 1950s, when the team won three Rio state league titles and earned the nickname the "Steamroller," Flamengo had to wait more than 25 years for their next great era. Inspired by Zico and his strike partner, Nunes, the team won the Rio Championship (the Carioca) in 1978, 1979, and 1981, and the Brazilian National Championship in 1980, 1982, and 1983. In 1981 it captured the Copa Libertadores and one month later went on to claim the World Club Cup, beating Liverpool 3–0.

▶ Gabriel Barbosa kisses the trophy in 2020 after Flamengo secured their second Campeonato Brasileiro Série A in a row.

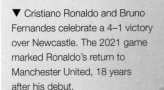

▼ Cristiano Ronaldo and Bruno Fernandes celebrate a 4–1 victory over Newcastle. The 2021 game marked Ronaldo's return to Manchester United, 18 years after his debut.

MANCHESTER UNITED
ENGLAND • FOUNDED: 1878
STADIUM: OLD TRAFFORD

Sir Alex Ferguson, the Premiership's longest-serving and most successful manager, led Manchester United to a unique triple in English soccer when it won the Premier League, the FA Cup, and the UEFA Champions League in 1999. Forty years earlier a Manchester United team coached by Sir Matt Busby—another Scot who became a knight—had captured the hearts and minds of fans everywhere. The story began in the mid-1950s. Great things were expected of the young "Busby Babes" team that had won two league titles (in 1956 and 1957) and included, among other talents, the young England stars Roger Byrne and Duncan Edwards. But in 1958 a tragic plane crash in Munich, Germany, killed 23 people on board, including eight members of the Manchester United first team. Busby had to build a new team, which contained tough defenders like Nobby Stiles, young midfielders such as Brian Kidd, and two survivors from the Munich crash, Bobby Charlton and central defender Bill Foulkes. Although often playing in midfield, Charlton formed a glittering attacking trio with Denis Law and George Best. Busby's team won the league title in 1965 and 1967, but the pinnacle of their achievements came in the 1968 European Cup. After beating Real Madrid in the semifinal, Manchester United faced Benfica in the final. Two goals from Charlton, one from Best, and one from the 19-year-old Kidd secured a memorable 4–1 victory. The "Red Devils," as the team is nicknamed, had become the first English team to win the European Cup.

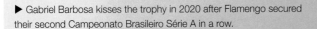

◀ Bobby Charlton (right) carries the trophy with teammate Shay Brennan after Manchester United's defeat of Benfica to win the European Cup in 1968.

▶ Inter forward Lautaro Martinez in action in a 5–1 Serie A win over Sampdoria in 2021.

INTERNAZIONALE (INTER MILAN)
ITALY • FOUNDED: 1908
STADIUM: GIUSEPPE MEAZZA (SAN SIRO)

Also known as Inter Milan, Internazionale was formed by a group of former AC Milan players. During the rule of dictator Benito Mussolini, the club was forced to change its name to Ambrosiana-Inter, but switched it back in 1942. Argentinian coach Helenio Herrera joined Inter in 1960 and pioneered a new tactical system, playing a sweeper behind a back four and using fast-moving defenders to build attacks. Known as the catenaccio (door bolt) system, it was seen as negative and defensive by some. But Inter won Serie A in 1963, 1965, and 1966 and also triumphed over Real Madrid in 1964 and the mighty Benfica in 1965 to win the European Cup twice. They added the World Club Cup to their list of honors in 1964 and 1965, but did not add to their European tally until the 1990s, when they won the UEFA Cup three times. In 2006, Inter was controversially awarded the Italian league title when Juventus were stripped of the trophy. Inter followed up with four further Serie A titles in 2007, 2008, 2009, 2010, and a fifth in 2021, when 24 goals and 11 assists by Romelu Lukaku helped break Juventus's league dominance.

SLAVIA PRAGUE
CZECH REPUBLIC
FOUNDED: 1892
STADIUM: SINOBO STADIUM

Enjoying golden spells in the 1930s, 1940s, and 1990s, Slavia Prague have often been overshadowed by their city rivals, Sparta. That has changed in recent years, however. Bolstered by new owners, the Red and Whites—whose colors have not changed since their formation—won the Czech First League in 2017, followed by league success again in 2019 and 2020. Despite the loss of midfield lynchpin Tomáš Souček and enterprising fullback Vladimír Coufal—both to West Ham in 2020—Slavia achieved a league and cup double in 2021. The team also fared relatively well in the 2020–21 Europa League, with wins over Bayer Leverkusen, Nice, Leicester City, and Rangers, before defeat at the quarterfinal stage to Arsenal.

◀ Slavia's Jakub Hromada holds off Leicester City's Youri Tielemans during a 2021 Europa League clash.

SANTOS
BRAZIL • FOUNDED: 1912 • STADIUM: VILA BELMIRO

Santos are most famous as being Pelé's club. The team had won few honors before he began playing for them in 1956, at age 15. During Pelé's 19 years at the club, Santos won the São Paulo Championship ten times and the Copa Libertadores twice, in 1962 and 1963. They also won the World Club Cup in those years, the first with an extraordinary 5–2 win away at Benfica, which included a sensational hat trick from Pelé. Santos have fared less well in the years since, but a number of bright young stars emerged in this century. The club took a gamble on many of these players in the 2002 Brazilian National Championship, fielding a team with an average age of only 22. With 17-year-old midfielder Diego and 18-year-old striker Robinho especially prominent, Santos rolled back the years and delighted many neutral fans by winning the competition.

◀ Santos defender Lucas Verissimo (right) clashes with Luiz Adriano of Palmeiras in the 2020 final of the Copa Libertadores. Due to the COVID-19 pandemic, the match was played in 2021.

▼ The Dick, Kerr Ladies team pictured during their historic and successful 1922 tour of North America.

BOCA JUNIORS
ARGENTINA • FOUNDED: 1905
STADIUM: LA BOMBONERA

Best known in Europe as the club for which Diego Maradona played, Boca Juniors were founded by a group of Italian immigrants and an Irishman, Patrick MacCarthy. With their Buenos Aires neighbors River Plate, they form one of the fiercest rivalries in world soccer. Boca have the edge when they play against each other and have won two more Copa Libertadores than River. Boca had a strong resurgence at the end of the 1900s. Beginning in May 1998 they went 40 league games unbeaten to set an Argentinian record. The run helped them win the Clausura and Apertura league titles in 1999, a feat that was followed by an incredible four Copa Libertadores triumphs in 2000, 2001, 2003, and 2007, as well as two Intercontinental Cups in 2000 and 2003.

◀ Boca Juniors forward Norberto Briasco (left) battles for the ball with Patronato defender Facundo Cobos in an Argentinian Primera División match in 2021.

DICK, KERR LADIES
ENGLAND • FOUNDED: 1917
NO STADIUM

W. B. Dick and John Kerr owned a railroad and tram equipment-making factory in Preston, northwest England. During World War I, women began to work in factories, taking the jobs of the men serving in the war. In 1917 the women at Dick, Kerr challenged their male coworkers to a game of soccer and went on to organize games against male and female opponents to raise money for war charities. By 1920 Dick, Kerr Ladies were playing matches to sell-out crowds. One game against St. Helen's Ladies attracted 53,000 spectators to Everton's Goodison Park. In 1921, at the peak of their popularity, Dick, Kerr Ladies played 67 games, and a tour of the United States the following year saw the team win three and tie three out of nine games against male teams. The Football Association felt threatened by a team that, in some cases, was attracting bigger crowds than the men's game. In 1921 the FA banned all women from playing soccer on the fields of its member clubs. Incredibly, the ban remained in force for 50 years. As a result, support for women's soccer dwindled, and by 1926 Dick, Kerr Ladies had disbanded. Yet the team left an important legacy by showing that women could play competitive, entertaining soccer.

AC MILAN
ITALY • FOUNDED: 1899
STADIUM: GIUSEPPE MEAZZA (SAN SIRO)

AC Milan's first period of notable success came in the 1950s, when a trio of Swedish stars—Gunnar Gren, Nils Liedholm, and Gunnar Nordahl—followed by Uruguayan striker Juan Alberto Schiaffino, helped them to four Serie A titles. Nordahl remains the club's highest scorer, with an amazing 210 goals in 257 games. The 1960s saw AC Milan emerge as one of the leading clubs in Europe, winning two European Cups and a Cup-Winners' Cup trophy. A period of decline followed, which included an enforced relegation in 1980 after a betting scandal. Milan's fortunes were revived by the arrival of a new chairman, Silvio Berlusconi, in 1986. The wealthy media tycoon appointed Arrigo Sacchi as coach the following year. An exciting team was assembled, which included the superb Dutch trio of Ruud Gullit, Marco van Basten, and Frank Rijkaard, alongside Franco Baresi, Roberto Donadoni, and Paolo Maldini. Milan won Serie A in 1988 and went on to win it five times during the 1990s. Starting in 1991, Milan went unbeaten in Serie A for an incredible 58 games. In Europe, Milan beat Real Madrid 5–0 and then Steaua Bucharest 4–0 in the final to collect the European Cup in 1989—a competition they also won in 1990, 1994, and 2003, and in which they were runner-up in 1993, 1995, and 2005. They won their seventh Champions League title in 2007. In Italy, Milan claimed the Serie A title for the 18th time in 2011.

▲ Kaka sprints away from Liverpool's defense during the 2007 Champions League final. Milan beat Celtic, Bayern Munich, and Manchester United on the way to the final.

RIVER PLATE
ARGENTINA • FOUNDED: 1901
STADIUM: MONUMENTAL

River Plate are one of Argentina's leading teams. In the late 1930s, they moved to a wealthy suburb of Buenos Aires which, along with a team of expensive players, led to their nickname, the Millionaires. River are renowned for their attacking style. In the late 1940s, their powerful forward line became known as La Maquina (the Machine), and the club has produced a succession of world-class attackers, including Omar Sivori, Mario Kempes, Hernan Crespo, Javier Saviola, and the legendary Alfredo di Stefano. River Plate have won 36 Argentinian league titles, yet it was not until 1986 that they triumphed in the Copa Libertadores. The team had made the final twice previously (in 1966 and 1976) before a squad featuring Norberto Alonso, Juan Gilberto Funes, and the great Uruguayan striker Enzo Francescoli beat America Cali of Colombia. River have enjoyed three further Copa Libertadores triumphs, the latest in 2018, in which they beat fierce rivals Boca Juniors 5–3 in the final.

▶ Striker Rafael Santos Borre celebrates scoring for River Plate against LDU Quito in the 2020 Copa Libertadores. The club reached the semifinal in that year, and the final in the year before.

MAMELODI SUNDOWNS
SOUTH AFRICA • FOUNDED: 1970
STADIA: LUCAS MORIPE / LOFTUS VERSFELD

Formed by a group of friends in Pretoria and formerly owned by a pair of doctors, Sundowns have enjoyed great success under the ownership of millionaire businessman Patrice Motsepe. He experimented with foreign coaches including Johan Neeskens, Hristo Stoichkov, and former France manager Henri Michel, but it was the arrival of former player and South Africa national team coach Pitso Mosimane in 2012 that triggered the most sustained period of success in the club's history. Eleven league titles have come since 1998, including four in a row up to 2021. The club also finished runner-up three times during that period, and in 2012 defeated Powerlines in a Nedbank Cup game by a record 24–0 margin. The year 2016 was a landmark one for "The Brazilians," so named for their yellow and blue uniforms. Having reached the final of the CAF Champions League in 2001, they went one step further, defeating Egyptian giants Zamalek 3–1 on aggregate in the two-legged final. The win meant Sundowns became only the second South African team (following Orlando Pirates) to win the continent's biggest club prize.

◀ Midfielder Thapelo Morena strikes the ball on the volley as the Sundowns play title rivals Kaiser Chiefs in 2019.

MOST CONSECUTIVE LEAGUE CHAMPIONSHIPS		
15	Tafea FC (Vanuatu)	1994–2008
14	Lincoln (Gibraltar)	2003–16
14	Skonto Riga (Latvia)	1991–2004
13	Al-Faisaly (Jordan)	1959–66, 1970–74
13	BATE Borisov (Belarus)	2006–18
13	Rosenborg (Norway)	1992–2004
11	Al-Ansar (Lebanon)	1988, 1990–99
11	Dinamo Zagreb (Croatia)	2006–16
11	Loto Ha'apai FC (Tonga)	1998–2008
11	Nauti (Tuvalu)	1980–90

PARIS SAINT-GERMAIN
FRANCE • FOUNDED: 1970 • STADIUM: PARC DES PRINCES

Formed to provide an elite club in Paris to challenge for trophies, PSG were initially owned by businesspeople and around 20,000 fans. The Coupe de France in 1982 was the club's first major piece of silverware; they have won the trophy 13 more times since. Their first Ligue 1 title came in 1986, but only one further success and six runner-up spots followed in the 1990s and early 2000s. In 2012, the Emir of Qatar became PSG's owner. This triggered a glut of big-money signings, starting with the French transfer record being broken for Javier Pastore ($56 million). Several signings of $45 million or more followed, including the world-record fee of $263 million to sign Neymar, and around $216 million for Kylian Mbappé. Edinson Cavani ($84 million) remains the club's all-time top scorer, with 200 goals. Between 2013 and 2021, PSG won seven out of nine Ligue 1 championships. In 2016, a record 9–0 thrashing of Troyes confirmed their status as Ligue 1 champions again with eight games still to play. While a 2020 runner-up spot is their highest Champions League placing, a staggering 20 domestic cups won since 2012, in addition to the league titles, confirms their status as France's leading club, augmented by the summer 2021 signings of Lionel Messi, Sergio Ramos, Nuno Mendes, and Gianluigi Donnarumma.

◀ PSG's Ángel di María chases down the ball. The winger has made over 300 appearances since joining the club in 2015.

▲ Fluminense players celebrate a 3–1 victory over their local rivals Flamengo in 2021. Games between these Rio de Janeiro clubs take place at their shared stadium, the Maracanã.

FLUMINENSE
BRAZIL • FOUNDED: 1902
STADIUMS: LARANJEIRAS, MARACANÃ

Founded in 1902, Fluminense have traditionally been supported by the middle classes, while their fierce Rio de Janiero rival, Flamengo, drew support from the working class. Games between the two teams always guarantee big crowds. One "Flu vs. Fla" match in 1963 attracted a world-record attendance for a club game, with 177,656 fans crammed inside the enormous Maracanã Stadium. Fluminense also competes in Rio's oldest local-rivalry game, the Classico Vovô (Grandpa Derby), with Botafogo, cofounders of the Rio league. Despite being the home club of a series of Brazilian soccer legends, including Didi during the 1950s and Carlos Alberto and Roberto Rivelino in the 1960s and 1970s, Fluminense have always disappointed on the international stage. They have never won a major South American competition. However, they have achieved a lot in Brazil, winning the Rio Championship title 31 times. One of their most impressive runs came when the Tricolores—so nicknamed for their green, red, and white colors—won three Rio Championships in a row from 1983 to 1985. Fluminense have also won the Brazilian National Championship four times, and won the inaugural Primeira Liga in 2016.

ARSENAL
ENGLAND • FOUNDED: 1886
STADIUM: EMIRATES

First known as Dial Square FC, this club was formed by workers from the Royal Arsenal munitions factory in Woolwich, south London—hence the team's nickname, the "Gunners." After a move to the north of the city in 1913, Arsenal's rise to the top of the English game coincided with the appointment of Herbert Chapman as coach in 1925. Chapman was highly innovative both on and off the field, and he built a counterattacking team featuring inside forwards Alex James and David Jack and winger Cliff Bastin, whose 178 goals for the club remained a record for more than 50 years. Arsenal were league runner-up in Chapman's first season and won the title in 1931 with a point total that would not be beaten for 30 years. Runner-up in 1932, the team then claimed three league titles in a row (1933–35) and two FA Cups (1930 and 1936). Despite a league and FA Cup double in 1971, the closest Arsenal have come to their earlier dominance has been under French coach Arsène Wenger. With a team boasting Thierry Henry, Dennis Bergkamp, and Patrick Vieira, they won three Premier League titles and four FA Cups from 1998 to 2005. Arsenal were unbeaten through the 2003–04 season, recording a total of 49 league games without defeat, a record in English soccer. They have won the FA Cup a record 14 times in total.

FACT FILE
Under Herbert Chapman, "The Arsenal" became just "Arsenal," allegedly to make them appear at the top of an alphabetical list of Division One clubs. Chapman also successfully campaigned for Gillespie Road subway station, close to the ground, to be renamed "Arsenal."

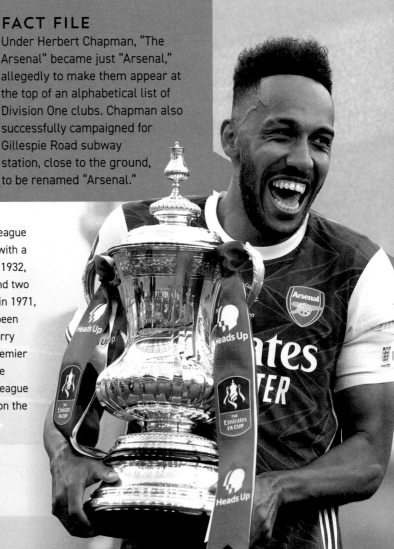

► Arsenal striker Pierre-Emerick Aubameyang celebrates with the trophy at Wembley after his team's record-breaking victory over Chelsea in the 2020 FA Cup final.

CORINTHIANS WOMEN
BRAZIL • FOUNDED: 1997, REFOUNDED 2016
STADIUM: PARQUE SÃO JORGE

Sport Club Corinthians Paulista Futebol Feminino were disbanded in 2009 and then reformed as a short-lived partnership with Audax before Corinthians went it alone. Inspired by stellar performances from players such as Tamires Dias de Britto, club captain Grazi, and young goal scorer Gabi Nunes—who struck 77 times in her first 115 matches for the club—the team has truly prospered. It has won the Campeonato Paulista twice (2019, 2020), the Campeonato Brasileiro twice (2018, 2020), and the Copa do Brasil once (2016). It scooped the continental prize, the Copa Libertadores Femenina, in 2017 and 2019, announcing the team as a major force in women's soccer.

◥ Victória (left) and Tamires of Corinthians celebrate a goal in the 2020 Women's Copa Libertadores semifinal.

▲ Juve forward Paulo Dybala celebrates a Champions League goal against Lokomotiv Moscow in 2019.

▲ Striker Hakan Sükür (center) scored more than 290 goals for Galatasaray in over 500 games.

GALATASARAY
TURKEY • FOUNDED: 1905
STADIUM: ALI SAMI YEN

Turkey's three biggest clubs—Galatasaray, Fenerbahçe, and Besiktas—are all based in Istanbul, and their passionate fans are fierce and occasionally violent rivals. Galatasaray have won the league title 22 times (three more than Fenerbahçe), the latest being in 2019, as well as the Turkish Cup 18 times, including victory over Akhisarspor in 2019. They are the best-known Turkish club overseas, partly because of their competitive performances in Europe during the 1990s. Visiting foreign teams often encounter an intimidating atmosphere—from "Welcome to Hell" banners displayed at the airport by fans, to a stadium that turns into a cauldron of color and noise on game nights. Galatasaray went unbeaten at home in Europe from 1984 to 1994, the year in which they tied 3–3 at Old Trafford to knock Manchester United out of the Champions League. In 2000 the team won their first major European trophy by beating Arsenal to win the UEFA Cup.

JUVENTUS
ITALY • FOUNDED: 1897
STADIUM: DELLE ALPI

Formed by high school students in Turin, Juventus used to play in pink shirts until they switched to black-and-white stripes in 1903. The club won five consecutive league titles from 1931 to 1935, and its successful 1980s team won Serie A four times and the 1985 European Cup. Financed by the wealthy Agnelli family, owners of the Fiat car company, Juventus spent lavishly on top-class players in the 1990s, including Roberto Baggio, Gianluca Vialli, Attilio Lombardo, Angelo di Livio, Fabrizio Ravanelli, and Christian Vieri. After capturing the UEFA Cup twice in the early 1990s, Juve won an Italian league and cup double in 1995 and beat Ajax to win the Champions League in 1996. The team lost the final of that competition in 1997 and 1998, but its fans could console themselves with Serie A titles in both years. Following a game-fixing scandal, Juventus were stripped of the 2005 and 2006 Serie A titles and relegated to Serie B for the first time. The team bounced back into Serie A in 2009 and built a new era of dominance, winning its ninth Serie A title in a row in 2020, its 14th Supercoppa Italiana in 2021, and reaching Champions League finals in 2015 and 2017.

BAYERN MUNICH
GERMANY • FOUNDED: 1900
STADIUM: ALLIANZ ARENA

Germany's most famous club was formed in 1900 by rebels who had split from their former club, MTV 1879. The new team beat their old side 7–1 in the first game between the clubs. Although Bayern won a league title in 1932, by the early 1960s they were one of West Germany's less popular clubs and did not achieve a place in the Bundesliga when it was formed in 1963. But the team earned promotion soon after and by the late 1960s was a dominant force in the domestic game. At the forefront were future soccer legends such as Sepp Maier, Franz Beckenbauer, and Gerd Müller, who was the Bundesliga's top scorer in seven seasons (1967, 1969–70, 1972–74, and 1978). With that squad, Bayern won German Cups in 1966 and 1967 and a European Cup-Winners' Cup in 1967. In the early 1970s Bayern's stars were joined by more world-class players such as Paul Breitner and Uli Hoeness. The team won three Bundesliga titles in a row and three consecutive European Cups from 1974 to 1976. Success has continued with 2012–13 proving a stellar season—including a notable Bundesliga, German Cup, and Champions League triple under outgoing coach Jupp Heynckes. In 2021, Bayern celebrated winning their 31st Bundesliga title, their ninth in a row. The year before the team had secured their sixth European Cup/Champions League crown.

▶ Bayern's Kingsley Coman celebrates after scoring the only goal of the Champions League final against PSG in 2020.

▶ Benfica players pose during the 1968–69 season. Having reached the final of the European Cup in 1968, the team started its next campaign with an 8–1 win over Iceland's Valur but was eventually knocked out by Ajax in the quarterfinals.

ZENIT SAINT PETERSBURG
RUSSIA • FOUNDED: 1925
STADIUM: PETROVSKY STADIUM

Founded by a group of local metal workers, Zenit originally played in the Soviet league and in the 1950s could count on the support of famous classical composer Dmitri Shostakovich in the stands. The breakup of the Soviet Union saw Zenit, known as the Blue-and-Whites, enter the Russian league, which they won for the first time in 2007—with Andrei Arshavin the team's standout performer. Six further league titles followed, including three in a row (2019, 2020, and 2021). The club frequently competes in the Champions League, but in 2008 Zenit won the UEFA Cup for the first time and beat Manchester United later the same year to lift the UEFA Super Cup.

BENFICA
PORTUGAL • FOUNDED: 1904
STADIUM: ESTADIO DA LUZ

Benfica remains Portugal's most famous and successful club, despite the long periods of glory enjoyed by rivals Porto and Sporting Lisbon. Their greatest era was undoubtedly the 1960s, which began under the management of Hungarian Bela Guttmann. The team played with a mix of speed, power, and skill, typified by the midfielder Mario Coluna and the brilliant Eusebio. Benfica began the decade by defeating Barcelona 3–2 to win the 1961 European Cup. The following year, facing the mighty Real Madrid in the final, they found themselves 3–1 down to a Ferenc Puskas hat trick but fought back to beat the Spanish giant 5–3. Benfica featured in five European Cup finals during the 1960s and won eight out of ten league championships. Defending another league title in the 1972–73 season, Benfica went unbeaten through 30 league games, scoring 101 goals in the process.

LOS ANGELES GALAXY
U.S. • FOUNDED: 1995
STADIUM: DIGNITY HEALTH SPORTS PARK

A founding member of Major League Soccer (MLS), the Los Angeles Galaxy are one of its most successful teams, with five MLS Cups (2002, 2005, 2011, 2012, 2014) and four MLS Supporters' Shields trophies (1998, 2002, 2010, 2011). In addition, the team has won the Lamar Hunt U.S. Open Cup twice (2001, 2005) and, in 2000, the CONCACAF Champions League. Attracting homegrown talents such as Cobi Jones and Landon Donovan, the Galaxy have also bought in foreign stars, including David Beckham and, in 2018, Zlatan Ibrahimović. After previously playing at the Rose Bowl and Titan Stadium, the team has played since 2005 at Dignity Health Sports Park.

▲ Mexican midfielder Jonathan dos Santos joined LA Galaxy in 2017. He scored the winning goal against the United States in the 2019 Gold Cup.

ANDERLECHT
BELGIUM • FOUNDED: 1908
STADIUM: LOTTO PARK

Anderlecht took 39 years to win their first league title in 1947 but have won 33 more since, along with 21 runner-up spots, to make them Belgium's most successful team. Such consistency saw the club qualify for European competition every year from 1964 to 2007. A golden period during the 1970s under the management of Raymond Goethals saw Franky van der Elst and Arie Haan play behind a talented strike force of Benny Nielsen and Robbie Rensenbrink. Four Belgian Cups, two European Cup-Winners' Cups, and two European Supercups were won during this period in great, attacking style.

▶ Anderlecht and Belgium forward Francis Amuzu controls the ball during a Belgian Pro League tie with Royal Antwerp in 2021.

VFL WOLFSBURG WOMEN
GERMANY • FOUNDED: 2003
STADIUM: AOK STADION

After relegation, promotion, and rebuilding in the mid-2000s, *Die Wölfinnen* (The She-wolves) won a remarkable treble in 2012–13. They won their first DFB-Pokal Frauen cup competition, their first Frauen-Bundesliga title, and the Women's Champions League. Wolfsburg repeated their league and Champions League feats the following year, which included twin 14–0 and 13–0 thrashings of Pärnu JK. Emphatic results were often achieved by the tactical excellence of Alexandra Popp and the free-scoring play of Conny Pohlers and Martina Müller. Wolfsburg added to their success throughout the 2010s, with a further seven cup wins and five league titles. The 2017 signing of Pernille Harder helped maintain the team's momentum as it battled fierce rivals Bayern Munich for domestic bragging rights.

◀ Members of the Wolfsburg team pose for photos after winning the DFB-Pokal Frauen in 2021. Striker Ewa Pajor holds the trophy.

OLYMPIQUE LYONNAIS FÉMININ
FRANCE • FOUNDED: 1970
STADIUM: PARC OLYMPIQUE LYONNAIS

Aligned to Olympique Lyonnais since 2004, this team has become known for pacy, powerful, and skillful women's soccer. OL Feminin have been dominant in France, winning a record 14 league titles in a row up to 2020. They have also won nine Coupe de France Féminine. In 2011, the team secured their first Women's Champions League title. Propelled by a free-scoring attack led by prolific Norwegian striker Ada Hegerberg and anchored by a tough defense, OL Féminin have won six further Champions League titles and finished runner-up twice, to make them the most successful women's club in Europe.

▲ OL Féminin celebrate their 2020 Champions League win. The team features French stars such as Wendie Renard and Amandine Henry and talented imports such as Chilean goalkeeper Christiane Endler (center).

◀ ES Tunis's Anice Badri (right) battles for the ball during the 2019 CAF Super Cup against Raja Casablanca.

ESPERANCE SPORTIVE TUNIS
TUNISIA • FOUNDED: 1919
STADIUM: EL-MENZAH

With a distinctive uniform that gave the team its nickname—the Blood and Golds—Esperance have long been one of the leading clubs in Tunisia and North Africa. Consecutive Tunisian league wins in 1993 and 1994 paved the way for their 1994 African Champions League triumph, where, in front of a delirious home crowd, the team beat the Egyptian holders Zamalek 3–1. In 1997 Esperance began a record-breaking league run. Seeing off the challenge of leading rivals such as Etoile Sportive du Sahel and Club Africain, the team captured an incredible seven straight league championships. No Tunisian club had won more than three in a row before, and many of the team's best players were part of the Tunisia squad that won the 2004 African Cup of Nations on home soil. The club went on two more back-to-back league-winning runs: four from 2009 to 2012 and five from 2017 to 2021, along with their fourth African Champions League in 2019.

▼ Peñarol's Facundo Torres (left) battles for the ball with Fagner of Corinthians in the 2021 Sudamericana.

PEÑAROL
URUGUAY
FOUNDED: 1891
STADIUM: CAMPEÓN DEL SIGLO

Along with Nacional, Peñarol dominate Uruguayan soccer. Peñarol are marginally the most successful, with 50 titles, the latest in 2018, leaving them four ahead of their rivals. In addition, the team has finished league runner-up 41 times. The club's first golden era came in the 1960s. Led by Ecuadorian striker Pedro Spencer, the team won three Copa Libertadores (1960, 1961, and 1966) and two World Club Cups (against Benfica in 1961 and Real Madrid in 1966). Peñarol's team of the 1980s added to this tally, winning two more Copa Libertadores and, in 1982, beating Aston Villa to win a third World Club Cup. Peñarol hold a number of Copa Libertadores records: the largest win (11–2 against Valencia of Venezuela in 1970), the highest aggregate win (14–1 versus Everest of Ecuador in 1963), and the most consecutive participations in the competition (15 between 1965 and 1979).

LIVERPOOL
ENGLAND • FOUNDED: 1892
STADIUM: ANFIELD

In 1959 Liverpool were struggling in the English second division and had been knocked out of the third round of the FA Cup by amateur team Worcester City. Then Bill Shankly arrived as manager. He was a passionate, no-nonsense Scot who went on to build a successful Liverpool team that won the league championship three times and lifted the UEFA Cup in 1973. One year later he resigned, and Bob Paisley—Shankly's assistant for 15 years—was promoted to manager. Paisley's Liverpool won 19 major trophies in nine years, making him the most successful British coach of the 1900s. The club won six league titles and three League Cups thanks to a watertight defense, a quick, accurate passing game, and intelligent attacking by players such as Kevin Keegan, Steve Heighway, John Toshack, and Kenny Dalglish. A UEFA Cup win in 1976 was followed by European Cup triumphs in 1977 and 1978, making Liverpool the first British team to successfully defend the trophy. In 1981 the club beat Real Madrid to win the European Cup for a third time, and a fourth win came (after penalties) in 1984 against Italian team Roma. Two further Champions League titles followed (in 2005 and 2019), the latter under the leadership of the team's popular German coach, Jürgen Klopp. Klopp's Liverpool team, led by his three-pronged attacking spearhead of Roberto Firmino, Mo Salah, and Sadio Mané, were on imperious form in 2019–20, when the Reds finished 18 points ahead of Manchester City to win their first league title since 1990.

FACT FILE
Between January 1978 and January 1981, Liverpool set an all-time record of 85 home games unbeaten in all competitions. Included in this run were an incredible 63 home league matches in a row.

◀ Ajax star Ryan Gravenberch holds off Oussama Tannane of Vitesse in the 2021 Dutch Cup final. Ajax won 2–1, with Gravenberch scoring the opening goal.

▲ Joël Matip and Virgil van Dijk hold the Champions League trophy after Liverpool's 2–0 defeat of Tottenham Hotspur in 2019.

AJAX
NETHERLANDS • FOUNDED: 1900 • STADIUM: AMSTERDAM ARENA

Rinus Michels arrived as Ajax's coach in 1965, saved the team from relegation, and transformed the club with his brand of "total soccer," where the emphasis was on fluid play and players interchanging positions freely. In 1969, Ajax became the first Dutch club to reach the final of the European Cup and triumphed in the competition in 1971, 1972, and 1973. The stylish team was led by Ruud Krol, Johan Neeskens, and Johan Cruyff, with the club providing the bulk of the Netherlands' 1974 World Cup final-reaching squad. In total, Ajax have won 35 Eredivisie and 20 KNVB Cups, one Cup Winners' Cup, and the UEFA Cup in 1992. A further night of European glory came in 1995, when a young Ajax team won the Champions League. The club continues to be a production line of promising young talent and won two Dutch league and cup doubles in three years (2019 and 2021).

COLO COLO
CHILE • FOUNDED: 1925 • STADIUM: DAVID ARELLANO

With around 60 percent of the country's soccer fans following them, Colo Colo are easily the most popular and successful of all the Chilean club teams. The team has won a record 32 league championships (14 more than fierce rivals Universidad de Chile) as well as the Copa Chile 13 times. Under their coach Arturo Salah, Colo Colo captured league titles in 1986 and 1989, before former Yugoslavia under-20 coach Mirko Jozic took up the manager's post during the 1990 season. The team completed a sequence of three league titles in a row in 1991, the same year that they enjoyed fantastic success abroad. In 1973, Colo Colo had been the first Chilean team to contest a final of the premier South American club cup competition, the Copa Libertadores. In 1991, the club went one stage further, beating the mighty Argentinian team River Plate in the semifinals and the cup holders Olimpia 3–0 on aggregate to win the trophy. While further international success has been restricted to a runner-up spot in the Copa Sudamericana in 2006, the club won nine league titles between 2006 and 2017.

◄ Pablo Solari (right) celebrates his winning goal for Colo Colo in a 2021 relegation playoff match versus Universidad de Concepcion.

MANCHESTER CITY
ENGLAND • FOUNDED: 1887 (1894 RENAMED MANCHESTER CITY) STADIUM: CITY OF MANCHESTER STADIUM

City won the first of their six FA Cups back in 1904 and their first English league title in 1937. The team then spent many years as also-rans until Joe Mercer became manager in 1965 and it won the league, FA Cup, and European Cup-Winners' Cup in a three-year spell. The club bounced between divisions for much of the 1980s and 1990s but has remained in the Premier League since 2002. City were bought by the Abu Dhabi United Group in 2008 and investment poured in. Some of the expensive signings weren't successful, but others—including David Silva, Vincent Kompany, and Sergio Agüero—had a major, long-term impact. City clinched their first English league title since 1968 in 2012 and have since been crowned EPL champion four more times (2014, 2018, 2019, 2021) and reached the Champions League final in 2021.

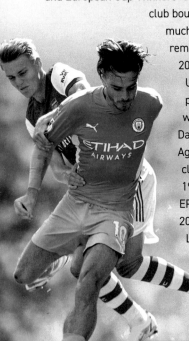

◄ Manchester City's record signing Jack Grealish shields the ball from Arsenal's Martin Ødegaard. Grealish cost City over $138 million in 2021.

CELTIC
SCOTLAND • FOUNDED: 1888 STADIUM: CELTIC PARK

With 51 league titles, Celtic have dominated Scottish soccer for decades alongside their Glasgow-based rivals, Rangers. But before Jock Stein's arrival as manager in 1965, Celtic hadn't won the league for 11 years. Stein built a homegrown team, all of whom hailed from Glasgow and the surrounding area. The team was full of youth, pace, and adventure with tricky winger Jimmy Johnstone, prolific strikers Steve Chalmers, Bobby Lennox, and Willy Wallace, and a defensive rock behind in Billy McNeill. Celtic won nine Scottish league championships in a row (1967–74), yet contested the 1967 European Cup Final as underdogs. Against the odds, Celtic recovered from a goal down to beat the Italian giants Internazionale 2–1 and become the first British team to win the trophy. The "Lions of Lisbon" narrowly failed to repeat their achievement after reaching the final again in 1970. It would be 33 years before Celtic played in another European final, losing 3–2 to Porto in the 2003 UEFA Cup.

► Celtic and Rangers clash in a 2021 Old Firm match—the fiercest rivalry in Scottish soccer. The clubs have met over 425 times in the competition.

DYNAMO KYIV

UKRAINE • FOUNDED: 1927
STADIUM: NATIONAL SPORT KOMPLEX OLIMPIYSKIY

Originally the soccer team of the Soviet secret police, Dynamo Kyiv were the first club outside Moscow to win the Soviet league championship. A player on that 1961 squad, Valery Lobanovsky, became Kyiv's coach 13 years later. He led the club through its greatest era, which began spectacularly with back-to-back Soviet league titles. In 1975, Kyiv won the Cup-Winners' Cup, becoming the first Soviet team to win a European competition. They also beat Bayern Munich 3–1 to win the European Supercup. In total, Lobanovsky (in three separate spells) managed Kyiv to eight league titles, six Soviet Cups, and two European Cup-Winners' Cups. In 1991, after the breakup of the Soviet Union, Kyiv played in the newly formed Ukrainian league. The team has dominated there, winning 16 league titles, including the 2020–21 competition.

◥ Dynamo Kyiv midfielder Vitaliy Buyalskyi holds off Villarreal's Etienne Capoue during a 2021 Europa League match. Buyalskyi was made club vice-captain for the 2021–22 season.

REAL MADRID

SPAIN • FOUNDED: 1902
STADIUM: BERNABEU

Real Madrid are one of the world's most famous and successful teams. They have won 34 league titles, eight more than rival Barcelona and 23 more than their neighbor, Atlético Madrid. In the 1940s and 1950s, Real's president, Santiago Bernabeu, began to transform the club with foreign players and a huge desire to win the newly formed European Cup competition. Real did not disappoint, capturing not only the first European Cup in 1956 but the next four as well. The team included two of the world's outstanding attacking talents in Ferenc Puskas and Alfredo di Stefano, as well as pacy winger Paco Gento, central defenders Marcos Marquitos, and Juan Zarraga, and attacking midfielder Hector Rial. From 1957 to 1965, Real remained unbeaten at home in 121 Spanish league games and won five La Liga titles in a row (1961–65). A transformed team captured the European Cup for a sixth time in 1966. Today, Real are one of the world's richest clubs, with a habit of buying soccer's most famous and expensive players, such as Zinedine Zidane, James Rodriguez, Cristiano Ronaldo, and Gareth Bale. Real have won seven La Liga titles in the 21st century, including the 2019–20 competition, and the team has taken its European Cup and Champions League triumphs to a total of 13, plus four Club World Cups.

▶ Real Madrid players celebrate their 2020 Spanish Super Cup victory, the 11th time that they won the trophy.

SNAPSHOT
LES BLEUS
TRIUMPH AGAIN

France was where the idea of a World Cup was formed, yet the country had never won the competition until 1998. That triumphant team, featuring global superstars such as Zinedine Zidane, had been captained by the hardworking defensive midfielder Didier Deschamps. Twenty years later, in 2018, Deschamps was head coach of the French team, packed full of outstanding attacking flair but with questions about their ability to perform on the biggest stage of all. Doubts also surrounded Deschamps's player selection, as he left talented attackers Karim Benzema, Anthony Martial, and Alexandre Lacazette out of his squad. After topping its group, France beat Argentina 4–3, with two goals for striker Kylian Mbappé, who finished as the tournament's second-highest scorer alongside his strike partner, Antoine Griezmann. Victories over Uruguay and Belgium took France to the final, in which they prevailed over Croatia 4–2 in the highest-scoring final since 1966.

The French team, captained by goalkeeper Hugo Lloris, celebrates with the 2018 World Cup trophy after a victory over Croatia in front of over 78,000 fans at Moscow's Luzhniki Stadium.

SOCCER DREAMS

From Beijing to Buenos Aires, Manchester to Mexico City, millions of children, teenagers, and adults play soccer for fun, sport, and exercise. Many are content to take part at an amateur level, but for some, the dream of emulating the stars they read about, watch, and worship is a passion.

FACT FILE
In 2015, Vanuatu's U23 team beat Micronesia by a record score of 46–0. It was the second heavy defeat for Micronesia, which earlier that year lost 38–0 to Fiji.

▲ USC Trojans take on UCLA Bruins in the NCAA Division I, the pinnacle of the U.S. women's college game.

YOUTH TEAMS AND COMPETITIONS

As young players approach the pinnacle of the game, there are international matches for schoolboys and schoolgirls, as well as under-17 and youth competitions. These reach a peak with the FIFA U-20 World Cup. At the 1991 tournament, Portugal swept to the title with a midfield containing teenagers João Pinto, Rui Costa, and Luis Figo. Argentina won five of the ten competitions held between 1993 and 2011, while Erling Haaland scored nine goals in a single game at the 2019 competition, which was won by Ukraine with South Korea second and Ecuador third. FIFA's Under-17 World Cup has also unearthed its own stars, from Landon Donovan to Phil Foden, the most valuable player of the 2017 tournament.

Some players are thrown onto their club or national team at a very early age. Steven Appiah was 14 when he debuted for Ghana; Ellie Carpenter 15 when she first appeared for the Australian women's team; and Pelé 16 when he turned out for Brazil.

YOUNG DREAMS

In most countries, young players can play at a regional, county, or state level in organized youth team competitions. Major soccer clubs run youth teams and soccer academies and also send scouts to watch games in the hope of spotting new talent. Young players may be invited to an open day or trial, where scouts and coaches can observe them in action at close hand. A club may then offer a contract or a place in its youth academy to a promising player. Famous academies exist at Barcelona, Bayern Munich, and Porto. One of the most famous is Ajax's De Toekomst youth academy, which has been responsible for a host of great players—from Johan Cruyff and Dennis Bergkamp in the past to Christian Eriksen, Frenkie de Jong, and Sven Botman in recent years.

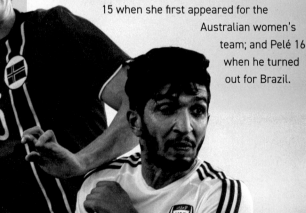

▶ Martin Ødegaard was just 15 when he played in the top Norwegian league for Strømsgodset and made his debut for Norway (pictured). By the age of 17 he had played for Real Madrid, before moving to Arsenal for $41 million in 2021.

▼ Jadon Sancho was just 14 when he was transferred for about $100,000 from Watford to Manchester City. He was 17 when sold to Borussia Dortmund for around $10 million, and age 21 when sold to Manchester United for $100 million in 2021.

HANDLING REJECTION

For millions of wannabes, the hope of playing professional soccer remains just a dream. As players rise through the soccer ranks, the vast majority find that their talents are surpassed by others and they are unable to progress further. Some talented young players are rejected because coaches believe their slight build or lack of height would put them at a disadvantage. As youngsters, Antoine Griezmann was rejected by Lyon, Roy Keane by Brighton, and Marcus Rashford by Manchester City, all for being too small.

Rejection is hard to take for many junior players, but it spurs some on to train harder and smarter and overcome barriers to prove their doubters wrong. Argentinian wide player Javier Zanetti was turned down by Independiente's youth academy for not being robust enough to play professional soccer. He eventually signed for Italian giant Inter Milan, for which he played a record 858 matches. In 2002, a very young Harry Kane was released from Arsenal's youth academy. He joined Tottenham's academy two years later and went on to become one of the world's most feared center forwards.

▼ Blind soccer matches last for 50 minutes. Here, Tomonari Kuroda of Team Japan holds off Spain during a Paralympic match in 2021.

SOCCER FOR ALL

Soccer can be enjoyed in all climates and conditions and by people of all ages and abilities. It is also played competitively by people with disabilities that range from being wheelchair-bound to having impaired hearing. At the 2017 Deaflympics, Turkey won the men's gold and Russia the women's gold. Amputee soccer is played by outfield players using crutches, but no artificial leg, and by goalkeepers who are single-arm amputees. Soccer for blind and visually impaired athletes uses a special ball. It contains a noise-making device that produces a distinctive sound as the ball moves. Teams consist of four blind outfield players, a goalie (who can be partially sighted), and five substitutes. In 2004, the sport made its debut at the Paralympics. Brazil has won all five Paralympic tournaments so far, including in 2021, when the team beat Argentina in the final.

FACT FILE

In 2014, Gloriana Villalobos made her debut for Costa Rica at the age of 14. The following year she appeared at the 2015 Women's World Cup.

A PRO'S LIFE

Viewed from the outside, a professional soccer player's life seems glamorous, exciting, and rewarding. But behind the appearances in top games, on television shows, and at celebrity events lies much hard work and sometimes frustration and disappointment.

MAKING THE GRADE

Only a tiny handful of talented players get to play professional soccer. In 2019, a study showed that just 180 out of the 1.5 million boys playing youth soccer in England will ever play a single minute in the Premier League. Even getting signed by a big club as a youth player is no guarantee of success. Most players do not make the grade and either drop out of pro soccer or have to move down a division or two to play first-team soccer. Jamie Vardy was released by Sheffield Wednesday at age 16 and played in non-league soccer until he was 25 before being signed by Leicester City, with whom he won the Premier League and FA Cup.

LOANED OUT

In many top leagues, clubs loan out to other clubs many of their young players, as well as some senior players who currently don't feature in the manager's plans. Some are loaned to lower-division or overseas clubs, although in some leagues, players are loaned out to rivals. In 2021–22, for example, Atalanta took central defender Merih Demiral on loan from rivals Juventus but loaned out a staggering 62 of their own players. In the same season, Chelsea sent out on loan more than 20 players, including Conor Gallagher to Crystal Palace and Tiémoué Bakayoko—on his fourth loan spell since joining for around $50 million in 2017—who was loaned out to AC Milan until 2023. If they play well, a loaned player may be signed permanently, or their parent club may bring them back onto the first-team squad.

◄ Nathaniel Chalobah reached the Chelsea substitutes bench at the age of 15 but played just ten Chelsea league games over the next seven years, as he went on six season-long loans.

► Alexia Putellas left Barcelona's youth academy at age 12. After spells at Levante and Espanyol, she rejoined Barça six years later and has now scored more than 150 goals for the club.

REWARDS AND RESPONSIBILITIES

Top players are globally famous and multimillionaires. Some put their celebrity to good use, helping charities and schools and publicizing worthy causes. They often have to deal with the media, give interviews, and make appearances for their club or sponsors. What can be harder for young players to handle is the way in which the press can invade their private lives. Photographers and reporters may besiege a player's home and follow their family and friends. Soccer players are seen as important role models for young people, and any wrongdoing, such as being fined for speeding, snubbing autograph hunters, or partying, attracts a lot of negative media attention.

◀ Lionel Messi has won FIFA's Ballon d'Or a record seven times (2009–12, 2015, 2019, and 2021).

▶ Marcus Rashford receives an honorary degree from Alex Ferguson in recognition for his campaign against child poverty.

FACT FILE

Not all injuries are caused on the field. Heerenveen leftback Rami Kaib broke his jaw eating a raw carrot in 2021. Twenty years earlier, Spanish goalie Santiago Canizares missed the World Cup after dropping a bottle of aftershave on his foot!

TRAINING, INJURIES, AND RECOVERY

A typical week for a soccer player involves training, resting, going to team functions, and traveling to one or more games. Training usually involves a mixture of fitness, strength, and flexibility exercises to boost a player's stamina, pace, and sharpness. Players also practice skills and tactics—improving their heading or working on free kicks and other set plays, for example. Soccer is a high-speed contact sport in which impacts, bad tackles, and falls cause significant numbers of injuries, especially leg muscle tears and ankle and knee joint problems. At any one time, it is not unusual for a top team to have between three and nine of their leading players injured or on the way back to full fitness. An injured player's recovery may involve surgery and recovery before full rehabilitation can start. This is usually headed by the club's physiotherapists and other members of the medical and fitness teams. It can be a long, frustrating period on the sidelines, with the player hungry for action as they gradually build up strength and mobility in the injured body part. During this time, the player is aware that a veteran, young star, or newly transferred player may seize their chance and establish themselves on the team. They also have the worry of suffering a reoccurrence of the injury—as happened to England women's captain Steph Houghton in 2022, just a few weeks after making her comeback from a tendon injury that had kept her out for four and a half months.

◀ Recovery from an injury can be a difficult and lonely time as players miss key games. England captain Steph Houghton looks on as she battles an Achilles tendon injury, while Raul Jimenez of Wolves trains after eight months out with a fractured skull.

THE PLAYERS' STAGE

Without stadiums, soccer would still be played, but games would be far quieter and a lot less exciting. Stadiums spring to life on game days, when they are transformed from empty silent steel and concrete structures into a seething sea of color and noise.

GREAT STADIUMS

The mighty Maracanã Stadium in Rio de Janiero, Brazil, holds the official world record for a soccer crowd—in 1950, around 199,850 people watched a World Cup game there between Brazil and Uruguay. In 2014, the Maracanã became only the second venue, after Mexico City's Azteca Stadium, to have hosted the World Cup final twice. Many of the world's biggest soccer stadiums were built to host the World Cup or European Championships—from the Centenario in Uruguay, the venue for the first World Cup in 1930, to Poland's National Stadium that hosted EURO 2012 matches. Eight venues were used for the 2022 World Cup in Qatar, seven of which were newly built. These included the 80,000-capacity Lusail Stadium that hosted the final of the tournament.

BEHIND THE SCENES

The forgotten people of soccer are often the staff who run a stadium and ensure that the day of a match goes smoothly. We tend to think of them only when there is a problem, such as crowd trouble or a field that is unfit for play. The club or stadium owner liaises with police and local authorities and employs stewards to prevent field invasions, violence, and other problems. Box office staff do their best to ensure that tickets are sold and distributed correctly, while turnstile operators, program sellers, and food and drink vendors all work at a soccer stadium on a game day.

The ground staff are in charge of the goals, the field, and its markings. They work especially hard when the field is in poor condition because of bad weather—clearing snow, thawing out the field, or soaking up excess moisture. Before the game, the referee examines the field and talks to the ground staff before deciding whether the game can go ahead.

◀▼ Ground staff prepare the goal nets and clear snow before a match.

FACT FILE
A railroad runs between the field and seats of Slovakian club Tartan Čierny Balog. The fans' view is sometimes obscured by puffs of smoke from the steam trains that run along it!

◥ The Timsah Arena is green and shaped like a crocodile's head. Completed in 2015, it's the home of Turkish club Bursaspor and seats around 45,000.

FACT FILE

Pelé scored both his first international goal and, in 1969, the 1,000th goal of his professional career at the Maracanã Stadium.

STADIUM INNOVATION

Stadium tragedies (see page 103) have prompted governments and soccer authorities to bring in stricter rules and safety measures. Most spectators stood in the past, but now large stadiums are usually seating only. New stadium designs include features like electronic ticketing, solar panels, and other energy-conscious innovations. Inside, hybrid fields may have grass reinforced with plastic fibers and undersoil heating—consisting of hundreds of yards of pipes through which warm water runs—to keep them from freezing. Many of these stadiums form part of a hotel, leisure, or shopping complex.

The United States staged the first indoor World Cup qualifier (at the Seattle Kingdome) and the first indoor World Cup finals match (at the Pontiac Silverdome). Stadiums with a sliding roof have become more and more popular, allowing the venue to host music concerts and other indoor events. The Johan Cruyff Arena was opened in 1996 as Ajax's new stadium. The first European stadium with a retractable roof, it seats 55,000 spectators. The Millennium Stadium in Cardiff, Wales, and London's Wembley Stadium also have sliding roofs. Inside a new stadium, fans may find a removable field, corporate boxes for business entertaining, and giant screens. The 72,000-seat Zenit Arena in Russia has two giant LED TV screens, 100 ft. (30.7m) long and 33.5 ft. (10.2m) high, which replay action from the game, interviews, and stadium messages.

▲ Benfica's dramatic Estádio da Luz has hosted two UEFA Champions League finals as well as EURO 2004 matches.

▼ The state-of-the-art Zenit Arena was opened in 2017.

FACT FILE

At the 1986 World Cup, eagle-eyed officials spotted that the field markings at the edge of the penalty area for the France-Hungary game were in the wrong place. They had to be hastily repainted.

FANS AND TEAMS

Dreams are not only held by players and coaches. Everyone connected to a club or national team hopes that their side will achieve glory and success, especially the fans.

FOLLOWING A TEAM

For millions of fans, following their club or national team is a lifelong passion. Fans may chant for a manager to leave or be unhappy with certain players or the team's performance, but their love of the club tends to remain. Dedicated fans go to great lengths to follow their team, putting up with poor weather, great expense, and long hours of traveling to away games. Many fans spend a lot of their income every season on getting to as many games as possible and buying replica shirts and other merchandise—from T-shirts and scarfs to club-branded toothpaste and credit cards.

Every loyal fan loves to feel the rush of excitement as they approach their home turf, chant with the crowd, and witness the start of a match. What comes next is a 90-minute rollercoaster ride of highs and lows, ending at the final whistle and followed by a postgame examination of what went right and wrong, before hope and expectancy build for the next game.

TOP TEN AVERAGE LEAGUE ATTENDANCES (2017–18)

1	Borussia Dortmund	79,496
2	Bayern Munich	75,000
3	Manchester United	74,976
4	Tottenham Hotspur	67,953
5	Barcelona	66,603
6	Real Madrid	66,161
7	FC Schalke 04	61,197
8	Arsenal	59,323
9	Inter Milan	57,529
10	Celtic	57,523

▲ Draped in scarves, a Bayern Munich fan celebrates his team's Bundesliga title in 2016.

▼ Senegal fans drum up the atmosphere during their team's 2–1 victory over Poland at the 2018 World Cup.

FACT FILE

Charlotte FC set an MLS regular-season attendance record in 2022 as 74,479 fans flocked to the Bank of America Stadium to watch the match against the LA Galaxy.

FANS AND THE MEDIA

Television coverage and Internet streaming have opened up the game to millions of new fans. Some fans, however, criticize TV for concentrating on the top teams and moving matches to different days and new starting times. TV companies spend a fortune on buying the rights to show live games and highlights from the top leagues. Back in the studio, famous former players and managers comment on the action, while reporters and statisticians provide interviews and highly detailed analyses of matches.

Coverage of soccer in other media has boomed, too. Fans manage their own teams in computer simulations or fantasy soccer leagues, while results, news, and video clips are sent to their smartphones and tablets. They can read about their club in books, magazines, fanzines, and blogs. The rise of radio phone-ins and social media has allowed fans to voice their opinions on games, players, managers, and referees.

▲ South African defender Janine van Wyk poses for a selfie with fans at the 2019 Women's World Cup.

MORE THAN A GAME

Fans look forward to certain matches in particular—a clash between two teams at the top of the league table, for example. A game between a small club and a top team allows fans to dream of a famous giant-killing victory. In March 2022, North Macedonian fans went wild when their team, a lowly 67th in the FIFA rankings, knocked reigning European champions Italy out of the World Cup qualifying playoffs with a last-gasp winner in the 92nd minute.

The most passionate of all games tend to be matches between two neighboring teams. Most clubs have some form of local rivalry game, but certain rivalries have passed into soccer folklore. Among them are the Milan contest between Internazionale and AC Milan and, in Greece, the battle between Olympiakos and Panathinaikos. One of the most intense local rivalries in South America is between Argentina's Boca Juniors and River Plate. For some fans, beating their local rivals can be even more important than league or cup success.

Some of the biggest rivalries are not between neighboring teams but between the top clubs in the country. Spain's Superclassico, for example, is contested by two teams that are 300 mi. (500km) apart—Real Madrid and Barcelona.

▲ A face-painted fan cheers on the Netherlands at EURO 2020.

▶ Ettie the chicken whips up the crowd at the 2019 Women's World Cup. The first World Cup mascot was Willie the lion in 1966.

WHEN FANS TURN BAD

Fighting between fans has sadly occurred since soccer's early days. Attempts to stop violence and hooliganism—through policing, video surveillance, seating-only stadiums, and lifetime exclusions for identified culprits—has reduced trouble in many stadiums, but not all. A 2021 Slovak Super Liga match between fierce rivals Spartak Trnava and Slovan Bratislava was abandoned after fans of both teams started fighting on the field.

Sometimes players and officials are the target of violence. In 2013, AC Milan's Kevin-Prince Boateng walked off the field, followed by the rest of both teams, after he and other black players were racially abused by some fans. In 2012, a Dutch referee's assistant was attacked by teenagers from Nieuw Sloten B1, one of the teams taking part. He died the next day. These deeply disturbing events should not mask the fact that the vast majority of games are peaceful and attended by fans who are there for the soccer, not fighting or abuse.

BIG BUSINESS

When it comes to the world's biggest leagues, soccer is big, big business. In 2020, the top five leagues in Europe generated around $17.1 billion of annual revenue. The pressure to achieve success, though, has seen some clubs overspend and fall deeply into debt.

VALUE FOR MONEY?

Spending huge sums can seem essential to top clubs, but it does not guarantee success. Tottenham Hotspur spent around $540 million on players in the five seasons up to 2021–22, yet they last won a league championship in 1961. Both Paris Saint-Germain and Manchester City have spent lavishly. PSG holds the record for the largest transfer fee—$216 million for Neymar—and City have spent over $1.8 billion on transfers since 2008. While both have won domestic honors, neither club has ever won the UEFA Champions League.

Less wealthy clubs can still succeed. The entire Leicester City squad that won the 2015–16 English Premier League cost under $90 million—less than Chelsea paid for one goalkeeper, Kepa Arrizabalaga, in 2018. Porto is outside of the top 50 richest soccer clubs, yet they won the UEFA Champions League in 2004, the UEFA Europa League in 2011, and Portuguese league titles in 2018 and 2020.

MONEY MATTERS

In the past, soccer clubs received most of their money from selling programs, tickets, food, and drinks. Today these items contribute just 13 percent of the income of clubs in La Liga and the English Premier League, and only 11 percent of club income in Ligue 1, Serie A, and the Bundesliga. Sales of shirts and other merchandise, as well as sponsorship and advertising deals with companies, accounts for 30–40 percent. The lion's share of revenue for big clubs comes from selling broadcasting rights to television in particular, but also to radio and Internet services. In the 2020–21 season, for example, Atlético Madrid received around $185 million in La Liga TV rights alone.

Some clubs succeed through the backing of a wealthy country, company, or individual, such as Chelsea's former chairman Roman Abramovich, Inter Milan owner Zhang Jindong, and the Agnelli family, who own Inter's rivals Juventus. Theoretically, the richest club in the world by benefactor is now Newcastle United following the club's $409 million purchase by Saudi Arabia's state-owned Public Investment Fund in 2021.

Some top clubs have run up huge debts through the collapse of business deals, high stadium construction costs, or the Covid pandemic causing competitions to be canceled or games played without paying fans. Most debts, though, are run up through excessive transfer fees and wages that don't result in success. Some teams go into administration and have to drop down many divisions or reform as a new team. Others struggle on. In 2021, Barcelona was more than $1.5 billion in debt. The year before, another Spanish club, Malaga CF, released their entire first-team squad to play elsewhere in order to survive.

▶ Lille defenders Sven Botman (left) and José Fonte cost a total of $9 million but helped guide Lille to the Ligue 1 title in 2021, conceding just 23 goals.

▶ Tottenham's new stadium cost around $1.3 billion and has left the club with one of the largest debts in European soccer.

FACT FILE
French striker Karim Benzema has a release clause in his Real Madrid contract. He can leave if another club bids more than $1.3 billion for him.

◀ Lionel Messi is thought to earn more than $30 million a year by endorsing products and through sponsorship deals.

PLAYER POWER

Spiraling transfer fees can be a lifeline to smaller, struggling clubs, because selling just one young talent for many millions can keep the club afloat for seasons. But for other clubs, the cost of keeping pace with richer rivals is huge. In summer 2021, Ligue 1 clubs spent $465 million on transfers. Bundesliga teams spent $490 million, Serie A clubs $720 million, and English Premier League teams an eye-watering $1.57 billion.

With big fees often come big wages. PSG spent $487 million on wages in 2021, with star players such as Kylian Mbappé and Neymar reported to be on at least $400,000 per week. That's what an average MLS player earns as a salary in a year, and four times the salary of a typical player in Australia's A-League. The women's game is even more underfinanced. While marquee signings may be paid $260,000 a year, typical NWSL and Women's Super League players earn around $45,000–$60,000 a year. Away from the bigger leagues, players are often semiprofessional. They are paid expenses or a small fee to play but need to work a second job to make ends meet.

FACT FILE
In 1999, Romanian club Nitramonia Fagaras were so cash-strapped that they could not pay a $20,000 gas bill. They had to transfer two players, Gabor Balazs and Ioan Fatu, to Gazmetan Medias (the gas company's soccer club) as payment.

◀ Despite their wealth, big clubs don't always get their own way. Fan protests forced Europe's elite teams to scrap their Super League project in 2021.

◀ In 2021, Chelsea paid a club-record fee of $135 million for Romelu Lukaku, a player they owned in 2011–14 but loaned out to other clubs before selling. Following further transfers to Manchester United and Inter Milan, a record $375 million has been spent in fees on this Belgian striker.

SOCCER NIGHTMARES

Soccer sadly has a dark side. With passions running high on and off the field, and with so much at stake in big matches, the game has sometimes lurched into a nightmare world of cheating, abuse, violence, and even death.

FACT FILE
In 2013, the players and officials of four Nigerian second-division teams were banned for life for game-fixing after two highly suspect scores. Police Machine FC won 67–0 and Plateau United Feeders recorded a 79–0 victory on the same day.

CUT OFF IN THEIR PRIME

A number of players have died suddenly through on-field collisions or because of a medical problem. In 2003, during a Confederations Cup match against Colombia, Cameroon's 28-year-old midfielder Marc-Vivien Foé collapsed and died shortly afterward. According to FIFA's Sudden Death Report, 614 amateur or professional players died between 2014 and 2018, mostly of heart attacks.

In 2019, Cardiff City's Argentinian striker, Emiliano Sala, died in a plane crash before he had played a game for the Welsh club. Other plane crashes have wiped out entire teams, including Bolivia's most popular team, The Strongest, in 1969; 18 members of the Zambian national squad in 1993; and Brazilian club Chapecoense in November 2016. One of the most famous air crashes was the 1958 Munich disaster that killed eight Manchester United players and 11 officials and journalists.

GAME–FIXING AND CHEATING

In England in 1909 George Parsonage was banned for life after asking for a $240 sign-on fee when he joined Chesterfield (the maximum allowed was $48). This looks tiny compared to today's examples of corruption, bribery, and game-fixing. In 1999 the former head coach of Romania's Dynamo Bucharest, Vasile Ianul, was sentenced to 12 years in jail for stealing more than $2.5 million from the team. German soccer was rocked in 2004 when referee Robert Hoyzer owned up to fixing games. He was sentenced to more than two years in jail. In 2006, after a game-rigging scandal, Juventus was relegated to Serie B, while AC Milan, Lazio, Fiorentina, and Reggina Calcio were fined, removed from European competitions, and had league points deducted. Further game-fixing or corruption scandals have rocked South Korean soccer in 2013 and Greek and Italian soccer in 2015. Four Swedish players received long bans for game-fixing in 2021.

▼ After scoring an own goal in a 2–1 loss to the U.S. at the 1994 World Cup, Colombian defender Andrés Escobar was murdered—shot 12 times by an unknown gunman.

▲ Denmark players form a barrier around Christian Eriksen after he suffered a heart attack at EURO 2020. Remarkably, he returned to action just 259 days later for Premier League team Brentford.

STADIUM DISASTERS

Crumbling stadiums, overcrowding, poor safety rules, and bad crowd control have caused many stadium disasters. The worst ever soccer tragedy occurred in Lima, Peru, in 1964 when over 300 fans were killed and more than 500 injured in panic stampedes and riots. Two major disasters occurred in 1985—a wooden stand at Bradford City's field caught fire, killing 56 people, while the European Cup final also ended in tragedy. A wall collapsed at the Heysel Stadium in Belgium and a riot flared when some Liverpool fans charged at Juventus fans. One Belgian and 38 Italian spectators died as a result. In January 2022, a crush outside Olembe Stadium before the African Cup of Nations match between Cameroon and Comoros resulted in eight deaths.

▶ Brazilian midfielder Oscar was banned for eight games for provoking this mass brawl between Shanghai and Guangzhou in 2017.

POOR ROLE MODELS?

Most professional players are dedicated to the game and are considered excellent role models to young people. Some, however, abuse their position by their actions on or off the field or have been convicted of crimes related to drugs, assault, or theft. A handful of players have even fought with fans, most famously Eric Cantona, who kung fu kicked a Crystal Palace fan in 1995.

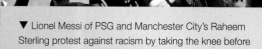

▼ Lionel Messi of PSG and Manchester City's Raheem Sterling protest against racism by taking the knee before a 2021 Champions League game.

RACISM

After concerted efforts by anti-racism groups, from Kick Racism Out to FARE (Football Against Racism in Europe), racism was thought to be declining in soccer. The truth, sadly, is different. There has been a rise in the number of non-white players, officials, and fans suffering racist abuse both at games and on social media. On occasion, teams have been punished for their fans' racism with fines and being forced to play games in empty stadiums. In 2021, UEFA handed Hungary a two-game crowd ban and a $216,000 fine after a section of fans abused England's Raheem Sterling and Jude Bellingham in a World Cup qualifier. However, many people feel that governments and soccer authorities are doing nowhere near enough, and punishments are often criticized as slow or too lenient. Some famous players have taken to social media to publicize incidents and to urge people to speak out and report racism when it occurs. In a handful of instances, players and teammates have walked off the field in protest.

Lionel Messi holds the Copa América and savors finally winning a senior trophy with the Argentinian national team. He was joint top goal scorer at the tournament and named its most valuable player.

SNAPSHOT
FINALLY, FINALLY, MESSI

It had been a long wait but, 16 years after his senior-team debut, Lionel Messi had finally won a major international trophy with Argentina—the 2021 Copa América. He sunk to his knees at the final whistle as his team defeated its fiercest rival, Brazil, 1–0 in the iconic Maracanã Stadium. Messi had endured a quiet final, but his role in the march to the Maracanã had been immense, as he scored or provided the assist for nine of Argentina's 11 goals.

Messi had burst onto the international scene at the 2005 FIFA World Youth Championship alongside Sergio Agüero and Fernando Gago. There, he celebrated his 18th birthday and scored six goals, winning the Golden Boot and netting a further award as its best player. Two of his goals came in the final as Argentina narrowly defeated Nigeria. At the start of what would be a glittering club career in which he won 35 cups or titles with Barcelona, it was inconceivable that it might be his only trophy in Argentinian colors. There was an Olympic gold medal in an under-23s tournament in 2008, but that failed to make up for the heartbreak of reaching four major international finals—three Copa Américas and the 2014 World Cup—only to finish as runner-up on each occasion. For Messi and Argentina, which had not won the Copa since 1993, it would be a case of fifth time lucky.

THE WORLD CUP

Exhibition or charity games are entertaining, but for a soccer game to have meaning it has to be part of a wider competition. Soccer has spawned hundreds of different competitions, but none can compete in global interest and prestige with the World Cup. From small beginnings with 13 competing countries, it has grown to the point where 207 nations attempted to qualify for the 2022 competition.

▲ Austria is in on goal in a first round tie against France in 1934. Austria won 3–2 in what was the first World Cup match to go to extra time.

URUGUAY 1930
FINAL
URUGUAY 4 · ARGENTINA 2
SEMIFINALS
URUGUAY 6 · YUGOSLAVIA 1
ARGENTINA 6 · U.S. 1
Games **18** · Goals **70** · Goals per game **3.89**

It took 19 minutes for France's Lucien Laurent to write his name in the record books as the scorer of the first World Cup goal. France beat Mexico 4–1, but it was their only victory and, like Belgium and Romania, they went out at the group stage. Four European teams made the long trip to South America by boat, but only Yugoslavia reached the semifinals. It and the U.S. were thrashed in the semis by Uruguay and Argentina respectively. Argentina boasted the best forward of the competition, Guillermo Stabile, but Uruguay—on home soil and as reigning Olympic champions— were firm favorites. In the final, the team came back strongly after Argentina had taken a 2–1 lead, to become the first World Cup winners.

▶ Uruguay captain Jose Nasazzi (left) and Argentina's Manuel Ferreira exchange team pennants before the 1930 World Cup final.

ITALY 1934
FINAL
ITALY 2 · CZECHOSLOVAKIA 1
SEMIFINALS
ITALY 1 · AUSTRIA 0
CZECHOSLOVAKIA 3 · GERMANY 1
Games **17** · Goals **70** · Goals per game **4.12**

In 1934, the South American teams had not forgotten the lack of European entrants for the first World Cup. As a result, world champions Uruguay chose not to defend their title, while Brazil and Argentina sent understrength teams to Italy. Yet 32 nations, mostly European, were eager to enter the competition. With 16 spaces available, qualification games began in June 1933. Italy's 4–0 win over Greece marked the first and only time that a World Cup host has had to play a qualifier to get into the finals. Egypt was the first nation outside of the Americas or Europe to qualify, but following one round of knockout games, the eight remaining teams were all European. After a 7–1 thrashing of the United States, Italy's goals dried up, and they just barely sneaked past Spain and Austria on their way to the final. In that game, Italy's Luisito Monti (formerly of Argentina) became the only player to have appeared in a World Cup final for different countries. Against a battling Czech team, a goal five minutes into extra time from Italy's Angelo Schiavio secured the Jules Rimet trophy for the hosts.

◀◀ Italy and Hungary in action in the 1938 final.
◀ The poster for the tournament in France—the last World Cup to be held before the Second World War.

WORLD CUP GOLDEN BOOT WINNERS (GOALS)

1930	Guillermo Stabile, Argentina (8)
1934	Oldrich Nejedly, Czech. (5)
1938	Léonidas da Silva, Brazil (8)
1950	Ademir Menezes, Brazil (9)
1954	Sandor Kocsis, Hungary (11)
1958	Just Fontaine, France (13)
1962	Garrincha, Brazil; Vava, Brazil; Valentin Ivanov, U.S.S.R.; Leonel Sanchez, Chile; Florian Albert, Hungary; Drazan Jerkovic, Yugoslavia (4)
1966	Eusebio, Portugal (9)
1970	Gerd Müller, West Germany (10)
1974	Gregorz Lato, Poland (7)
1978	Mario Kempes, Argentina (6)
1982	Paolo Rossi, Italy (6)
1986	Gary Lineker, England (6)
1990	Salvatore Schillaci, Italy (6)
1994	Hristo Stoichkov, Bulgaria; Oleg Salenko, Russia (6)
1998	Davor Suker, Croatia (6)
2002	Ronaldo, Brazil (8)
2006	Miroslav Klose, Germany (5)
2010	Thomas Müller, Germany; Wesley Sneijder, Netherlands; Diego Forlán, Uruguay; David Villa, Spain (5)
2014	James Rodriguez, Colombia (6)
2018	Harry Kane, England (6)

FRANCE 1938
FINAL
ITALY 4 · HUNGARY 2
SEMIFINALS
ITALY 2 · BRAZIL 1
HUNGARY 5 · SWEDEN 1
Games **18** · Goals **84** · Goals per game **4.67**

With the threat of war looming over Europe, Spain and Austria were forced to pull out of the tournament. But the 1938 World Cup did feature the first team from Asia, the Dutch East Indies (now Indonesia), as well as a Cuban team that sprang a major shock by beating Romania in a replay. Sweden thrashed Cuba 8–0 but were then on the receiving end of a 5–1 semifinal mauling by the first great Hungarian team. The other semifinal saw one of the great managerial blunders when the Brazil coach, Adhemar Pimenta, either because of arrogance or through injury fears, rested his star player, Léonidas da Silva. Léonidas had lit up the tournament, most notably in an epic 6–5 thriller against Poland in which he became the first player to score four goals in a World Cup final game, only for Poland's Ernest Wilimowski to do the same five minutes later. Without the tournament's top scorer, Brazil crashed to defeat against Italy, who went on to become champions for the second time.

FACT FILE
At the 1930 World Cup, not one of the 18 games was tied. Neither was there a playoff game to decide third place.

BRAZIL 1950
FINAL POOL
URUGUAY 5 PTS · BRAZIL 4 PTS
SWEDEN 2 PTS · SPAIN 1 PT
Games **22** · Goals **88** · Goals per game **4.00**

The only World Cup to feature a final pool of four instead of a final, the 1950 tournament started poorly. Scotland and Turkey withdrew, only 13 nations attended, and the mighty Maracanã Stadium was not ready to host the first match. But the competition built in excitement and drama as the goals flowed, often from the cleats of the hosts who, after topping their group, ran rampant in the final pool stages, scoring seven against Sweden and six against Spain. Before that point, there had been several notable shocks, including the United States' 1–0 defeat of a highly qualified England team. The final pool format could have been a letdown, but the outcome went down to the very last game, with Uruguay and Brazil separated by one point and playing in front of around 199,850 fans. Despite falling a goal behind to the favorites, Uruguay won the game 2–1 to lift the World Cup once again.

▲ Brazilian goalie Moacir Barbosa gathers the ball during a 1950 group game against Yugoslavia. The match, watched by more than 142,000 spectators in the Maracanã, ended in a 2–0 victory for Brazil.

SWITZERLAND 1954
FINAL
WEST GERMANY 3 · HUNGARY 2
SEMIFINALS
WEST GERMANY 6 · AUSTRIA 1
HUNGARY 4 · URUGUAY 2
Games **26** · Goals **140** · Goals per game **5.38**

As the home of the headquarters of FIFA, which was celebrating its 50th birthday, Switzerland was an obvious host for the 1954 tournament. It featured newcomers such as Turkey, South Korea, and the western half of a divided Germany (which had been barred from the 1950 competition). The fans saw plenty of drama and goals, none more than in Austria's 7–5 defeat of Switzerland (the highest-scoring game in the history of the World Cup finals). Hungary, boasting the incredible talents of Ferenc Puskas, Sandor Kocsis, and Nandor Hidegkuti, was the most menacing team, scoring an incredible 27 goals in only five games. At its third World Cup, Uruguay thrashed Scotland 7–0 and beat England 4–2 to reach the semifinals. It was the only team never to have been beaten in the World Cup until they came up against Hungary, which won 4–2 and went into the final as favorite. West Germany, however, overturned the odds to record a highly emotional victory.

▼ Members of West Germany's triumphant 1954 team are carried off the field after two goals from Helmut Rahn and one from Max Morlock secured the country's first World Cup.

FACT FILE
Two pairs of brothers have played on winning teams in a World Cup final—Fritz and Ottmar Walter of West Germany (1954) and England's Jack and Bobby Charlton (1966).

SWEDEN 1958
FINAL
BRAZIL 5 · SWEDEN 2
SEMIFINALS
BRAZIL 5 · FRANCE 2
SWEDEN 3 · WEST GERMANY 1
Games **35** · Goals **126** · Goals per game **3.60**

Fifty-five countries entered the 1958 qualifying tournament, and some big names, including Italy, the Netherlands, Spain, and Uruguay, failed to qualify. All four U.K. home nations (Scotland, England, Northern Ireland, and Wales) reached the finals—the only time this has happened. England had lost key players in the Munich aircrash (see page 77) but was the only team to hold a rampant Brazilian squad to a tie and to stop them from scoring. It was the World Cup's first 0–0 tie. Yet it was the two smaller British nations, Wales and Northern Ireland, that qualified for the quarterfinals, with the Irish sensationally beating a strong Czech team. Free-scoring France and Brazil quickly emerged as the favorites, and their semifinal clash was an epic in which the 17-year-old Pelé blasted a hat trick in Brazil's victory. France had to be content with a 6–3 mauling of West Germany to secure third place. Just Fontaine's four goals in that game propelled him to the Golden Boot with 13 goals in total, a record to this day. The host, Sweden, had quietly seen off Hungary, the Soviet Union, and West Germany to reach the final, but the team was no match for Brazil, which triumphed 5–2 to win the tournament for the first time.

▲ Brazil, pictured after the team's 1958 final win, during which a 17-year-old Pelé (front row, center) scored two of Brazil's five goals.

▶ Jairzinho scores Brazil's third goal in the 1970 final to become the first player to score in every game at a World Cup tournament.

CHILE 1962

FINAL
BRAZIL 3 · CZECHOSLOVAKIA 1
SEMIFINALS
BRAZIL 4 · CHILE 2
CZECHOSLOVAKIA 3 · YUGOSLAVIA 1
Games 32 · Goals 89
Goals per game 2.78

Chile was a controversial choice to host the World Cup, with its small population and its infrastructure damaged by an earthquake in 1960. As it turned out, most of the problems happened on the field. A series of bad-tempered matches occurred in the first round, including the infamous "Battle of Santiago," during which armed police had to split up warring Chilean and Italian players. Chile made it through to a semifinal against Brazil by beating the Soviet Union, while two strong Eastern European teams, Yugoslavia and Czechoslovakia, battled it out in the other semifinal. The Brazilians lost Pelé to injury after only two games, but in Garrincha and Vava they had two of the best players of the competition. Brazil duly won the final with a team featuring eight World Cup winners from the 1958 tournament.

MEXICO 1970

FINAL
BRAZIL 4 · ITALY 1
SEMIFINALS
BRAZIL 3 · URUGUAY 1
ITALY 4 · WEST GERMANY 3
Games 32 · Goals 95 · Goals per game 2.97

For many seasoned soccer observers, the 1970 World Cup remains the best. Much of the brutal, physical play seen in the 1962 and 1966 tournaments was absent. In its place were fascinating tactical and skillful contests between the world's greatest teams. Although the tournament was the first to feature red and yellow cards, no player was sent off, and some of the games have passed into soccer legend. These include a chess-like battle between Brazil and England that the South Americans narrowly won 1–0; Italy's 4–1 defeat of Mexico; and Italy's amazing 4–3 victory against West Germany in the semifinal. Brazil powered through the rounds, with stars such as Jairzinho, Pelé, and Rivelino attacking with flair. In the final against Italy they were unstoppable, recording their third World Cup win and claiming the Jules Rimet trophy for good.

FACT FILE
Vava's goal in the 1962 final, added to his pair of goals in the 1958 final, make him the only player to have scored in the finals of successive World Cups.

▼ Soviet goalie Lev Yashin saves at the feet of German striker Uwe Seeler in the 1966 semifinal. West Germany ran out 2–1 winners.

ENGLAND 1966

FINAL
ENGLAND 4 · WEST GERMANY 2
SEMIFINALS
ENGLAND 2 · PORTUGAL 1
WEST GERMANY 2 · SOVIET UNION 1
Games 32 · Goals 89 · Goals per game 2.78

The 1966 World Cup was a well-organized tournament and the first to feature a mascot (World Cup Willie). West Germany and Portugal were the most free-scoring teams in a competition characterized by defensive play. Two huge shocks occurred early on—Brazil was eliminated by Portugal, and newcomer North Korea knocked out Italy with a stunning 1–0 victory. The North Koreans won the support of many neutral fans, and the team's quarterfinal meeting with Portugal was a classic. North Korea was 3–0 up within 20 minutes before Portugal, inspired by the tournament's eventual top scorer, Eusebio, hit back to win 5–3. In the semifinal, Eusebio's 82nd-minute strike could not stop England going through to meet West Germany in what proved to be an epic final. The Germans went ahead, then England scored twice to lead until a surprise last-minute German goal took the game into extra time. Geoff Hurst scored two more goals to secure a dramatic victory for the host nation (see page 72).

WEST GERMANY 1974
FINAL
WEST GERMANY 2 · NETHERLANDS 1
THIRD-PLACE PLAYOFF
POLAND 1 · BRAZIL 0
Games **38** · Goals **97** · Goals per game **2.55**

Ninety-nine nations attempted to qualify for the 1974 tournament, which would see the winners lift a new trophy—the FIFA World Cup. Spain, France, and England all failed to reach the tournament, while Zaire, Haiti, East Germany, and Australia made their debuts. Changes to the competition format meant that there would be no semifinal games. Instead, the winners of the two second-round groups would contest the final, and the group runners-up would play off for third place. The Netherlands, exhibiting their brand of "total soccer," swept aside Bulgaria (4–1), Uruguay (2–0), Brazil (2–0), and Argentina (4–0) to top Group A and reach the final. Poland was the surprise package. Propelled by the goals of striker Gregorz Lato, the team came second in Group B after narrowly losing 1–0 to West Germany. The West Germans started slowly, but with Franz Beckenbauer in charge and Gerd Müller on fine form, they made the final. There, they overcame the setback of a first-minute Dutch goal from a penalty to win the World Cup for a second time.

> ▶ Italy forward Luigi Riva heads the ball above Arsene Auguste of Haiti. The Haitians were at the World Cup finals for the first time in their history.

FACT FILE
On June 14, 1974, Carlos Caszely of Chile became the first player to receive a red card in a World Cup tournament.

ARGENTINA 1978
FINAL
ARGENTINA 3 · NETHERLANDS 1
THIRD-PLACE PLAYOFF
BRAZIL 2 · ITALY 1
Games **38** · Goals **102** · Goals per game **2.68**

A colorful and at times controversial tournament, the 1978 World Cup may have lacked some stand-out stars, but it was rarely short of soccer drama. The hosts found themselves in the toughest of groups with France, Hungary, and a young Italian team that beat them, but Argentina made it through to the second group stage. Tunisia caused a shock by tying with holder West Germany and beating Mexico 3–1 to become the first African team to win a World Cup finals game. Austria, with its star striker Hans Krankl, played strongly in the early stages, beating Spain, Sweden, and West Germany. But it was crushed 5–1 by a Dutch team that lacked Johan Cruyff, who had pulled out of the tournament for family reasons. Scotland's campaign held promise but went askew when it failed to beat Iran and lost to Peru. Then the team roused itself, however, to beat the Netherlands 3–2. In the second group stage, Italy, Argentina, Brazil, and the Netherlands emerged as frontrunners. Much controversy centered on the Argentina-Peru game. As the last Group B match, it would determine whether Argentina or Brazil reached the final. Peru had played well earlier in the tournament, winning its group ahead of the Netherlands, so its 6–0 loss to Argentina was suspicious. It meant that Brazil was knocked out without being defeated, while Argentina progressed to the final, in which they beat the Netherlands.

> ▶ Hugo Sánchez, Mexico's most famous player, during his team's surprise defeat to Tunisia in 1978.

SPAIN 1982
FINAL
ITALY 3 · WEST GERMANY 1
SEMIFINALS
ITALY 2 · POLAND 0
WEST GERMANY 3 · FRANCE 3 (5–4 PENALTIES)
Games **52** · Goals **146** · Goals per game **2.81**

In 1982, the format of the tournament changed again so that 24 countries would appear at the finals. Teams played in six groups of four, with the top 12 teams playing in four groups of three to determine the semifinalists. Belgium beat the holder Argentina to win its group, while England topped its group ahead of France. Surprise packages Northern Ireland and Algeria beat Spain and West Germany respectively. Poland made the semifinals, but the host, Spain, went out after just one win. The toughest second-round group, containing Brazil, Argentina, and Italy, saw the Italians go through, beating Brazil in a 3–2 thriller. West Germany beat France in an equally exciting semifinal but could not stop the Italians from winning their third World Cup.

MEXICO 1986
FINAL
ARGENTINA 3 · WEST GERMANY 2
SEMIFINALS
ARGENTINA 2 · BELGIUM 0
WEST GERMANY 2 · FRANCE 0
Games **52** · Goals **132** · Goals per game **2.54**

Colombia had been due to host the 1986 World Cup, but troubles in that country meant that it had to withdraw. When Mexico stepped in, it became the first nation to host the tournament twice. More than 120 nations battled for the 24 places in the finals, in which Canada and Iraq both made their debuts. Morocco became the first African nation to reach the second round when it won a group that contained Portugal, Poland, and England. Denmark looked promising until it was thrashed 5–1 by Spain, while Belgium squeezed past the Soviet Union 4–3 in one of the best games of the tournament. The quarterfinals were extremely close games. Three went to penalty shoot-outs, while the fourth game saw England face Argentina. Maradona arrived at the World Cup as the world's most expensive player and a heavily marked man. His incredible dribbling and scoring skills made him the best player of the tournament. In the quarterfinal, his two goals (one a deliberate handball, the other a magnificent solo effort—see pages 54–55) sank England and he repeated the feat against Belgium in the semifinal. In the final, West Germany went 2–0 down, rallied to 2–2, but were beaten by a late Argentinian goal.

FACT FILE
The fastest send-off in World Cup history occurred in 1986, when Uruguay's José Batista was dismissed against Scotland after just 55 seconds.

▶ Diego Maradona is sent flying over West German goalie Harald Schumacher during the final of the 1986 World Cup. The Argentinian legend was sensational as he helped his country win the trophy for a second time.

ITALY 1990
FINAL
WEST GERMANY 1 · ARGENTINA 0
SEMIFINALS
WEST GERMANY 1 · ENGLAND 1
(4-3 PENALTIES)
ARGENTINA 1 · ITALY 1 (4-3 PENALTIES)
Games **52** · Goals **115** · Goals per game **2.21**

This fondly remembered World Cup had moments of great theater, from veteran Cameroon striker Roger Milla's dance at the corner flag to Costa Rica's joy at defeating both Scotland and Sweden to qualify for the second round. Sadly, the tournament also saw much negative soccer and a record number of bookings (164), as well as 16 send-offs. Cameroon was the talk of the tournament, beating Romania and Colombia to set up a quarterfinal against England. Cameroon went 2-0 up, but two Gary Lineker penalties and a third England goal in extra time saw the neutrals' favorites go out.

The Netherlands arrived as European Champions but failed to win a match, while Brazil and the Soviet Union also disappointed. The semifinals were both full of drama, but the final was deeply forgettable. West Germany beat Argentina courtesy of an 85th-minute penalty, while Pedro Monzon was the first of two send-offs for Argentina and the first player to be red-carded in a World Cup final.

▼ Midfielder Emmanuel Petit celebrates as France beats Croatia 2-1 to secure a place in the 1998 World Cup final against Brazil.

UNITED STATES 1994
FINAL
BRAZIL 0 · ITALY 0 (3-2 PENALTIES)
SEMIFINALS
BRAZIL 1 · SWEDEN 0
ITALY 2 · BULGARIA 1
Games **52** · Goals **141** · Goals per game **2.71**

Some feared that the crowds at the 1994 World Cup would be small in a country where male soccer is not a dominant sport. But it proved to be a lively and well-attended tournament. Attacking play had been encouraged by the adoption of the back-pass rule (see page 24) and three instead of two points for a win in the group games. Despite losing many players since the breakup of the Soviet Union, Russia recorded the biggest win, 6-1 against Cameroon, with Oleg Salenko scoring five goals—the most by one player in a World Cup match. Maradona went home after he failed a drug test, and the Republic of Ireland shocked Italy with a 1-0 win in the group stages. The Bulgarians were terrific, beating Argentina, knocking out Germany, and finishing fourth overall. European teams dominated the quarterfinals, yet it was Brazil that beat the Netherlands, Sweden, and Italy to lift the World Cup trophy for a record fourth time.

FRANCE 1998
FINAL
FRANCE 3 · BRAZIL 0
SEMIFINALS
FRANCE 2 · CROATIA 1
BRAZIL 1 · NETHERLANDS 1 (4-2 PENALTIES)
Games **64** · Goals **171** · Goals per game **2.67**

With places at this tournament increased to 32, newcomers included Jamaica, Japan, and South Africa. Iran caused a shock in its first World Cup for 20 years by beating the United States. Nigeria upset the odds with a 3-2 defeat of Spain that effectively knocked out the European team. Despite 22 red cards, the competition was enthralling, with Croatia, Denmark, Brazil, France, and the Netherlands playing attacking soccer. England narrowly went out, losing on penalties to Argentina in one of the best games of the tournament. Croatia progressed and won against Germany 3-0 in the quarterfinal. For the second World Cup in a row, Italy was knocked out on penalties, this time to France at the quarterfinal stage. A France-Brazil final was an exciting prospect, but Ronaldo was sick before the game and was extremely subdued. France won with relative ease, aided by two goals from Zinedine Zidane.

SOUTH KOREA AND JAPAN 2OO2

FINAL
BRAZIL 2 · GERMANY 0
SEMIFINALS
BRAZIL 1 · TURKEY 0
GERMANY 1 · SOUTH KOREA 0
Games **64** · Goals **161** · Goals per game **2.52**

An amazing 193 nations attempted to qualify for the first World Cup held in Asia. Surprise failures included the Netherlands, Uruguay, and Colombia. A shock came in the opening game, in which Senegal beat the World Cup holder, France, 1–0. France then lost to Denmark and exited the tournament, as did Russia, Poland, and Portugal. Cheered on by passionate crowds, the South Koreans were headline news, knocking out Italy, Spain, and Portugal to reach the semifinals, along with Turkey, which eventually finished third. The final saw Brazilian striker Ronaldo turn back the years to score two goals that defeated Germany.

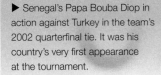

▶ Senegal's Papa Bouba Diop in action against Turkey in the team's 2002 quarterfinal tie. It was his country's very first appearance at the tournament.

GERMANY 2OO6

FINAL
ITALY 1 · FRANCE 1 (5–3 PENALTIES)
SEMIFINALS
ITALY 2 · GERMANY 0 (AFTER EXTRA TIME)
FRANCE 1 · PORTUGAL 0
Games **64** · Goals **147** · Goals per game 2.3

Despite a thrilling opening match (with Germany winning 4–2 over Costa Rica), this tournament saw defenses on top and a record card count (345 yellow and 28 red). Italy's miserly defense, led by Fabio Cannavaro, let in just one goal on the way to the first all-European final since 1982. Elsewhere, only one (Ghana) of the five African nations present progressed from their group, while Australia, Oceania's first team at a World Cup since 1982, surprisingly qualified from a group featuring Brazil, Japan, and Croatia. In the final, Zinedine Zidane—playing his last competitive match—scored a penalty kick, only for Italian defender Marco Materazzi to equalize. During extra time, Zidane was sent off for head-butting Materazzi in the chest. With the game ending in a stalemate, Italy won a tense penalty shoot-out to secure the World Cup for a fourth time.

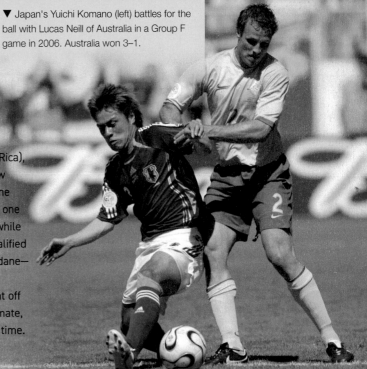

▼ Japan's Yuichi Komano (left) battles for the ball with Lucas Neill of Australia in a Group F game in 2006. Australia won 3–1.

SOUTH AFRICA 2010
FINAL
SPAIN 1 · NETHERLANDS 0
(AFTER EXTRA TIME)
SEMIFINALS
NETHERLANDS 3 · URUGUAY 2
SPAIN 1 · GERMANY 0
Games **64** · Goals **145**
Goals per game **2.27**

The first tournament to be held in Africa will be remembered as a noisy, colorful affair, with some 3.18 million spectators attending matches in ten stadiums. Serbia and Slovakia made their tournament debuts but failed to progress from their group, a fate which also befell Cameroon, Denmark, Italy, and France.

The Germans would score the most goals (16) in the tournament, but they finished in third place after being knocked out in the semifinals. The Netherlands were also on a roll, taking their World Cup and World Cup qualifying winning run to 13 games when they knocked out Brazil in the quarterfinals. Spain lost their very first game 1–0 against Switzerland, but they won each one of their four knockout games 1–0, including a tense final against the Netherlands, to claim their very first World Cup.

▲ Spanish goalie Iker Casillas intercepts the ball before Dutch striker Robin van Persie can pounce during the 2010 final.

▶ Russian striker Artem Dzyuba celebrates scoring against Spain in the Round of 16 at the 2018 World Cup. His team would go on to win the tie in a thrilling penalty shoot-out.

▼ Bastian Schweinsteiger (left) and Lukas Podolski celebrate with the trophy after Germany's fourth World Cup win. The champions scored 18 times in seven games, conceding only four goals.

BRAZIL 2014
FINAL
GERMANY 1 · ARGENTINA 0 (A.E.T.)
SEMIFINALS
GERMANY 7 · BRAZIL 1
ARGENTINA 0 · NETHERLANDS 0 (4–2 PENALTIES)
Games **64** · Goals **171** · Goals per game **2.67**

The first World Cup in Brazil for 64 years saw the debut of Bosnia & Herzegovina, goal line technology, and vanishing foam to mark out distances for free kicks. Defending champion Spain crashed out at the group stage after being thrashed 5–1 by the Netherlands and losing 2–0 to Chile. In Group D, Uruguay and Costa Rica progressed, knocking out England and Italy, while Algeria got through the group stage for the first time ever. The host's hopes were crushed in an extraordinary semifinal in which Germany scored five times in just 20 minutes to win 7–1. They met Argentina in the final, where a Mario Götze goal made Germany the first European team to win a World Cup in the Americas. Colombia's James Rodriguez won the Golden Boot with six goals, while Lionel Messi was awarded the Golden Ball as the tournament's best player.

RUSSIA 2018

FINAL
FRANCE 4 · CROATIA 2
SEMIFINALS
FRANCE 1 · BELGIUM 0
CROATIA 2 · ENGLAND 0
Games **64** · Goals **169** · Goals per game **2.64**

With this celebration of soccer and fandom, Russia proved a welcoming host. The soccer often dazzled and entertained, with only one of the 64 games—France against Denmark—ending in a goalless tie. With a population of less than 340,000, Iceland became the smallest country to play in a World Cup. They failed to qualify out of their group, as did all the African nations and the defending champion, Germany. Losing to both Mexico and South Korea, it was the first time Germany had failed to qualify from its group since 1938. The host team, however, fared better, progressing from its group then beating Spain in a penalty shoot-out that gripped spectators around the world. Exciting young stars like Kevin de Bruyne and Kylian Mbappé helped propel Belgium and France to the semifinals, while England recorded its biggest World Cup win ever, overpowering Panama 6–1. England's Harry Kane would win the Golden Boot as top scorer, while Luka Modric won the Golden Ball as the tournament's best player. But the glory and a second World Cup win went to France.

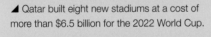

▲ Qatar built eight new stadiums at a cost of more than $6.5 billion for the 2022 World Cup.

▼ Mali's Ibrahim Kone celebrates scoring against Kenya in a 2022 World Cup qualifier. His country was aiming to make it to the tournament for the first time in its history.

HOPING TO HOST

Six nations expressed an interest in hosting the first World Cup, held in 1930, and ever since, countries have prepared their bid many years in advance to try and secure the World Cup within their borders. The tournament was first held in Africa in 2010 and was hosted in the Middle East—in Qatar—for the first time in 2022. Only one tournament has been co-hosted (Japan/South Korea in 2002), but the 2026 World Cup will feature three hosts—Canada, the United States, and Mexico—with an expanded format containing 48 teams.

THE WOMEN'S WORLD CUP

Given how popular women's soccer is today, it is hard to believe that many countries only lifted their ban on women's competition in the 1970s. Asia was the first continent to hold a competition: in 1975, New Zealand defeated Thailand in the final of the AFC Women's Championship (now the AFC Women's Asian Cup). In the 1980s, increased lobbying and the success of Italy's invitational women's tournament, the Mundialito, led to FIFA running a test event in China in 1988. Three years later, the world's elite female soccer players returned to take part in the very first Women's World Cup.

▲ Carla Overbeck (center) celebrates with the 1999 U.S. team she captained. Overbeck was also part of the winning team in 1991.

CHINA 1991
FINAL
U.S. 2 · NORWAY 1

The first Women's World Cup was a great success and proof that women's soccer had a major global audience. Twelve teams from all six FIFA confederations took part, and 65,000 spectators watched the final between the U.S. and Norway. The U.S. ran out 2–1 winners, with both their goals coming from Michelle Akers. Akers was awarded the Golden Shoe after scoring ten goals in the tournament.

▶ U.S. forward Wendy Gebauer skips to avoid a challenge from Japan's Kyoko Kuroda at the 1991 World Cup.

SWEDEN 1995
FINAL
NORWAY 2 · GERMANY 0

The tournament's 26 games saw plenty of goals. Brazil was thrashed 6–1 by Germany, which then lost a 3–2 thriller to Sweden. The U.S. and China shared the spoils in an epic 3–3 encounter, and Norway powered through their group, putting 17 goals past Canada, England, and Nigeria, before knocking out the U.S. at the semifinal stage. Sweden's Ingrid Jonsson became the first woman to referee a FIFA final, in which Norway scored two first-half goals to secure the world crown.

UNITED STATES 1999
FINAL
U.S. 0 · CHINA 0 (5–4 PENALTIES)

Expanded to 16 teams, the tournament was a huge success and saw Nigeria become the first African team to reach the quarterfinals. The U.S., with Mia Hamm, Brandi Chastain, and Tiffeny Milbrett all playing superbly, had to work hard to overcome both Germany and Brazil. China, in contrast, cruised to the final. Played in front of more than 90,000 fans at the Rose Bowl, the final was a very tense affair. The game went to penalties, with Briana Scurry saving Ying Liu's spot kick to see the Unites States win the shoot-out 5–4.

UNITED STATES 2003
FINAL
GERMANY 2 · SWEDEN 1

Relocated to the U.S. from China at the last minute due to the SARS virus epidemic, the 2003 tournament was predicted to be a successful swansong for many of the United States' veteran players. However, a vibrant, attacking German team, led by the tournament's leading scorer, Birgit Prinz, knocked them out in the semifinals. In a memorable final, a golden goal by substitute Nia Kuenzer secured Germany its first Women's World Cup.

CHINA 2007
FINAL
GERMANY 2 · BRAZIL 0

The tournament got off to a record start, with Germany thrashing Argentina 11–0 in Group A while Brazil, led by top scorer Marta, mauled New Zealand 5–0 and China 4–0 in Group D. These two teams, along with Norway and the U.S., made it out of their groups and into the semifinals, where Brazil handed a surprise 4–0 defeat to the U.S. to join Germany in the final. Two second-half goals from Birgit Prinz and Simone Ladehr propelled Germany to their second World Cup final victory in a row.

CANADA 2015
FINAL
U.S. 5 · JAPAN 2

Canada hosted a competition expanded from 16 to 24 teams. All games were played on artificial turf, which caused player complaints, but otherwise the tournament was a great success. Compelling matches and stunning displays showcased women's elite soccer. There were mismatches— Switzerland defeated Ecuador 10–1, while Germany thrashed the Ivory Coast 10–0—but many other games were tight affairs. Australia defeated a highly rated Brazilian team in the quarterfinals, lost narrowly to Japan, but beat Germany in the playoff to finish third overall.

The United States met holder Japan in a repeat of the 2011 final, and the game was memorable for U.S. midfielder Carli Lloyd's spectacular hat trick, which included an incredible shot from the halfway line.

▲ Germany's Celia Sasic (left) shared the 2015 Golden Boot (six goals) with Carli Lloyd of the U.S.

GERMANY 2011
FINAL
JAPAN 2 · U.S. 2 (3–1 PENALTIES)

An exciting, well-staged tournament saw almost a million spectators watch matches between the 16 teams, which included Colombia and Equatorial Guinea for the first time. Two quarterfinals went to penalty shoot-outs, with France defeating England and Brazil losing to the U.S. after an epic match. The U.S. went down to ten players after a red card in the 65th minute, but managed to take the game into extra time and equalized in the 122nd minute. The U.S. went through to the final, where they came up against the newest force of women's soccer. Japan, led by the tournament's best player, Homare Sawa, became the first team from Asia to win a World Cup.

▼ U.S. striker Abby Wambach (right) battles with Japan's Saki Kumagai during the 2011 final.

▶ Delphine Cascarino of France is tracked by South Korea's Sohyun Cho in 2019.

FRANCE 2019
FINAL
U.S. 2 · NETHERLANDS 0

France 2019 was the biggest Women's World Cup ever, with global television audiences passing one billion. There were goals galore as host France kicked off with an emphatic 4–0 win over South Korea, the first of 52 matches and 146 goals in total. The U.S. entered the competition as defending champions and firm favorites. They did not disappoint, hammering Thailand with a record-breaking score of 13–0 in their opening match and a record-breaking five goals in one game for striker Alex Morgan. The U.S. knocked out Spain, France, and England on their way to the final, where they beat the Netherlands 2–0 in their fourth World Cup win. U.S. co-captain Megan Rapinoe stole the headlines, bagging the Golden Ball for best player and the Golden Boot for six goals. More history was made when Brazilian legend Marta scored against Italy, bringing her World Cup record to 17 goals, more than any other player.

THE EUROPEAN CHAMPIONSHIPS

FACT FILE
Midfielder Michel Platini holds the record for the most goals scored in a European Championships. He scored nine of France's 14 goals in the 1984 competition.

The European Championships began in 1958 as the UEFA European Nations Cup but struggled to attract teams to compete. However, today it is the largest international soccer competition behind the World Cup. It is also held every four years.

HOSTS AND WINNERS

Year	Host	Final
1964	Spain	Spain 2–1 U.S.S.R.
1968	Italy	Italy 2–0 Yugoslavia (after replay)
1972	Belgium	West Germany 3–0 U.S.S.R.
1976	Yugoslavia	Czechoslovakia 2–2 W. Germany (5–3 pen.)
1980	Italy	West Germany 2–1 Belgium
1984	France	France 2–0 Spain
1988	West Germany	Netherlands 2–0 U.S.S.R.
1992	Sweden	Denmark 2–0 Germany
1996	England	Germany 2–1 Czech Republic
2000	Belgium / Neth.	France 2–1 Italy
2004	Portugal	Greece 1–0 Portugal
2008	Austria / Switz.	Spain 1–0 Germany
2012	Poland / Ukraine	Spain 4–0 Italy
2016	France	Portugal 1–0 France
2020	Europe-wide	Italy 1–1 England (3–2 pen.)

GROWING COMPETITION

Early tournaments consisted of qualifying rounds, with just four teams progressing to a mini tournament of semifinals and a final. By 1980, this was extended to eight teams, and it doubled again for the 1996 tournament, the first held in England. Before expansion, many talented teams missed out on the tournament, such as the Soviet Union in 1984 and Spain and Italy in 1992. EURO 2016 saw further growth, with 24 teams taking part. Five nations made their EURO debuts at this tournament, with Iceland and Wales (the latter reaching the semifinals) making the biggest impact.

SURPRISE WINNERS

EURO 1992 saw Denmark record a memorable triumph. They had failed to qualify, and most of their players were on vacation when UEFA invited them to the tournament following Yugoslavia's disqualification. With little time to prepare, the Danes defeated the Netherlands and Germany to win the most unlikely of European Championship crowns. In 1976, Czechoslovakia surprised everyone by beating the World Cup holders, West Germany, in the final. EURO 2004 began with shocks aplenty when Spain and Italy were knocked out early, followed by Germany, which had been held to a tie by minnows Latvia. Greece had defeated the tournament host Portugal in the opening match, only to face them again in the final. Greek forward Angelos Charisteas scored his third goal of EURO 2004 in the 57th minute, as Greece won 1–0 to secure its first major international trophy.

◀ Denmark celebrates in 1992. ▶ Spain's Jordi Alba tussles with Mario Balotelli of Italy in 2012. ▶▶ Ronaldo lifts the trophy as Portugal players toast their 2016 victory.

FACT FILE

Spanish leader General Franco, a critic of communism, refused the Soviet team entry into Spain to play its qualifying game for the 1960 competition. The Soviets were awarded a win.

EURO 2020

Postponed for a year due to the Covid-19 pandemic, this was the first tournament with no single or shared hosts, but with games spread out across the continent. Spain's helter-skelter 5–3 defeat of Croatia, Switzerland knocking out France, and Germany's 4–2 defeat of Portugal were among the highlights. England had suffered knockout infamy at the hands of Iceland in 2016, but five years later, Gareth Southgate's well-drilled team cruised past Germany, Ukraine, and Denmark to reach the final. There England faced an Italian team whose tight defense, well marshaled by veteran Giorgio Chiellini, saw them prevail in a tense tussle that went to penalties. Italian goalkeeper Gianluigi Donnarumma—the player of the tournament—twice proved a penalty shoot-out hero to give the Italians their first EURO title for 53 years.

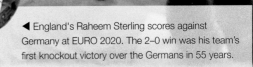

◀ England's Raheem Sterling scores against Germany at EURO 2020. The 2–0 win was his team's first knockout victory over the Germans in 55 years.

WOMEN'S EUROS

Starting in 1984 with just four invited teams, the women's EUROs has expanded, with 16 teams taking part for the first time in 2017. That tournament was won by the Netherlands, the fourth time a host nation had triumphed. They joined Norway (1987, 1993) and Sweden (1984) as the only teams to stop Germany, which has dominated the competition with an astonishing eight tournament wins. The 2022 tournament, held in England, featured four groups of four teams, including Northern Ireland, which qualified for the first time.

▶ Norway's Maria Thorisdóttir (left) and Daniëlle van de Donk of the Netherlands in action at EURO 2017.

THE OLYMPICS

Until the emergence of the World Cup, the Olympics provided soccer's leading world competition. Soccer appeared in the 1896 games as an exhibition event and became a full Olympic sport 12 years later. With the exception of the 1932 Los Angeles Games, it has featured at every Olympics since. The competition was boosted in the 1990s by the admittance of professional stars and the emergence of African soccer, which produced two Olympic gold medalists in Nigeria and Cameroon.

AMATEURS ONLY

For most of its history, Olympic soccer was played by amateurs only. The rise of professional soccer in the 1920s meant that many of the world's best professionals were unable to appear at the Games. State-run teams from Eastern Europe dominated the Olympics after World War II—from 1952 to 1988, every Olympic winner came from Eastern Europe, with the exception of the 1984 French team, while Hungary remains the only team to have won soccer gold three times. But as the Olympics began to accept professional athletes in other sports, so it changed the rules for soccer. Professionals who were part of their national under-23 teams appeared at the 1992 games. In 1996 the rule was relaxed to allow each team to field three professional players over the age of 23. At Sydney 2000, Chile, led by 33-year-old striker Ivan Zamorano, won bronze. Zamorano's six goals made him the top scorer at the Games.

EMERGING PLAYERS

Great professional players have emerged from the Olympics. For example, French midfielder Michel Platini and Mexican legend Hugo Sanchez burst onto the international scene at the 1976 Montreal games. The 1996 Brazil team included Rivaldo and Ronaldo. The 1952 Olympics in Helsinki, Finland, saw the arrival of a stunningly good Hungarian team. Featuring players such as Ferenc Puskas, Nandor Hidegkuti, and Sandor Kocsis, the Hungarians conceded two goals but scored 20 on their way to the gold medal. These players went on to form the core of the Hungarian team that lit up international soccer through the 1950s (see page 68).

▼ Mexico's Oribe Peralta is mobbed after scoring the winner in the 2012 Olympic final against Brazil.

FACT FILE

The first official Olympic tournament, in 1908, saw a record average of eight goals per game. This tally was helped by Denmark's 17–1 thrashing of France. Sophus Nielsen scored ten times, including three goals within the first six minutes!

▶ Cameroon's Samuel Eto'o in the gold-medal match at Sydney 2000. His team's win secured his country's first Olympic gold medal.

OLYMPIC WOMEN

Women's soccer finally became part of the Olympics at the 1996 Atlanta Games, after many years of lobbying for inclusion. With no time for a qualifying competition, the top eight nations at the 1995 Women's World Cup were invited to take part, with the exception of England, which was ineligible to compete. The final saw China beaten 2–1 by the United States in front of 76,481 spectators, a world record for a women's sporting event at that time. Five nations—the U.S., China, Germany, Norway, and Brazil—shared all the medals until 2012, when powerful Canadian and Japanese teams emerged. But the qualification system now in place will ensure that Asia, Africa, and Oceania are all represented at future Olympics.

▶ Canada midfielder Julia Grosso (left) scored the decisive penalty kick in a shoot-out to win gold for Canada at Tokyo 2020.

2016 AND 2020 GAMES

The 2016 tournament saw new winners in both competitions. In the men's, Neymar was the hero for Brazil, scoring the winning penalty kick in a shoot-out to defeat Germany in the final. The Germans gained consolation from their female colleagues, who defeated Sweden 2–1 in front of 52,000 spectators to win gold for the first time. The 2020 competition, delayed for a year due to the Covid-19 pandemic, offered plenty of drama, from the Netherlands women's team thrashing China 8–2 to Canada's Jessie Fleming scoring the penalty kick that knocked the favorite U.S. out at the semifinal stage. In the men's tournament, Mexico had enjoyed a 4–1 win over France and a 6–3 victory against South Korea, but could not find the net against eventual champion Brazil, losing to that team in a penalty shoot-out.

▼ Dani Alves, the oldest player in the tournament at 38, shows off his gold medal after Brazil's triumph at Tokyo 2020.

COPA AMÉRICA

▼ Peruvian striker Gianluca Lapadula (right) and Ecuador's Robert Arboleda in a 2021 Copa América Group B match. Lapadula scored the first of Peru's two goals in the game, which ended 2–2.

The oldest continental cup competition, the Copa América has been played under a bewildering array of names and formats ever since the first tournament, a three-way affair between Argentina, Uruguay, and Chile in 1910. One thing has remained constant—its status as a major soccer prize for the nations of South America.

CUP DOMINATION

The Copa América has had to contend with clubs reluctant to release players and the increasing popularity of international club competitions. Yet it still maintains a strong appeal. There have been 47 Copa America competitions, eight of which have been unofficial but are counted for the records. The tournament has been dominated by the "big three" South American nations of Argentina, Brazil, and Uruguay. Fifteen Copas passed until another country, Peru, won it. Since then, Argentina and Uruguay (both with 15 titles) have maintained a strong grip. Brazil has won eight times; Paraguay and Peru twice; and Bolivia, Chile, and Colombia have each won once.

INVITED GUESTS

In 1993, the Copa was expanded to 12 teams. Teams are invited from outside South America, including Mexico (runner-up twice), the U.S., Costa Rica, and Honduras—which caused a sensation in 2001 by beating Brazil 2–0 in the quarterfinals. Mexico appeared for the sixth time at the 2015 Copa, tying 3–3 with host Chile, which progressed to the final after beating Uruguay and Peru in the quarters and semis. Chile defeated Argentina 4–1 on penalties to win their very first Copa, and won the tournament again the next year.

▶ Chile's Gonzalo Jara (left) and Arturo Vidal hold the trophy after winning the centenary edition of the Copa América in 2016.

COPA AMÉRICA WINNERS

1910*	Argentina	1942	Uruguay	1989	Brazil
1916*	Uruguay	1945*	Argentina	1991	Argentina
1917	Uruguay	1946*	Argentina	1993	Argentina
1919	Brazil	1947	Argentina	1995	Uruguay
1920	Uruguay	1949	Brazil	1997	Brazil
1921	Argentina	1953	Paraguay	1999	Brazil
1922	Brazil	1955	Argentina	2001	Colombia
1923	Uruguay	1956*	Uruguay	2004	Brazil
1924	Uruguay	1957	Argentina	2007	Brazil
1925	Argentina	1959*	Argentina	2011	Uruguay
1926	Uruguay	1959	Uruguay	2015	Chile
1927	Argentina	1963	Bolivia	2016	Chile
1929	Argentina	1967	Uruguay	2019	Brazil
1935*	Uruguay	1975	Peru	2021	Argentina
1937	Argentina	1979	Paraguay		
1939	Peru	1983	Uruguay	* unofficial
1941*	Argentina	1987	Uruguay	tournament

AFRICA CUP OF NATIONS

When first held in 1957, the tournament was contested by just three of Africa's nine independent nations: Sudan, Ethiopia, and the eventual winner, Egypt. Since then, the number of nations has risen sharply, and now teams strive to qualify for one of the 24 places at the finals.

UPS AND DOWNS

The Africa Cup of Nations has had to endure its ups and downs, with poor playing facilities in some countries, hostilities between nations, and major controversies. These continue into the modern era. Nigeria, one of Africa's top teams, was expelled from the 1998 tournament after the team had refused to travel to the 1996 competition. Since the early 1990s, the best teams in the competition have relied on calling back as many of their foreign-based stars as possible. In 2006, for example, not one player on the Ivory Coast and Cameroon squads was based in his home country. Four years later, Cameroon striker Samuel Eto'o notched his 18th goal, making him the tournament's all-time leading goal scorer.

◀ Sadio Mané of Senegal (right) battles Egypt's Emam Ashour in the 2021 final. Mané scored the winning penalty in the shoot-out that gave Senegal victory.

AFRICA CUP OF NATIONS WINNERS

1957	Egypt	1990	Algeria
1959	Egypt	1992	Ivory Coast
1962	Ethiopia	1994	Nigeria
1963	Ghana	1996	South Africa
1965	Ghana	1998	Egypt
1968	Congo-Kinshasa	2000	Cameroon
		2002	Cameroon
1970	Sudan	2004	Tunisia
1972	Congo-Brazzaville	2006	Egypt
		2008	Egypt
1974	Zaire	2010	Egypt
1976	Morocco	2012	Zambia
1978	Ghana	2013	Nigeria
1980	Nigeria	2015	Ivory Coast
1982	Ghana	2017	Cameroon
1984	Cameroon	2019	Algeria
1986	Egypt	2021	Senegal
1988	Cameroon		

WINNERS AND LOSERS

Champions have come from around the continent—from Africa's northernmost country, Morocco (winner in 1976), to its southernmost nation, South Africa, which returned from the international wilderness to win an emotional competition in 1996. Nine tournament finals have ended in penalty shoot-outs, including the 2015 tournament, when the Ivory Coast defeated Ghana 9–8 despite missing their first two penalty kicks. One of the most unlucky nations has to be Zambia, which lost an entire team in a tragic 1993 plane crash (see page 102), yet miraculously reached the final the following year. Zambia finally triumphed in 2012, after a period of dominance by Egypt—three wins in a row—which took them to the top of the winners' table with seven cups. The 2017 final was contested by the cup's most successful teams, Egypt (7 titles) and Cameroon (5 titles), while Algeria won its second title in 2019. The delayed 2021 edition saw Egypt in the final once again, this time against Senegal. After a tense penalty shoot-out, Senegal won the trophy for the very first time.

◀ Guinea's Issiaga Sylla holds off Algeria captain Riyad Mahrez in 2019. Mahrez scored a vital 95th-minute winner in the semifinal and led his team to the title with victory over Senegal.

ASIAN GAMES AND ASIAN CUP

Asia is the one continent that has two major soccer competitions for its nations—the Asian Games and the Asian Cup. Both tournaments are held every four years, but in cycles that keep them two years apart.

◄ Japan's Maya Yoshida out-jumps Almoez Ali of Qatar in the 2019 Asian Cup final.

THE ASIAN GAMES

The Asian Games is a multisport competition in which soccer is just one of a number of events. South Korea has shared the title twice, after the final was tied. After a self-imposed exile from the Asian Games in the mid-1990s, Iran powered to victories in 1998 and 2002. By the 2002 games, the tournament had become an under-23 competition, with teams allowed to field up to three over-age players. The 2018 competition saw South Korea win again.

THE ASIAN CUP

First held in 1956 with just four teams, the Asian Cup has grown in importance, with 46 nations entering qualifying for the 2023 tournament. Japan is the competition's most successful team, winning the cup four times, followed by Iran and Saudi Arabia with three titles. Israel was a major force in the early years. The team was in the final of the first four Asian Cups, winning in 1964. In 1975, however, Israel was expelled from the Asian Football Confederation, and it joined UEFA in 1992.

China became hosts for the first time in 2004, when the tournament was expanded to include 16 teams. The Japan versus China final attracted enormous interest. The match was broadcast live to 60 nations; in China alone, the television audience was more than 250 million.

Australia entered the fray from 2007 onward, finishing runner-up in 2011 but triumphing in 2015, defeating South Korea 2–1 in the final. They joined other recent first-time champions, including Iraq in 2007 and, sensationally, Qatar in 2019. The Qataris went through the entire tournament unbeaten and, propelled by nine goals from Almoez Ali, reached the final, where they defeated Japan 3–1.

◄ Iranian players run a lap of honor after their surprise defeat of Japan to win the 2002 Asian Games.

ASIAN GAMES AND ASIAN CUP WINNERS

Games winners (since 1962)		Cup winners	
1962	India	1956	South Korea
1966	Burma	1960	South Korea
1970	Burma and	1964	Israel
	South Korea	1968	Iran
1974	Iran	1972	Iran
1978	North Korea and	1976	Iran
	South Korea	1980	Kuwait
1982	Iraq	1984	Saudi Arabia
1986	South Korea	1988	Saudi Arabia
1990	Iran	1992	Japan
1994	Uzbekistan	1996	Saudi Arabia
1998	Iran	2000	Japan
2002	Iran	2004	Japan
2006	Qatar	2007	Iraq
2010	Japan	2011	Japan
2014	South Korea	2015	Australia
2018	South Korea	2019	Qatar

CONCACAF CHAMPIONSHIP

GOLD CUP WINNERS

Canada   2000

Mexico   1993, 1996, 1998, 2003, 2009, 2011, 2015, 2019

U.S.   1991, 2002, 2005, 2007, 2013, 2017, 2021

Of all the soccer-playing regions of the world, North America, Central America, and the Caribbean Islands have had the most complex history of competitions. Five different tournaments have been open to them, starting with the CCCF Championship in 1941.

THE GOLD CUP

For a number of years, competition in the CONCACAF zone was used as a direct way of qualifying for the World Cup. In 1991, the tournament was renamed the Gold Cup, which from 2019 features 16 teams in the finals. Every Gold Cup has been hosted by the U.S., either alone or jointly with Mexico. Teams from outside CONCACAF have often been invited to play. In 1996, the Brazilian under-23 squad lost to Mexico in the final. South Korea was a guest in 2000, but lost out on a quarterfinal place to Canada on the toss of a coin. Canada went on to beat another guest, Colombia, in the final. Qatar was the invited guest for the 2021 tournament and reached the semifinal, only to fall to the eventual winner, the United States. It was the seventh victory for the host, one behind its great rival, Mexico. In recent years, the two teams' dominance has been threatened by an enterprising Jamaican team that knocked the U.S. squad out of the 2015 tournament and Mexico out of the 2017 competition, and reached the semifinals in 2019.

▲ U.S. defender Shaq Moore (right) gets past Haiti's Duckens Nazon in a 2021 Gold Cup match.

▶ New Caledonia (in red) defends against New Zealand's Chris Wood in the 2016 OFC Nations Cup.

THE OFC NATIONS CUP

Oceania's competition is the smallest and youngest of the continental championships. It has been held nine times since 1973, now every four years. The 2004 tournament saw a major surprise as the Solomon Islands beat New Zealand to make the final, losing to Australia. The 2012 Cup saw further surprises, with New Caledonia knocking out New Zealand and Tahiti emerging as champions. New Zealand triumphed in 2016, defeating Papua New Guinea on penalties in the final.

SOCCER LEAGUES

Clubs compete in leagues that are made up of several divisions. Rules, numbers of teams, and the length of a league season vary around the world. Many top leagues—in Spain, Italy, France, and Germany, for example—have 18 or 20 teams.

NUMBERS AND BREAKS

The top divisions of Sweden and Russia contain 16 teams, while Australia has 12 and Latvia just ten. In most leagues the teams play each other twice, home and away, during a season. In Denmark, the 12 teams play each other three times. Scotland's top division has an unusual format—there are 12 teams, but the season lasts for 38 games. Teams play each other three times, before the league turns into two groups of six for a further round of matches. Some leagues—in Argentina and Mexico, for example—are split into two short seasons every year. League teams in Spain, France, Germany, Hungary, and some other countries take a midwinter break, while in northern European nations, such as Norway and Finland, the league season begins in the spring. England's Women's Super League (WSL) has risen from eight clubs in 2015 to 12 by 2019.

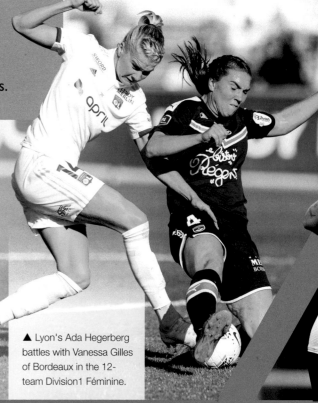

▲ Lyon's Ada Hegerberg battles with Vanessa Gilles of Bordeaux in the 12-team Division1 Féminine.

PROMOTION AND RELEGATION

While leagues in Australia and the U.S. guarantee each team a place for the following season, most leagues have a system of promotion and relegation, with top and bottom teams switching places for the new season. In Uruguay, relegation and promotion are determined by the performance of teams over two seasons. In Austria, one team is promoted and one relegated each season. In Hungary, the Czech Republic, and South Korea, two teams go up and down, while in France, Spain, Egypt, and Ghana it is three. In Germany, the third-place team in the second division contests a two-game playoff with the team finishing 16th in the Bundesliga, to determine who will play in the top division the following season. Other nations, such as Italy and England, hold a playoff series featuring semifinals and a final to determine which of four teams will be promoted along with others that won automatic promotion above them. In Italy, playoffs are also used to determine which team joins three other relegated teams from Serie A. Playoff systems are criticized for turning a whole season into a lottery over one, two, or three games, but many people think they maintain interest and add drama.

◀ VfL Osnabruck captain Marc Heider is dejected after his team's relegation to the German 3. Liga in 2021.

HARD FALLERS

Just as clubs can rise, so can they fall. In the 2021–22 season, 15 former champions of the French league (with 31 titles between them) played outside the top division. A slide down the divisions can be sudden or gradual. Deportivo La Coruña won the Spanish League in 2000 and the Intertoto Cup in 2008 yet were relegated twice in three years, so that come 2021, they were playing in the third tier of Spanish soccer. Napoli was home to Diego Maradona and was one of Italian soccer's aristocrats, winning the league title in 1987 and 1990 and finishing runner-up in the two intervening years. Yet by the early 2000s the team was bankrupt and playing in Serie C, two divisions down from the top flight.

Rarely, however, has a downturn been more dramatic than that experienced by Manchester City or Tasmania 1900 Berlin. In 1937, Manchester City was the English league champion. In the following season, the team scored 80 league goals, more than any other squad, but was relegated. Tasmania 1900 Berlin was joint first in the early stages of the 1965–66 Bundesliga season. By the end, the team was at the bottom and holder of a series of unenviable records for a season, including fewest wins (two), most losses (28), most goals against (108), and lowest points total (eight).

▼ Al-Ahly (in white) are Africa's most successful club team, with 42 Egyptian league titles.

◄ KV Mechelen have been promoted to or relegated from the Belgian First Division A 25 times.

FAST RISERS

Some leagues have been dominated by a small number of teams throughout their history. For 43 seasons from 1932, the Uruguayan league title was won by either Peñarol or Nacional (Defensor were the champions in 1976). Scotland's Glasgow Rangers hold the world record for the most league championships, with a staggering 55 titles, four more than their arch rivals, Celtic. In some leagues small teams have risen dramatically from humble beginnings to become champions or contenders. In Europe, the now mighty Bayern Munich team was not considered successful enough to join the Bundesliga in the early 1960s, but since then the team has become one of the pillars of German soccer.

FACT FILE

In 2017, newly promoted team Génération Foot won the Senegal Premier League by 13 points. The previous year's champions, U.S. Gorée, finished bottom and were relegated.

► Jesús Medina in action for New York City FC on their way to winning the 2021 MLS Cup. It was the fast-rising club's first trophy, having joined the MLS just six years earlier.

▶ Inter Milan striker Lautaro Martinez is challenged in a 2021 clash with Serie A debutants Spezia Calcio.

SERIE A

For decades, Serie A was considered the ultimate test for the world's top players. Some clubs have since struggled with the results of their former lavish spending on players. Winning Serie A is sometimes referred to as the *scudetto* (small shield), as the champions' strip the following season bears a small coat of arms in Italian colors. Internazionale, for example, won the UEFA Cup in 1994 but could only manage 13th place in the league. Juventus are the most successful Serie A club, with 35 titles, followed by Internazionale (19), AC Milan (18), and Genoa (nine). In the 2021–22 season, only three former champions—Casale, Novese, and Pro Vercelli—were playing in lower divisions.

THE BUNDESLIGA

Starting in 1965, the Bundesliga is considered one of the powerhouses of club soccer and a breeding ground for innovative coaches. It is the best-supported league in world soccer, with an average attendance during the 2018–19 season of 43,358 spectators per game—astonishing considering the league included SC Freiburg, whose stadium can only hold 24,000. Bayern Munich are the Bundesliga's most successful team by far, with 30 titles, followed by Borussia Dortmund and Borussia Mönchengladbach (five each) and Werder Bremen (four). Polish striker Robert Lewandowski's 308 goals puts him well ahead of current rivals but still far behind the legendary Gerd Müller's record of 365 Bundesliga goals.

◣ Pedri of Barcelona (right) challenges Real Madrid's Nacho Fernandez as the La Liga giants meet in 2020.

▲ Borussia Dortmund's superstar striker Erling Haaland breaks through the Bayern Munich defense in a 2021 Bundesliga encounter.

LA LIGA

The Spanish league banned foreign players between 1963 and 1973, but since then it has been the home of some of the world's greatest soccer stars, from Johan Cruyff and Lionel Messi to current stars Luis Suárez, Jan Oblak, and João Félix. The league can be highly competitive but is mostly dominated by Real Madrid and Barcelona. La Liga has two professional divisions and a series of amateur divisons. Unlike other national leagues, the reserve teams of the major clubs play in the lower divisions, not in a separate reserves league. Real Madrid and Barcelona remain La Liga's most wealthy and successful clubs, with 60 league titles between them.

ENGLISH PREMIER LEAGUE

In the early 1990s, England's first division clubs broke away from league control to form the Premier League. Money has flooded into the top clubs' coffers and a wide gap has opened up between established teams and newly promoted teams that may find it hard to stay up. Manchester United won 13 of the first 21 titles. Their battle for supremacy was fought initially against clubs like Arsenal and Chelsea, before Manchester City, with five recent titles up to 2021, and Liverpool joined the fray. Currently featuring many of the world's most elite players, such as Kevin de Bruyne and Mo Salah, its matches attract massive worldwide TV audiences.

◄ James Milner of Liverpool (left) and Man City's Phil Foden in 2021.

▼ The U.S.'s National Women's Soccer League has been home to many of the world's very best female players, including high profile U.S. internationals such as Megan Rapinoe and Alex Morgan. Below, Orlando Pride's Meggie Dougherty Howard holds off Caprice Dydasco of N.J./N.Y. Gotham City FC.

LIGUE 1

Despite having produced some of the world's greatest players, the French league has traditionally not been as well funded as others in Europe. Its homegrown stars, such as Paul Pogba and Karim Benzema, usually move abroad. Bolstered by PSG's extreme spending, this is now changing, with French teams highly competitive in Europe and home to some of the world's most exciting players. AS Saint-Étienne and Marseille have each won the league ten times, but more recently Lyon (Olympique Lyonnais), Lille, and PSG—which won seven titles between 2013 and 2020—have triumphed.

ASIAN LEAGUES

The first professional league in Asia was South Korea's K-League, which began with just five teams in 1983 and now features 22 teams split over two divisions. The league's most successful team is Seongnam Ilhwa Chunma, with seven titles. Japan's J.League kicked off in 1993 and now has two divisions. Kashima Antlers are the most successful squad, with eight titles, while the league was won in both 2020 and 2021 by Kawasaki Frontale. The Chinese Super League has been won by Guangzhou Evergrande eight times since it began in 2004.

MAJOR LEAGUE SOCCER (MLS)

An unusual league system with two parallel conferences, Eastern and Western, and no promotion or relegation, the MLS kicked off in 1996 with ten teams. It is now expanding to three times that size, with the likes of Austin and Charlotte joining recently, and St. Louis and Sacramento arriving in 2023. The league mixes homegrown players with foreign stars, which in the past included David Beckham and Thierry Henry, and currently features Javier Hernandez, Blaise Matuidi, and Carles Gil. The LA Galaxy, with five championships, and D.C. United with four, are the MLS's most successful teams.

FACT FILE

In the 1998 Swedish league championship, AIK Solna scored fewer goals than any of their 13 opponents (just 25 in 26 matches), yet still managed to win the title.

CLUB CUP COMPETITIONS

In 1872, Wanderers beat Royal Engineers by one goal to zero to win the first FA Cup—the oldest surviving major cup competition. Since that time, hundreds of cup competitions have been introduced all over the world. Some, such as the UEFA Super Cup and the African Super Cup, are contested between the winners of other cup competitions.

COPA LIBERTADORES

South America's first international club competition was staged by Chilean club Colo Colo in 1948 and won by Brazil's Vasco da Gama. However, it was not until 1960 that a regular competition, the Copa Libertadores, was set up. Peñarol of Uruguay won the first two contests, but the team was defeated in the final of the third by Santos, courtesy of two goals from Pelé. Today the Copa Libertadores begins with nine groups of four teams and culminates in knockout rounds ending, since 2019, in a single-match final. It is open to the highest-placed teams of each South American nation, and between 1960 and 1987, the previous winner received a bye until the semifinals of the competition. The Copa Libertadores has always outshone the national team competition—the Copa América—and other South American cups in popularity and passion.

Clubs from Argentina (25 times), Brazil (21 times), and Uruguay (8 times) have won the most Copas, with Independiente the leading winners with seven titles. There have been eight occasions when the champions came from elsewhere. In 2016, Colombia's Atlético Nacional triumphed, beating Independiente del Valle of Ecuador in the final. Two years later, another Colombian team, Atlético Huila, won the women's version of the competition, the Copa Libertadores Femenina, which has been held since 2009 and has been mostly won by Brazilian teams.

◄ The 2021 Copa Libertadores final was contested by Palmeiras and Flamengo.

▼ Tamires (left) and Victória of Corinthians with the Copa Libertadores Femenina trophy in 2021.

AROUND THE WORLD

The Copa Libertadores and the UEFA Champions League (see pages 133–134) are the most famous continental club competitions. The winners of these two events used to play each other in the Intercontinental Cup (later, the World Club Cup) but in 2000, a new competition, the FIFA Club World Cup, ran and eventually took over. It features the winners of each continent's leading club competition. The 2021 competition, held in the United Arab Emirates, featured seven teams and was won by Chelsea for the first time.

Africa's most prestigious competition is the African Champions League. In recent years, Tunisian, Moroccan, and Egyptian clubs have dominated, with Al-Ahly winning ten times, including the 2020 and 2021 competitions. The last sub-Saharan winners, Mamelodi Sundowns (2016), also hold the record for the biggest victory, an 11–1 thrashing of Côte d'Or FC from the Seychelles in 2019.

The Asian Champions League is highly competitive, with 24 different winners so far, from Thai Farmers Bank to Saudi Arabian club Al-Hilal—the leading winners with four titles.

▲ Al-Ahly's Aliou Dieng (left) is tackled by Mosa Lebusa of Mamelodi Sundowns in a 2021 African Champions League tie.

CUPS IN EUROPE

All European nations have at least one cup competition for clubs in addition to their leagues. Among the most famous are the Copa del Rey in Spain, first held in 1903, and the Coupe de France, which was first contested in 1917. The oldest surviving cup competition in the world is England's FA Cup, which celebrated its 150th birthday in 2021. Arsenal have reached the final the most times (21), winning on a record 14 occasions.

Between 1960 and 1999, national cup winners took part in a European-wide Cup-Winners' Cup, won most often by Barcelona, although their 1969 final loss to Slovan Bratislava (now of Slovakia) gave Eastern Europe its first major continental cup winner. From 1999, cup winners in Europe's strongest countries, as well as teams with high league finishes, gained automatic entry into the UEFA Cup—a large competition founded in 1971 to replace the Inter-Cities Fairs Cup. In 2009, the UEFA Cup was reformatted as the Europa League, with preliminary stages followed by 12 mini leagues, each containing four teams, then a 32-team knockout competition. With multiple entrants from the bigger nations, it is no surprise that ten UEFA Cup or Europa League finals have been contested by teams from the same country. Spanish clubs have won the most titles (13). Sevilla are the most successful team, with six victories, the latest in 2020.

► Villareal striker Paco Alcácer kisses the UEFA Europa League trophy after his team won the competition for the first time in 2021.

EUROPEAN CHAMPIONS

European club competitions date back to 1927, when the Mitropa Cup was first contested by the leading clubs of central Europe. Sparta Prague became its first winners. The last Mitropa Cup was won by Yugoslav team Borac Banja Luka in 1992, but by then the glamour of the Mitropa had long been eclipsed by the mighty European Cup, a competition that is now known as the UEFA Champions League.

▲ Inter players celebrate their win in 1964, a 3–1 victory over Real Madrid.

▼ The two greatest players of the Champions League era, Lionel Messi and Cristiano Ronaldo, vie for the ball in 2008.

EARLY DAYS

The European Champion Clubs' Cup, usually known as the European Cup, developed out of a meeting set up by Frenchman Gabriel Hanot. Italian, Spanish, French, and Portuguese club teams were eager to take part, as were teams from many other countries. The first European Cup, held in 1955–56, featured major names such as Real Madrid, Sporting Lisbon, Anderlecht, and AC Milan. Clubs that are less well known today also entered— Århus GF and FC Saarbrucken, for example. English league champions Chelsea, however, were forbidden from entering, but Scottish club Hibernian reached the semifinal. The first winners of the trophy were Real Madrid.

CHANGING CHAMPIONS

Real won the first five European Cups, before the tournament hit a golden age of competition in the 1960s, with Benfica, Internazionale, and AC Milan all winning the trophy. The 1970s saw both Ajax and Bayern Munich crowned champions three years in a row. English clubs won six European Cups in succession from 1977 but were banned from European competition for five years after the 1985 Heysel Stadium disaster (see page 103). There have been 18 Spanish winners, 13 English winners, and 12 Italian champions.

As the European Cup grew in intensity, it became harder to successfully defend the title. No team managed to retain their crown between AC Milan's win in 1990 and Real Madrid's in 2017. The first year that the final went into extra time was 1958, while the first penalty shoot-out in the final was in 1984. The two finals won by Eastern European teams, Steaua Bucharest (1986) and Red Star Belgrade (1991), both went to nail-biting penalty shoot-outs.

FACT FILE

Swedish striker Zlatan Ibrahimovic is the only player to have scored in Champions League games for six teams: Ajax, Juventus, Internazionale, Barcelona, AC Milan, and Paris Saint-Germain.

EUROPEAN CUP / CHAMPIONS LEAGUE WINNERS

1956	Real Madrid	1980	Nottingham Forest	2004	Porto
1957	Real Madrid	1981	Liverpool	2005	Liverpool
1958	Real Madrid	1982	Aston Villa	2006	Barcelona
1959	Real Madrid	1983	Hamburg	2007	AC Milan
1960	Real Madrid	1984	Liverpool	2008	Manchester United
1961	Benfica	1985	Juventus	2009	Barcelona
1962	Benfica	1986	Steaua Bucharest	2010	Internazionale
1963	AC Milan	1987	Porto	2011	Barcelona
1964	Internazionale	1988	PSV Eindhoven	2012	Chelsea
1965	Internazionale	1989	AC Milan	2013	Bayern Munich
1966	Real Madrid	1990	AC Milan	2014	Real Madrid
1967	Celtic	1991	Red Star Belgrade	2015	Barcelona
1968	Manchester United	1992	Barcelona	2016	Real Madrid
1969	AC Milan	1993	Marseille	2017	Real Madrid
1970	Feyenoord	1994	AC Milan	2018	Real Madrid
1971	Ajax	1995	Ajax	2019	Liverpool
1972	Ajax	1996	Juventus	2020	Bayern Munich
1973	Ajax	1997	Borussia Dortmund	2021	Chelsea
1974	Bayern Munich	1998	Real Madrid		
1975	Bayern Munich	1999	Manchester United		
1976	Bayern Munich	2000	Real Madrid		
1977	Liverpool	2001	Bayern Munich		
1978	Liverpool	2002	Real Madrid		
1979	Nottingham Forest	2003	AC Milan		

▶ Manchester United's Teddy Sheringham (left) and David Beckham. Sheringham scored the first of two injury-time goals to win the 1999 final.

▲ Gareth Bale scores a spectacular bicycle kick goal for Real Madrid against Liverpool in the 2018 final. He scored a second goal 20 minutes later and was made man of the match.

EXPANSION AND DOMINATION

The format of the European Cup remained almost unchanged for its first 35 years. Teams competed in knockout rounds, playing one match at home and one away. If the scores were tied after the two games, the team with more away goals would go through. For many years, the competition was open only to the league champions of each country. Today as many as four teams from each top league take part.

In 1992, everything changed. The competition was revamped as the UEFA Champions League. Group stages were introduced, guaranteeing qualifying teams a series of games and vast sums of television money. With a prize sum now in excess of $2 billion per season and almost $95 million guaranteed for winning, participating in the competition is essential for the financial health of Europe's top teams. Failure to qualify can be a financial disaster. The format has been tweaked and expanded on a number of occasions, with major changes planned for the 2024–25 season: the abandonment of groups in favor of one 36-club league, with teams each playing one match against ten different opponents and the top 16 progressing to the later stages.

MAGIC MOMENTS

Now the most-watched club competition in the world, the UEFA Champions League has provided fans with many astonishing games and moments. These have occurred at the group stage—such as in 1994 when Werder Bremen, down 3–0 after 65 minutes, roared back to triumph 5–3 against Anderlecht. They can also occur in the final, such as in 2005, when AC Milan entered the second half comfortably in the lead 3–0, only for their opponent, Liverpool, to stage a remarkable comeback victory. In the same year, Inter Milan's Dejan Stanković produced one of the best goals of the competition, striking a volley from just past the halfway line that sailed over Manuel Neuer into the Schalke net. Another German team, Bayer Leverkusen, found themselves on the receiving end of a Lionel Messi masterclass in 2012 as Barcelona's maestro scored five goals in a 7–1 rout. Messi has scored a staggering 125 goals so far in Champions League games, plus 41 goal assists. He is eclipsed only by his rival Cristiano Ronaldo, who has notched 140 goals and 48 assists in 182 matches, the most appearances of any player. He has won the competition five times. Since Inter Milan's 2010 triumph, all the winners have come from Germany, Spain, or England.

FACT FILE

Nineteen-year-old Erling Haaland scored a hat trick in the first half of his debut in the competition for Red Bull Salzburg versus Genk in 2018. For Borussia Dortmund, he was the 2020–21 Champions League top scorer, with ten goals.

▲▲ Goalkeeper Georgios Athanasiadis of minnows FC Sheriff celebrates his team's stunning Group D victory over 13-time champions Real Madrid in 2021.

▲ Sebastian Haller scores for four-time champions Ajax against Besiktas in 2021.

◄ Robert Lewandowski with the trophy after Bayern Munich's 2020 triumph.

FACT FILE

Eintracht Frankfurt have conceded the fastest goal in a women's final—scored by Marta after 12 seconds for Umeå in 2008. They have also scored the latest goal in a final—by Birgit Prinz after 93 minutes in 2006.

WOMEN'S CHAMPIONS LEAGUE

In 2001, UEFA founded the Women's Cup for leading women's clubs in Europe. Thirty-three clubs entered the competition, which saw Eintracht Frankfurt beat Swedish club Umeå IK 2–0 in the final. In early competitions, mismatches saw some one-sided scores—Armenia's CSC Yerevan conceding 18 goals in a 2001–02 group game, for example. At the elite end, competition was heating up with German, Swedish, and French teams to the fore and Russian, English, and Spanish squads not far behind.

The competition was rebadged as the UEFA Women's Champions League in 2009 and 53 clubs entered, with Potsdam defeating Lyon 7–6 on penalties in the final. The 2018 final again featured Lyon in the middle of an unprecedented run of five titles. After 90 tense minutes against Vfl Wolfsburg it was 0–0. By the end of extra time however, it was 4–1 to the French champions. One of their goals was scored by Ada Hegerberg, who notched 15 during the campaign—still a competition record. Lyon looked unstoppable season after season until they faced PSG in the 2021 quarterfinals and went out on away goals. PSG were then narrowly defeated by Barcelona, which routed Chelsea 4–0 in the final to record the first Spanish victory in the competition.

WOMEN'S CUP / WOMEN'S CHAMPIONS LEAGUE WINNERS

2002	Eintracht Frankfurt
2003	Umeå IK
2004	Umeå IK
2005	Turbine Potsdam
2006	Eintracht Frankfurt
2007	Arsenal
2008	Eintracht Frankfurt
2009	FCR 2001 Duisburg
2010	Turbine Potsdam
2011	Lyon
2012	Lyon
2013	Vfl Wolfsburg
2014	Vfl Wolfsburg
2015	Eintracht Frankfurt
2016	Lyon
2017	Lyon
2018	Lyon
2019	Lyon
2020	Lyon
2021	Barcelona

▲ Lieke Martens (top) celebrates after scoring for Barcelona in the second leg of the Champions League semifinal in 2021.

▶ Lyon's Ada Hegerberg with the trophy in 2019. The win over Barcelona was the French club's sixth Champions League title.

U.S. SOCCER

Soccer in the United States has a long history, with its first club team, Oneida in Boston, Massachusetts, having a roster of players as early as 1862.

The country's first major cup competition, the American Cup, began in 1885, the same year that an unofficial national team played its first game, against Canada. The United States joined FIFA in 1914, and a year earlier its governing body, the United States Soccer Federation, had been founded. In addition to sanctioning the majority of U.S. domestic leagues and competitions, it also awards the Soccer Athlete of the Year, the country's most illustrious soccer award.

PROFESSIONAL LEAGUES

Numerous attempts at establishing national leagues have come and gone, but Major League Soccer (MLS) is thriving, with increasing crowds, media interest, and team numbers in recent seasons. The league has expanded to 28 teams, with a flurry of new arrivals including Inter Miami CF (2020), Austin FC (2021), and Charlotte FC (2022), and with St. Louis City SC scheduled to join in 2023. Below the MLS is the National American Soccer League (NASL), and below that, the United Soccer League (USL).

USL teams in the past have performed well in the U.S. Open Cup, with three USL teams reaching the quarterfinal stages or further in 2017 and 2018.

Launching in 2009 with seven teams, Women's Professional Soccer took over from the defunct WUSA as the highest tier of women's club soccer in North America, but only survived three seasons. In 2013, the National Women's Soccer League (NWSL) kicked off. It now contains 12 teams after the arrival of San Diego Wave in 2021. The teams are split into three divisions—East, Central, and West—with the top six regular-season teams heading into an elimination playoff tournament to determine the champions.

INTERNATIONAL OUTLOOK

Despite tumult behind the scenes with the retirement of veteran star players and a failure to qualify for the 2018 FIFA World Cup, the U.S. men's team has been climbing the world rankings steadily. It has risen from 25th in 2018 to 13th in 2022, just two places behind Germany and one behind its greatest regional rival, Mexico. The team triumphed over Mexico at the CONCACAF Gold Cup in 2021 thanks to Miles Robinson's 117th-minute winner. Robinson was part of a back line that conceded just one goal all tournament. While the MLS is home to the majority of up-and-coming talent, some U.S. players have sought experience overseas. These include Weston McKennie, who joined Italian giants Juventus in 2020, and Christian Pulisic, whose $73-million move to Chelsea is the highest fee paid for a U.S. player.

At the start of 2022, the U.S. women's team celebrated its eighth consecutive year at the top of the world rankings. It went unbeaten in 2020 and lost just two out of 24 games in 2021, both at the Tokyo Olympics. This disappointment was tempered by FIFA Women's World Cup wins in 2015 and 2019, the latter followed by the retirement of coach Jill Ellis. The team also triumphed at the 2018 CONCACAF Gold Cup and won three SheBelieves Cups in a row (2020, 2021, 2022).

WEBSITES

ussoccer.com
The official home of U.S. soccer in its many forms.

nwslsoccer.com
The website of the NWSL, giving all the stats, news, and results from the competition.

mlssoccer.com
A huge collection of MLS history and team data. Also included are the rules of the game and coaching advice.

theguardian.com/football/series/the-100-best-footballers-in-the-world
Profiles of the 100 best players in the world, updated each year.

canadiansoccernews.com
All the news and opinion on Canadian soccer players and teams.

usyouthsoccer.org
News about young players and their coaches, plus upcoming competitions.

FACTS AND FIGURES

U.S. SOCCER ATHLETE OF THE YEAR

Men

1984	Rick Davis
1985	Perry van der Beck
1986	Paul Caligiuri
1987	Brent Goulet
1988	Peter Vermes
1989	Mike Windischmann
1990	Tab Ramos
1991	Hugo Perez
1992	Marcelo Balboa
1993	Thomas Dooley
1994	Marcelo Balboa
1995	Alexi Lalas
1996	Eric Wynalda
1997	Kasey Keller
1998	Cobi Jones
1999	Kasey Keller
2000	Chris Armas
2001	Earnie Stewart
2002	Brad Friedel
2003	Landon Donovan
2004	Landon Donovan
2005	Kasey Keller
2006	Oguchi Onyewu
2007	Clint Dempsey
2008	Tim Howard
2009	Landon Donovan
2010	Landon Donovan
2011	Clint Dempsey
2012	Clint Dempsey
2013	Jozy Altidore
2014	Tim Howard
2015	Michael Bradley
2016	Jozy Altidore
2017	Christian Pulisic
2018	Zack Steffen
2019	Christian Pulisic
2020	Weston McKennie
2021	Christian Pulisic

Women

1985	Sharon Remer
1986	April Heinrichs
1987	Carin Jennings-Gabarra
1988	Joy Biefield
1989	April Heinrichs
1990	Michelle Akers
1991	Michelle Akers
1992	Carin Jennings-Gabarra
1993	Kristine Lilly
1994	Mia Hamm
1995	Mia Hamm
1996	Mia Hamm
1997	Mia Hamm
1998	Mia Hamm
1999	Michelle Akers
2000	Tiffeny Milbrett
2001	Tiffeny Milbrett
2002	Shannon MacMillan
2003	Abby Wambach
2004	Abby Wambach
2005	Kristine Lilly
2006	Kristine Lilly
2007	Abby Wambach
2008	Carli Lloyd
2009	Hope Solo
2010	Abby Wambach
2011	Abby Wambach
2012	Alex Morgan
2013	Abby Wambach
2014	Lauren Holiday
2015	Carli Lloyd
2016	Tobin Heath
2017	Julie Ertz
2018	Alex Morgan
2019	Julie Ertz
2020	Sam Mewis
2021	Lindsey Horan

NATIONAL ASSOCIATION FOOTBALL LEAGUE (NAFL)

Following a failed attempt by baseball team owners to fill their stadiums in the off-season with a league in 1894, the NAFL started the following year. It struggled at first but received a boost when the U.S. won gold in soccer at the 1904 Olympics.

1895	Bayonne Centerville
1898	Paterson True Blues
1907	West Hudson
1908	Paterson Rangers
1909	Clark AA
1910	West Hudson
1911	Jersey AC
1912	West Hudson
1913	West Hudson
1914	Brooklyn FC
1915	West Hudson
1916	Alley Boys
1917	Jersey AC
1918	Paterson FC
1919	Bethlehem Steel
1920	Bethlehem Steel
1921	Bethlehem Steel

AMERICAN SOCCER LEAGUE (ASL) I AND II

Featuring teams mostly based on and near the East Coast, the ASL was the first U.S. league with major financial support, enough to attract players from Europe. In the mid-1920s the league boasted large attendances, but difficulties saw it fold in 1933. However, a successor, ASL II, formed the following year.

ASL I

1922	Philadelphia FC
1923	J & P Coats
1924	Fall River Marksmen
1925	Fall River Marksmen
1926	Fall River Marksmen
1927	Bethlehem Steel
1928	Boston Wonder Workers
1929	Fall River Marksmen
1930	Fall River Marksmen
1931	New York Giants
1932	New Bedford Whalers
1933	Fall River FC

ASL II

1934	Kearney Irish-Americans
1935	German-Americans
1936	New York Americans
1937	Scots-Americans
1938	Scots-Americans
1939	Newark Scots
1940	Newark Scots
1941	Newark Scots
1942	Philadelphia Americans
1943	Brooklyn Hispano
1944	Philadelphia Americans
1945	Brookhattan
1946	Baltimore Americans
1947	Philadelphia Americans
1948	Philadelphia Americans
1949	Philadelphia Nationals
1950	Philadelphia Nationals
1951	Philadelphia Nationals
1952	Philadelphia Americans
1953	Philadelphia Nationals
1954	New York Americans
1955	Uhrik Truckers (Philadelphia)
1956	Uhrik Truckers (Philadelphia)
1957	New York Hakoah
1958	New York Hakoah
1959	New York Hakoah
1960	Colombo
1961	Ukrainian Nationals (Philadelphia)
1962	Ukrainian Nationals (Philadelphia)
1963	Ukrainian Nationals (Philadelphia)
1964	Ukrainian Nationals (Philadelphia)
1965	Hartford Football Club
1966	Roma Soccer Club
1967	Baltimore St. Gerards
1968	Washington Darts
1969	Washington Darts
1970	Ukrainian Nationals (Philadelphia)
1971	New York Greeks
1972	Cincinnati Comets
1973	New York Apollo
1974	Rhode Island Oceaneers
1975	New York Apollo
1976	Los Angeles Skyhawks
1977	New Jersey Americans
1978	New York Apollo
1979	Sacramento Gold
1980	Pennsylvania Stoners
1981	Carolina Lightnin'
1982	Detroit Express
1983	Jacksonville Tea Men

NORTH AMERICAN SOCCER LEAGUE (NASL)

Two competing organizations were formed in the 1960s—the National American Soccer League (NASL) changed its name to the United Soccer Association (USA) to avoid a name clash with its rival, the National Professional Soccer League (NPSL). They merged in 1968 to form the North American Soccer League (NASL). The NASL peaked in the mid- to late 1970s, importing some of the big names in world soccer, including Pelé and George Best. Overexpansion, rising costs, and the lack of a TV deal saw the league fold in 1984.

1967	Oakland Clippers (NPSL Champions)
1968	Atlanta Chiefs
1969	Kansas City Spurs
1970	Rochester Lancers
1971	Dallas Tornado
1972	New York Cosmos
1973	Philadelphia Atoms
1974	Los Angeles Aztecs

1975 Tampa Bay Rowdies
1976 Toronto Metros-Croatia
1977 New York Cosmos
1978 New York Cosmos
1979 Vancouver Whitecaps
1980 New York Cosmos
1981 Chicago Sting
1982 New York Cosmos
1983 Tulsa Roughnecks
1984 Chicago Sting

NATIONAL PROFESSIONAL SOCCER LEAGUE

Starting as the American Indoor Soccer Association in 1984, this professional indoor league changed its name in 1990.

1992 Detroit Rockers
1993 Kansas City Attack
1994 Cleveland Crunch
1995 St. Louis Ambush
1996 Cleveland Crunch
1997 Kansas City Attack
1998 Milwaukee Wave
1999 Cleveland Crunch
2000 Milwaukee Wave
2001 Milwaukee Wave

MAJOR LEAGUE SOCCER (MLS)

After the great interest spawned by the U.S. hosting the 1994 World Cup, the MLS kicked off in 1996 with ten teams. Today the league is made up of 28 teams.

1996 D.C. United (OT)
1997 D.C. United
1998 Chicago Fire
1999 D.C. United
2000 Kansas City Wizards
2001 San Jose Earthquakes (OT)
2002 Los Angeles Galaxy (OT)
2003 San Jose Earthquakes
2004 D.C. United
2005 Los Angeles Galaxy
2006 Houston Dynamo
2007 Houston Dynamo
2008 Columbus Crew
2009 Real Salt Lake
2010 Colorado Rapids
2011 Los Angeles Galaxy
2012 Los Angeles Galaxy
2013 Sporting Kansas City
2014 Los Angeles Galaxy
2015 Portland Timbers
2016 Seattle Sounders
2017 Toronto FC

2018 Atlanta United FC
2019 Seattle Sounders FC
2020 Columbus Crew
2021 New York City FC

WOMEN'S SOCCER LEAGUES

The W-League was the first of three semiprofessional or professional leagues that arose in the U.S. in the 1990s. For a while it was divided into an upper and lower division (W-1 and W-2). It was joined by the WPSL and then the WUSA, which only lasted for three seasons. Women's Professional Soccer (WPS) began in 2009, with seven teams recruiting many of the world's leading female soccer players. The National Women's Soccer League began in 2013 with eight teams, four of which originally played in WPS.

W-League
1995 Long Island Lady Riders
1996 Maryland Pride
1997 Long Island Lady Riders
1998 Raleigh Wings
1999 Raleigh Wings
2000 Chicago Cobras
2001 Boston Renegades
2002 Boston Renegades
2003 Hampton Roads Piranhas
2004 Vancouver Whitecaps
2005 New Jersey Wildcats
2006 Vancouver Whitecaps
2007 Vancouver Whitecaps

Women's Premier Soccer League (WPSL)
1998 Silicon Valley Red Devils
1999 California Storm
2000 San Diego WFC
2001 Ajax Southern California
2002 California Storm
2003 Utah Spiders
2004 California Storm
2005 FC Indiana
2006 Long Island Fury
2007 FC Indiana

National Women's Soccer League (NWSL)
2013 Portland Thorns FC
2014 FC Kansas City
2015 FC Kansas City
2016 Western New York Flash
2017 Portland Thorns FC
2018 North Carolina Courage

2019 North Carolina Courage
2020 Canceled due to COVID-19 pandemic
2021 Washington Spirit

U.S. OPEN CUP CHAMPIONSHIP

One of the oldest soccer cup competitions in the Americas, the U.S. Open Cup dates back to 1914. Only one team, Greek-American of New York, has won the cup three times in a row (1967–69). Since 1996, a Women's Open Cup competition has also been played.

1914 Brooklyn Field Club
1915 Bethlehem Steel
1916 Bethlehem Steel
1917 Fall River Rovers
1918 Bethlehem Steel
1919 Bethlehem Steel
1920 St. Louis Ben Millers
1921 Brooklyn Robins Dry Dock
1922 St. Louis Scullins Steel
1923 Paterson FC/St. Louis Scullin Steel (cochampions)
1924 Fall River Marksmen
1925 Shawsheen (MA) Indians
1926 Bethlehem Steel
1927 Fall River Marksmen
1928 New York Nationals
1929 New York Hakoah
1930 Fall River Marksmen
1931 Fall River FC
1932 New Bedford Whalers
1933 St. Louis Stix, Baer & Fuller
1934 St. Louis Stix, Baer & Fuller
1935 St. Louis Central Breweries
1936 Philadelphia German-American
1937 New York Americans
1938 Chicago Sparta
1939 Brooklyn St. Mary's Celtic
1940 Baltimore SC/Chicago Sparta A & BA (cochampions)
1941 Pawtucket FC
1942 Pittsburgh Gallatin
1943 Brooklyn Hispano
1944 Brooklyn Hispano
1945 New York Brookhattan
1946 Chicago Vikings
1947 Fall River Ponta Delgada
1948 St. Louis Simpkins-Ford
1949 Pittsburgh Morgan SC
1950 St. Louis Simpkins-Ford
1951 New York German-Hungarians
1952 Pittsburgh Hamarville

1953 Chicago Falcons
1954 New York Americans
1955 SC Eintracht
1956 Pittsburgh Hamarville
1957 St. Louis Kutis
1958 Los Angeles Kickers
1959 San Pedro McIlvane Canvasbacks
1960 Philadelphia Ukrainian Nationals
1961 Philadelphia Ukrainian Nationals
1962 New York Hungarians
1963 Philadelphia Ukrainian Nationals
1964 Los Angeles Kickers
1965 New York Ukrainians
1966 Philadelphia Ukrainian Nationals
1967 New York Greek-American
1968 New York Greek-American
1969 New York Greek-American
1970 SC Elizabeth
1971 New York Hota
1972 SC Elizabeth
1973 Los Angeles Maccabee
1974 New York Greek-American
1975 Los Angeles Maccabee
1976 San Francisco AC
1977 Los Angeles Maccabee
1978 Los Angeles Maccabee
1979 Brooklyn Dodgers
1980 New York Pancyprian Freedoms
1981 Los Angeles Maccabee
1982 New York Pancyprian Freedoms
1983 New York Pancyprian Freedoms
1984 New York AO Krete
1985 San Francisco Greek-Americans
1986 St. Louis Kutis
1987 Washington Club España
1988 St. Louis Busch Seniors
1989 St. Petersburg Kickers
1990 Chicago AAC Eagles
1991 Brooklyn Italians
1992 San Jose Oaks
1993 San Francisco CD Mexico
1994 San Francisco Greek-Americans
1995 Richmond Kickers
1996 D.C. United
1997 Dallas Burn
1998 Chicago Fire
1999 Rochester Ragin' Rhinos
2000 Chicago Fire
2001 Los Angeles Galaxy
2002 Columbus Crew

2003	Chicago Fire
2004	Kansas City Wizards
2005	Los Angeles Galaxy
2006	Chicago Fire
2007	New England Revolution
2008	D.C. United
2009	Seattle Sounders FC
2010	Seattle Sounders FC
2011	Seattle Sounders FC
2012	Sporting Kansas City
2013	D.C. United
2014	Seattle Sounders FC
2015	Sporting Kansas City
2016	FC Dallas
2017	Sporting Kansas City
2018	Houston Dynamo
2019	Atlanta United FC
2019	Atlanta United FC
2020	Canceled due to COVID-19 pandemic
2021	Canceled due to COVID-19 pandemic

INDIVIDUAL AND TEAM RECORDS

Top league goal scorers

1975	Steve David	23
1976	Derek Smethurst	20
1977	Steve David	26
1978	Giorgio Chinaglia	34
1979	Giorgio Chinaglia	26
1980	Giorgio Chinaglia	32
1981	Giorgio Chinaglia	29
1982	Ricardo Alonso	21
1983	Roberto Cabanas	25
1984	Steven Zyngul	20
1985	Josue Partillo	8
1986	Brent Goulet	9
1987	Joe Mihaljevic	7
1988	Jorge Acosta	14
1989	Ricardo Alonso, Mirko Castilo	15
1990	Chance Fry	17
1991	Jean Harbour	17
1992	Jean Harbour	13
1993	Paulinho	15
1994	Paul Wright	12
1995	Peter Hattrup	11
1996	Roy Lassiter	27
1997	Jaime Moreno	16
1998	Stern John	26
1999	Stern John, Roy Lassiter, Jason Kreis	18
2000	Mamadou Diallo	26
2001	Alex Pineda	19
2002	Carlos Ruiz	23
2003	Carlos Ruiz, Taylor Twellman	15
2004	Amado Guevara	10
2005	Taylor Zwellman	17
2006	Jeff Cunningham	16

2007	Luciano Emilio	20
2008	Landon Donovan	20
2009	Jeff Cunningham	17
2010	Chris Wondolowski	18
2011	Dwayne De Rosario	16
2012	Chris Wondolowski	27
2013	Camilo Sanvezzo	22
2014	Bradley Wright-Phillips	27
2015	Sebastian Gicovinco	22
2016	Bradley Wright-Phillips	24
2017	Nemanja Nikolic	24
2018	Josef Martinez	31
2019	Carlos Vela	34
2020	Diego Rossi	12
2021	Valentin Castellanos	22

MLS Most Valuable Player

1997	Preki, Kansas City Wizards
1998	Marco Etcheverry, D.C. United
1999	Jason Kreis, FC Dallas
2000	Tony Meola, Kansas City Wizards
2001	Alex Pineda Chacón, Miami Fusion
2002	Carlos Ruiz, LA Galaxy
2003	Preki, Kansas City Wizards
2004	Amado Guevara, MetroStars (New Jersey)
2005	Taylor Twellman, New England Revolution
2006	Christian Gomez, D.C. United
2007	Luciano Emilio, D.C. United
2008	Guillermo Barros Schelotto, Columbus Crew
2009	Landon Donovan, LA Galaxy
2010	David Ferreira, FC Dallas
2011	Dwayne De Rosario, D.C. United
2012	Chris Wondolowski, San Jose Earthquakes
2013	Mike Magee, Chicago Fire
2014	Robbie Keane, Los Angeles Galaxy
2015	Sebastian Giovinco, Toronto FC
2016	David Villa, New York City FC
2017	Diego Valeri, Portland Timbers
2018	Josef Martinez, Atlanta United FC
2019	Carlos Vela, Los Angeles FC
2020	Alejandro Pozuelo, Toronto FC
2021	Carles Gil, New England Revolution

All-time MLS goal scorers (from 1996)

Chris Wondolowski	171
Landon Donovan	145
Jeff Cunningham	134
Jaime Moreno	133
Kei Kamara	130
Bradley Wright-Philips	117
Ante Razov	114
Jason Kreis	108
Dwayne De Rosario	104
Taylor Twellman	101
Edson Buddle	100

Leading international appearances (men)

Cobi Jones	164
Landon Donovan	157
Michael Bradley	151
Clint Dempsey	141
Jeff Agoos	134
Clint Dempsey	132
Marcelo Balboa	128
DaMarcus Beasley	126

Leading international goal scorers (men)

Clint Dempsey	57
Landon Donovan	57
Jozy Altidore	42
Eric Wynalda	34
Brian McBride	30

Leading international appearances (women)

Kristine Lilly	354
Carli Lloyd	316
Christie Pearce	311
Mia Hamm	276
Julie Foudy	274

Leading international goal scorers (women)

Abby Wambach	184
Mia Hamm	158
Carli Lloyd	134
Kristine Lilly	130
Alex Morgan	115
Michelle Akers	107
Tiffeny Milbrett	100

GLOSSARY

Advantage rule A rule that allows the referee to let play continue after a foul if it is to the advantage of the team that has been fouled against.

AFC The Asian Football Confederation, responsible for running soccer in Asia.

Agent A person who represents players and negotiates contracts and transfer moves.

Anchor A midfielder positioned just in front of, and who protects, the defense. An anchor player may allow other midfielders to push further forward.

Assist A pass that releases a player to score a goal. An assist can be a pass on the ground, a flick, or a cross from which a headed goal is scored.

Away goals rule A rule used in some cup competitions. If the scores are equal over two legs, the team that has scored more goals away from home wins.

Back pass rule A law stating that a deliberate pass backward by a player to his or her goalkeeper cannot be handled by the goalkeeper.

CAF The *Confédération Africaine de Football*, which runs soccer in Africa.

Cap Recognition given to a player for each appearance in an international game for his or her country.

Catenaccio A defensive tactical system in which a sweeper plays behind a solid defense.

Caution Another word for a yellow card (a warning from the referee to a player for a foul or infringement). A player who receives two yellow cards in a match is automatically shown a red card and sent off.

Central defender The defender who plays in the middle of the last line of defense.

Chip A pass lofted into the air from a player to a teammate or as a shot on goal.

CONCACAF The Confederation of North, Central American, and Caribbean Association Football, which runs soccer in North and Central America.

CONMEBOL The *Confederación Sudamericana de Fútbol*, which runs soccer in South America.

Counterattack A quick attack by a team after it regains possession of the ball.

Cross To send the ball from a wide position toward the center of the field, often into the opposition penalty area.

Cushioning Using a part of the body to slow down a ball in order to bring it under control.

Derby A match between two rival teams, often located in the same town or city.

Direct free kick A kick awarded to a team because of a serious foul committed by an opponent. A goal may be scored directly from the kick.

Dissent When a player uses words or actions to disagree with the referee's decision.

Distribution The way the ball is released by a goalkeeper or is moved around the field by a team.

Dribbling Moving the ball under close control with a series of short kicks or taps.

Drop ball A way of restarting play in which the referee releases the ball to a player of the team that last touched the ball. All other players must be at least 13.1 ft. (4 m) away.

Extra time A way of deciding a tied match. It involves two periods of additional play, usually lasting 15 minutes each.

FA (Football Association) The national soccer federation of England.

Feinting Using fake moves of the head, shoulders, and legs to deceive an opponent and put him or her off balance.

FIFA The *Fédération Internationale de Football Association*, the international governing body of soccer.

Formation The way in which a team lines up on the field in terms of the numbers of defenders, midfielders, and forwards.

Foul An action committed intentionally by a defender to stop an opponent who has a clear run on goal.

Fourth official An additional match official responsible for displaying added-on time, checking substitutions, and aiding the referee and his or her two assistants.

Friendly An exhibition game that is not part of a league or tournament play.

Futsal A type of five-on-five soccer, supported and promoted by FIFA.

Golden Boot An award given to the player who scores the most goals at a World Cup. It is also an annual award given to the top goal scorer in European club soccer.

Handball The illegal use of the hand or arm by a player.

Hat trick Three goals scored by a player in a single match.

Indirect free kick A kick awarded to a team because of a minor foul committed by an opponent. A goal cannot be scored from the kick unless the ball is first touched by a player other than the kicker.

Instep The part of a player's foot where his or her shoelaces lie.

Interception When a player gains possession of the ball by latching on to a pass made by the opposition.

Jockeying A defensive technique of delaying an attacker who has the ball.

Laws of the game The 17 main rules of soccer, established and updated by FIFA.

Libero *See sweeper.*

Man-to-man marking A system of marking in which a defender stays close to and goalside of a single opposition player.

Marking Guarding a player to prevent him or her from advancing the ball toward the goal, making an easy pass, or receiving the ball from a teammate.

MLS Major League Soccer, the American professional male league.

Narrowing the angle A technique in which a goalkeeper moves toward an attacker who has the ball in order to cut down the amount of goal the attacker can aim a shot at.

NWSL National Women's Soccer League, the American professional female league.

Obstruction When a player, instead of trying to win the ball, uses his or her body to prevent an opponent from playing it.

OFC The Oceania Football Confederation, which runs soccer in Oceania.

Offside A player is offside if he or she is closer to the other team's goal than both the ball and the second-to-last opponent at the moment that the ball is played forward.

Offside trap A defensive tactic used to trick opposition attackers by leaving them offside. Defenders who play the offside trap usually move upfield together, in a straight line, when the ball is played toward their goal.

Overlap To run outside and beyond a teammate down the side of the field in order to create space and a possible passing opportunity.

Overload When an attacking team has more players in the opposition's half or penalty area than the defending team. An overload often leads to a scoring chance.

Penalty shoot-out A method of deciding a tied match by a series of penalty kicks, all taken at one end of the field.

Playmaker A skillful midfielder or deep-lying attacker who coordinates the attacking movement of a team.

Playoff A match, pair, or series of matches used to decide a final placing. In the World Cup, the two losing semifinalists contest a single playoff game for third place. In many leagues, playoff matches are used to decide relegation and promotion issues.

Referee's assistant An official who assists the referee during the game by signaling for fouls, infringements, and offsides.

Reserve team A team made up of players who are not on the first team at a club or national team.

Scout A person employed by a soccer club who attends games and training sessions to look for up-and-coming players.

Set piece A planned play or move that a team uses when a game is restarted with a free kick, penalty kick, corner kick, goal kick, throw-in, or kickoff.

Shielding A technique used by the player with the ball to protect it from a defender who is closely marking them. The player in possession keeps his or her body between the ball and the defender.

Simulation Pretending to be fouled or feigning injury in order to fool the referee. A player found guilty of simulation by the referee receives a yellow card.

Stoppage time Time added to the end of any period of a game to make up for time lost during a major halt in play. Also known as added time or injury time.

Substitution Changing the team lineup on the field by replacing one player with another from the substitutes' bench.

Sweeper A defender who can play closest to his or her goal, behind the rest of the defenders, or in a more attacking role with responsibility for bringing the ball forward.

Tactics Methods of play used in an attempt to outwit and beat an opposition team.

Target man A tall striker, usually the player furthest upfield, at whom teammates aim their forward passes.

Through ball or pass A pass to a teammate that puts him or her beyond the opposition's defense and through on goal.

Total soccer A style of soccer in which players switch positions all over the field. It was made famous by the Dutch national team and Dutch clubs such as Ajax.

UEFA The Union of European Football Associations, which organizes soccer in Europe.

VAR Short for video assistant referee, this official can be instructed by a referee to review a major incident, such as a penalty or direct red card, on video screens to ensure the right decision is made.

Volley Any ball kicked by a player when it is off the ground.

Wall pass A quick, short pair of passes between two players that sends the ball past a defender. Also known as a one-two pass.

Wingback A defender on the sides of the field who, when the opportunity occurs, makes wide runs forward in attack.

WUSA The world's first professional soccer league for women, based in the United States.

Zonal marking A defensive system in which defenders mark opponents who enter their area of the field.

INDEX

Page numbers in **bold** refer to main entries.

ACKNOWLEDGMENTS

The publisher would like to thank the following for permission to reproduce their material. Top = *t*, bottom = *b*, center = *c*, left = *l*, right = *r*

Prelims and chapter 1
Page 1 LLUIS GENE/AFP/Gettyimages; 2 Matt McNulty—Manchester City/Gettyimages; 4bl Marcio Machado/Gettyimages; 4-5 Alex Pantling/Gettyimages; 5tr Daniel Beloumou Olomo/Gettyimages; 5br Kyodo News/Gettyimages; 6t Popperfoto/Gettyimages; 6bl Stray Toki/Shutterstock; 7t Laurence Griffiths/Gettyimages; 7br Reinhold Thiele/Gettyimages; 8l Alex Caparros—FIFA/Gettyimages; 8t Oli Scarff/Gettyimages; 8cl above Evgeniya Telennaya/Shutterstock; 8br Pressinphoto/Gettyimages; 9tr J. A. Hampton/Stringer/Gettyimages; 9cl below VANDERLEI ALMEIDA/AFP/Gettyimages; 9c Paris Saint-Germain Football/Stringer/Gettyimages; 10t Central Press/Stringer/Gettyimages; 10b MB Media/Gettyimages; 11l Darren Walsh/Gettyimages; 11r J.LEAGUE/Gettyimages; 12-13 Eric Alonso/Gettyimages.

Chapter 2
14r David Rogers/Gettyimages; 14l; Simon Stacpoole/Offside/Gettyimages; 15tr Kyle Ross/Icon Sportswire/Gettyimages; 15c The Asahi Shimbun/Gettyimages; 15bl Ivica Drusany/Shutterstock; 15br Manuel Queimadelos/Quality Sport Images/Gettyimages; 16t Tim Nwachukwu/Gettyimages; 16b Matt McNulty—Manchester City/Gettyimages; 17t PA Images / Alamy Stock Photo; 17c Angel Martinez - FIFA/FIFA/Gettyimages; 18c Matthias Hangst/Gettyimages; 18 bl TT News Agency / Alamy Stock Photo; 18br Silvia Lore/Gettyimages; 19cl OSCAR DEL POZO/AFP/Gettyimages; 19bl LOIC VENANCE/AFP/Gettyimages; 19br Clive Mason/Gettyimages; 20tr ANP Sport/Gettyimages; 20bl Hector Vivas/Stringer/Gettyimages; 21t Andrew Powell/Liverpool FC/Gettyimages; 21l Hector Vivas—FIFA/Gettyimages; 22tr Angel Martinez/Stringer/Gettyimages; 22c ANDREAS SOLARO/AFP/Gettyimages; 22bl Denis Doyle/Stringer/Gettyimages; 22br Harry Langer/DeFodi Images/Gettyimages; 23tr Jose Breton—Pics Action/Shutterstock; 23c Randy Litzinger/Icon Sportswire/Gettyimages; 23bl Andrew Powell/Liverpool FC/Gettyimages; 24t Paul Ellis—Pool/Gettyimages; 24c Randy Litzinger/Icon Sportswire/Gettyimages; 24b Pieter Stam De Jonge/ANP/Gettyimages; 25c Fred Kfoury III/Icon Sportswire/Gettyimages; 25b Buda Mendes/Gettyimages; 26bl Naomi Baker/Gettyimages; 26br Stu Forster/Gettyimages; 27t FRANCK FIFE/AFP/Gettyimages; 27c Alex Livesey—FIFA/Gettyimages; 27b JUSTIN TALLIS/AFP/Gettyimages; 28t Alex Livesey/Stringer/Gettyimages; 28c Michael Regan/Gettyimages; 28b CLIVE BRUNSKILL/POOL/AFP/Gettyimages; 29t LOIC VENANCE/AFP/Gettyimages; 29c FERENC ISZA/AFP/Gettyimages; 30-31 Paul Ellis/Gettyimages.

Chapter 3
32t Ed Lacey/Popperfoto/Gettyimages; 32bl ROMEO GACAD/Staff/Gettyimages; 32br Helios de la Rubia/Real Madrid/Gettyimages; 33t Quality Sport Images/Gettyimages; 33c Central Press/Stringer/Gettyimages; 33b Visionhaus/Gettyimages; 34t Jonathan Moscrop/Gettyimages; 34b Shaun Botterill—UEFA/Gettyimages; 35t Mike Finn-Kelcey/Gettyimages; 35br James Gill-Danehouse/Gettyimages; 35bl Laurence Griffiths/Gettyimages; 36tl Marco Luzzani/Stringer/Gettyimages; 36tr Popperfoto/Gettyimages; 36b Bob Thomas/Gettyimages; 37cl Popperfoto/Gettyimages; 37r Marc Atkins/Gettyimages; 37b Michel Barrault/Onze/Icon Sport/Gettyimages; 38r Ezra O. Shaw/Allsport/Gettyimages; 38tl Popperfoto/Gettyimages; 38b GES-Sportfoto/Gettyimages; 39t Matt McNulty—Manchester City/Gettyimages; 39br Pedro Ugarte/AFP/Gettyimages; 39bl Andrew Dieb/Icon Sportswire/Gettyimages; 40bl Simon

Stacpoole/Offside/Gettyimages; 40c Pressefoto Ulmer/ullstein bild/Gettyimages; 40br Shaun Botterill/Allsport/Gettyimages; 41tl Bob Thomas/Gettyimages; 41bl Alejandro Rios/DeFodi Images/Gettyimages; 42c MICHAEL URBAN/Staff/Gettyimages; 42br Pedro Fiúza/NurPhoto/Gettyimages; 43tl Valerio Pennicino/Gettyimages; 43tr Christian Liewig/TempSport/Corbis/Gettyimages; 43bl JEFF PACHOUD/AFP/Gettyimages; 43br Maddie Meyer - FIFA/Gettyimages; 44r John Powell/Liverpool FC/Gettyimages; 44cl Popperfoto/Gettyimages; 44bl Jan Kruger—UEFA/Gettyimages; 45tl Bob Thomas/Gettyimages; 45tr Hulton-Deutsch/CORBIS/Gettyimages; 45b Rafal Oleksiewicz/PressFocus/MB Media/Gettyimages; 46tl Alexandre Schneider/Gettyimages; 46tr Jamie McDonald/Staff/Gettyimages; 46tl Alexandre Schneider/Gettyimages; 47tl Alexander Hassenstein/Staff/Gettyimages; 47tr Ben Radford/Staff/Gettyimages; 47b Bride Lane Library/Popperfoto/Gettyimages; 48bl Mateo Villalba/Quality Sport Images/Gettyimages; 48tr Rolls Press/Popperfoto/Gettyimages; 48br Mark Kolbe/Staff/Gettyimages; 49t Professional Sport/Popperfoto/Gettyimages; 49bl Alessandro Sabattini/Gettyimages; 49br REPORTERS ASSOCIES/Gamma-Rapho/Gettyimages; 50t Alessandro Sabattini/Gettyimages; 50bl David Price/Arsenal FC/Gettyimages; 50br Bob Thomas/Gettyimages; 51t Alex Livesey—FIFA/Gettyimages; 51c Jed Jacobsohn/Gettyimages; 51bl Robyn Beck/AFP/Gettyimages; 51br Baptiste Fernandez/Icon Sport/Gettyimages; 52t Alessandro Sabattini/Gettyimages; 52bl Lars Baron/Gettyimages; 52r Marc Atkins/Gettyimages; 53l Matthias Hangst/Gettyimages; 53b Leo Mason/Popperfoto/Gettyimages; 54 Bob Thomas/Gettyimages; 55 Bob Thomas/Gettyimages.

Chapter 4
56l Dale MacMillan/Soccrates Images/Gettyimages; 56br David Cannon/ALLSPORT/Gettyimages; 57cl TF-Images/Gettyimages; 57bl Yusuf Ozcan/Anadolu Agency/Gettyimages; 57br Matthew Peters/Manchester United/Gettyimages; 58t Stu Forster/Staff/Gettyimages; 58b Adam Pretty/Staff/Gettyimages; 59t Mateo Villalba/Quality Sport Images/Gettyimages; 59cl Brad Smith/ISI Photos/Gettyimages; 60t David Ramos/Staff/Gettyimages; 60b Denis Doyle/Stringer/Gettyimages; 61t Alexander Hassenstein/POOL/AFP/Gettyimages; 62l Jimmy Bolcina/Photonews/Gettyimages; 62br Jean Catuffe/Gettyimages; 63tl Mike Hewitt/Gettyimages; 63tr Johnny Fidelin/Icon Sport/Gettyimages; 63ct Review News/Shutterstock; 63br VCG/Gettyimages; 64tr VI Images/Gettyimages; 64bl Michael Regan/Staff/Gettyimages; 64br PA Images / Alamy Stock Photo; 65tl Alex Livesey/Staff/Gettyimages; 65c PAUL ELLIS/AFP/Gettyimages; 65b Tottenham Hotspur FC/Gettyimages; 65br Alex Livesey—Danehouse/Gettyimages; 66-67 Richard Heathcote/Gettyimages.

Chapter 5
68bl Popperfoto/Gettyimages; 68br Jamie Sabau/Stringer/Gettyimages; 69l Tony Duffy/Allsport/Gettyimages; 69br Alex Pantling/Gettyimages; 70tr Brad Smith/ISI Photos/Gettyimages; 70br Shaun Botterill/Gettyimages; 71tr Alex Grimm/Gettyimages; 71bl STAFF/AFP/Gettyimages; 72t Rolls Press/Popperfoto/Gettyimages; 72br David Cannon/Allsport/Gettyimages; 73tr Eric Verhoeven/Soccrates Images/Gettyimages; 73cl Paul Popper/Popperfoto/Gettyimages; 73br Julian Finney/Gettyimages; 74tr Rolls Press/Popperfoto/Gettyimages; 74cr Popperfoto/Gettyimages; 74bl Visionhaus/Corbis/Gettyimages; 75b Allsport/Gettyimages; 75t Alex Grimm/Gettyimages; 76b LLUIS GENE/AFP/Gettyimages; 76tr KHALED DESOUKI/AFP/Gettyimages; 77tr Buda Mendes/Gettyimages; 77bc Popperfoto/Gettyimages; 77bl Clive

Brunskill/Gettyimages; 78tl Jonathan Moscrop/Gettyimages; 78bl Plumb Images/Leicester City FC/Gettyimages; 78/79t RICARDO MORAES/POOL/AFP/Gettyimages; 78/79b Marcelo Endelli/Stringer/Gettyimages; 79cr Gircke/ullstein bild Dtl./Gettyimages; 80tr Laurence Griffiths/Gettyimages; 80br Agustin Marcarian - Pool/Gettyimages; 81tr PHILL MAGAKOE/AFP/Gettyimages; 81bl John Berry/Gettyimages; 82tr Buda Mendes/Gettyimages; 82br Marc Atkins/Gettyimages; 83tr Juan Ignacio Roncoroni—Pool/Gettyimages; 83tr FABRICE COFFRINI/AFP/Gettyimages; 83cl Daniele Badolato—Juventus FC/Gettyimages; 84tr Laurence Griffiths—UEFA/Gettyimages; 84cr Rolls Press/Popperfoto/Gettyimages; 85tr Herman Dingler/BSR Agency/Gettyimages; 85bl Meg Oliphant /Stringer /Gettyimages; 85br Lars Baron/Gettyimages; 86tl Alejandro Rios/DeFodi Images/Gettyimages; 86c KARIM JAAFAR/AFP/Gettyimages; 86br Alexandre Schneider/Stringer/Gettyimages; 87cr Visionhaus/Gettyimages; 87bl Gerrit van Keulen/BSR Agency/Gettyimages; 88tl DRAGOMIR YANKOVIC/PHOTOSPORT/AFP/Gettyimages; 88bl Shaun Botterill/Gettyimages; 88br Ian MacNicol / Stringer/Gettyimages; 89tl Andrey Lukatsky/BSR Agency/Gettyimages; 89br FAYEZ NURELDINE/AFP/Gettyimages; 90-91 Shaun Botterill/Gettyimages.

Chapter 6
92l Andy Bao/Gettyimages; 92br Trond Tandberg/Gettyimages; 93l Pressinphoto/Icon Sport/Gettyimages; 93r The Asahi Shimbun/Gettyimages; 94l Francesco Pecoraro/Stringer/Gettyimages; 94r Urbanandsport/NurPhoto/Gettyimages; 95tl Aurelien Meunier/Stringer/Gettyimages; 95tr Tom Purslow/Manchester United/Gettyimages; 95bl Joe Prior/Visionhaus/Gettyimages; 95b Wolverhampton Wanderers FC/Gettyimages; 96r (above) Chris Ricco—UEFA/Gettyimages; 96r (below) Alexander Hassenstein—UEFA/Gettyimages; 96b Ali Atmaca/Anadolu Agency/Gettyimages; 97t Ross Kinnaird/Staff/Gettyimages; 97br FRANCOIS XAVIER MARIT/Staff/Gettyimages; 98t Matthias Hangst/Staff/Gettyimages; 98b Simon Stacpoole/Offside/Gettyimages; 99t Marianna Massey—FIFA/Gettyimages; 99l JOHN THYS/AFP/Gettyimages; 99b Marcio Machado/Gettyimages; 100bl DENIS CHARLET/AFP/Gettyimages; 100br Dignity 100/Shutterstock; 101tl Art Konovalov/Shutterstock; 101r Visionhaus/Gettyimages; 101bl OLI SCARFF/AFP/Gettyimages; 102bl David Cannon/Gettyimages; 102br Stuart Franklin/Staff/Gettyimages; 103t STR/Stringer/Gettyimages; 103b Visionhaus/Gettyimages; 104-105 Buda Mendes/Gettyimages.

Chapter 7
106tr Keystone-France/Gamma-Keystone/Gettyimages; 106bl Popperfoto/Gettyimages; 107tl Keystone/Gettyimages; 107t Popperfoto/Gettyimages; 107br ullstein bild/Gettyimages; 108tr ullstein bild/Gettyimages; 108bl Keystone-France/Gettyimages; 109tr Popperfoto/Gettyimages; 109bl Popperfoto/Gettyimages; 110tr STAFF/AFP/Gettyimages; 110bl Alessandro Sabattini/Gettyimages; 111b Bob Thomas/Gettyimages; 112bl Paul Popper/Popperfoto/Gettyimages; 113t Photo by Eric Renard/Onze/Icon Sport/Gettyimages; 113br Bob Thomas/Gettyimages; 114t Lars Baron/Gettyimages; 114bl Laurence Griffiths/Gettyimages; 115t Clive Rose/Gettyimages; 115bl KELLY AYODI/AFP/Gettyimages; 115br Joerg-Drescher/Shutterstock; 116t David Madison/Gettyimages; 116b Bob Thomas/Gettyimages; 117tr Steven Kingsman/Icon Sportswire/Corbis/Gettyimages; 117bl DANIEL ROLAND/AFP/Gettyimages; 117br Baptiste Fernandez/Icon Sport/Gettyimages; 118bl Shaun Botterill/Staff/Gettyimages; 118bc Alex Grimm/Gettyimages; 118br Matthias Hangst/Staff/Gettyimages; 119t Catherine Ivill/Gettyimages; 119b TF-Images/Gettyimages; 120l Gary Prior/Visionhaus/Gettyimages; 120r

Tommy Hindley/Professional Sport/Popperfoto/Gettyimages; 121l Zhizhao Wu/Gettyimages; 121b Alexander Hassenstein/Gettyimages; 122b LatinContent/Stringer/Gettyimages; 122t MB Media/Gettyimages; 123b Visionhaus/Gettyimages; 123t KENZO TRIBOUILLARD/AFP/Gettyimages; 124t Masashi Hara/Gettyimages; 124b KIM JAE-HWAN/AFP/Gettyimages; 125c Nick Tre. Smith/Icon Sportswire/Gettyimages; 125b Anthony Au-Yeung/Stringer/Gettyimages; 126t Baptiste Fernandez/Icon Sport/Gettyimages; 126b Nico Paetzel/TF-Images/Gettyimages; 127l Philippe Crochet/Photo News/Gettyimages; 127t Islam Safwat/NurPhoto/Gettyimages; 127b Steph Chambers/Staff/Gettyimages; 128t Gabriele Maltinti/Stringer/Gettyimages; 128c Alexandre Simoes/Borussia Dortmund/Gettyimages; 128b LLUIS GENE/AFP/Gettyimages; 129t Michael Regan/Staff/Gettyimages; 129b Roy K. Miller/ISI Photos/Gettyimages; 130l Agencia Gamba/Stringer/Gettyimages; 130r EITAN ABRAMOVICH/AFP/Gettyimages; 131t PHILL MAGAKOE/AFP/Gettyimages; 131b Boris Streubel—UEFA/Gettyimages; 132tr Popperfoto/Gettyimages; 132r Jasper Juinen/Staff/Gettyimages; 133r PATRICK HERTZOG/Gettyimages; 133l David Ramos/Quality Sport Images/Gettyimages; 134tr Diego Souto/Quality Sport Images/Gettyimages; 134cr MAURICE VAN STEEN/ANP/Gettyimages; 134b Matt Childs/Pool/Gettyimages; 135l Eric Alonso/Gettyimages; 135b Daniela Porcelli/Gettyimages.

Poster
Tc Alexandre Schneider/Gettyimages; tr Matthias Hangst/Gettyimages; bc Manuel Queimadelos//Quality Sport Images/Gettyimages; br Catherine Ivill/Gettyimages.